The Legend of Freud

The publication of this book was assisted by a bequest from Josiah H. Chase to honor his parents, Ellen Rankin Chase and Josiah Hook Chase, Minnesota territorial pioneers.

The Legend of Freud

Samuel Weber

University of Minnesota Press
Minneapolis

Copyright © 1982 by the University of Minnesota
All rights reserved.
Published by the University of Minnesota Press,
2037 University Avenue Southeast, Minneapolis, MN 55414
Printed in the United States of America.

Library of Congress Cataloging in Publication Data

Weber, Samuel, 1940-
    The legend of Freud.

Translation of: Freud-Legende.
    Includes bibliographical references and index.
    1. Psychoanalysis. 2. Freud, Sigmund, 1856-1939.
I. Title.
BF173.F85W2813   150.19'52   82-4759
ISBN 0-8166-1113-0   AACR2
ISBN 0-8166-1128-9 (pbk.)

Originally published as *Freud Legende: Drei
Studien zum Psychoanalytischen Denken,*
© 1979, Walter Verlag AG, Olten, Switzerland.
This English-language edition is a revision
of the German text; the translation is by
the author, Samuel Weber.

The University of Minnesota
is an equal-opportunity
educator and employer.

For

Jacques Derrida

In Admiration and Friendship

Contents

Foreword by Joseph H. Smith, M.D. xi

Preface xv

I. Psychoanalysis Set Apart 1
Going My Way 3
A Problem of Narcissism 8
Observation, Description, Figurative Language 17
Metapsychology Set Apart 32

II. The Other Part 63
The Meaning of the Thallus 65
The Joke: Child's Play 84
The Shaggy Dog 100

III. Love Stories 119
The Analyst's Desire: Speculation in Play 121
The *Fort!* 136
Speculation: The Way to Utter Difference 146

Notes 167

Index 177

*When breath threatened to fail me in the
struggle, I prayed the angel to desist,
and that is what he has done ever since.
But I did not turn out to be the stronger,
although ever since I noticeably limp.*

S. FREUD

Foreword

The main symptom of being—being with a small "b," i.e., just being and knowing it by having life and language or being had by life and language—takes the form of a search for origins, destiny, and ultimate purpose, for a foundation, for a central meaning or truth, for governing principles or a governing Being, by which we can establish and hierarchically organize our selves and our world. Jacques Derrida sees in this symptom what he variously refers to as the logocentric or phallocentric or ontotheological bias that pervades Western science and philosophy and Western religion. The symptomatic nature of their hold on us is indicated in that science and philosophy undermine religion, religion undermines science and philosophy (or ought to), and art undermines itself and all of the others. In fact, at their best, each undermines itself and exposes itself as a symptom. Each represses (and thus contains the traces of) what it overtly is not. The difference these traces reveal is covered over by difference being interpreted as the loss of a prior wholeness, i.e., the castration story. Origin and destiny are posited as a defense of the defensively (i.e., narcissistically) organized ego in relation to which any organized system of belief is the mirror image. Derrida, following (he claims) Nietzsche and Freud, questions such ontotheological foundations of Western thought. It is another radically decentering turn of the Copernican screw in the face of which Derrida marks out the following alternatives:

Turned toward the presence, lost or impossible, of the absent origin the structuralist thematic of broken immediacy is thus the sad, *negative*, nostalgic, guilty, Rousseauist aspect of the thought of play of which Nietzschean affirmation of the play of the world and the innocence of becoming, the affirmation of a world

of signs without fault, without truth, without anger, offered to an active interpretation—would be the other side [*Of Grammatology*, p. xiii]

The influence of Jacques Lacan's reading of Freud on Sam Weber's reading of Freud is here palpable. But it would be a mistake to consider Weber a Lacanian. The question that arises from these pages is more one of whether Freud was a Derridean. The book is dedicated to Derrida and is a remarkably intelligent Derridean reading of Freud. In my opinion, the thought of neither Lacan nor Derrida is destined to take over the world, but the questions they raise are of such compelling pertinence that I do not think any psychoanalyst can afford to remain blind to them. Weber's book, precisely because it focuses on the story of how Freud's story was constructed in, through, on, and by Freud, provides the best access for the psychoanalyst to Derrida's questions.

To quote Weber (p. vi): "Through the writings of Jacques Lacan and Jacques Derrida, the status of Freud's discourse itself has been put into question: not simply by applying the concepts and categories of psychoanalysis to the work of an individual, Freud, and thereby performing a psychoanalysis of the initiator of psychoanalysis, but by posing the problem of a theory which in deriving the functions of consciousness from the conflictual dynamics of the unconscious, cannot but dislocate the conceptions of *cognition* and of *truth* upon which theory has traditionally depended."

This is a way of phrasing Freud's own Copernican step and also states Weber's project: Freud is to be seen in series with Nietzsche and Derrida by his displacement of consciousness-as-central; by his means of discovering and validating that displacement by the method of free association; by the recurrence of revision and the repetition of transgressing or going beyond his own theoretical system—ultimately in "going beyond" the pleasure principle; in general, by his struggle against/for that which undermined his system. Weber, with virtually none of the neologistic jargon over which one must stumble in reading Lacan and Derrida, traces the traces of this struggle through Freud's thinking about dreaming, narcissism, jokes, and a beyond of the pleasure principle. But these are not to be found here under headings that might be expected from a conventional—whatever that would be—reading of Freud. The three sections, "Psychoanalysis Set Apart," "The Other Part," and "Love Stories," include the chapter titles "Going My Way . . . ," "The Meaning of the Thallus . . . ," (he *means* Thallus, not Phallus), "The Joke: Child's Play . . . ," "The Shaggy Dog . . ." and "The Analyst's Desire: Speculation in Play. . . ."

Freud, according to Weber, has been rendered less problematic than he actually was by the *Standard Edition*, in respect to which "the 'figure' of Freud which . . . emerges in this book should seem disfigured. . . . For it is only in remarking the differences between a Freud who has grown all too familiar, and another, less comforting figure, that his legend can regain the uncanny force we have 'known' all the time, but of which we *think* less and less" (p. vii).

Joseph H. Smith, M.D.

Preface

In his essay, "What is an Author?" Michel Foucault distinguishes between the foundation of scientific disciplines and the initiation of what he calls "discursive practices." "In a scientific discipline," he writes, "the founding act is on an equal footing with its future transformations: it is merely one among the many modifications it makes possible." The founder of a discipline establishes a clearly defined space, within which or with respect to which his successors work, developing the intrinsic implications of the doctrine, "rediscovering" analogies with "current forms of knowledge," or transposing the founding discourse "into totally new domains," a process Foucault designates as "reactivation." The case of discursive practices, however, is radically different:

The initiation of a discursive practice . . . overshadows and is necessarily detached from its later developments and transformations. . . . If we return [to it], it is because of a basic and constructive omission, an omission that is not the result of accident or incomprehension. In effect, the act of initiation is such, in its essence, that it is inevitably subjected to its own distortions. . . . The barrier imposed by omission was not added from the outside; it arises from the discursive practice in question, which gives it its law. . . . In addition, it is always a return to a text in itself . . . with particular attention to those things registered in the interstices of the text, its gaps and absences. We return to those empty spaces that have been masked by omission or concealed in a false and misleading plenitude.[1]

Foucault, who names Marx and Freud as examples of initiators of discursive practices, could have been paraphrasing the latter's remarks on the interpretation of dreams. To interpret dreams or any of the other articulations of the unconscious, Freud taught, is to "return" to a text that is not merely distorted, *entstellt*, but that distorts its distortions by producing a facade of "false and misleading plenitude." Such a "return," moreover, can only reveal these distortions by participating in them: by repeating them, which is to say, by transforming them.

If such self-dissimulating distortions have long been recognized as the privileged object of Freudian psychoanalysis, it is only recently that this domain has been extended to encompass the workings of psychoanalytic discourse itself. The writings of Jacques Lacan and Jacques Derrida have put into question the status of Freud's discourse itself, not simply by applying the concepts and categories of psychoanalysis to the work of an individual, Freud, and thereby performing a psychoanalysis of the initiator of psychoanalysis, but by posing the problem of a theory that, in deriving the functions of consciousness from the conflictual dynamics of the unconscious, cannot but dislocate the conceptions of cognition and of truth on which theory has traditionally depended.

The question that thereby imposes itself, and that this book seeks to address, is: can psychoanalytic thinking itself escape the effects of what it endeavors to think? Can the disruptive distortions of unconscious processes be simply recognized, theoretically, as an object, or must they not leave their imprint on the process of theoretical objectification itself? Must not psychoanalytical thinking itself partake of—repeat—the dislocations it seeks to describe?

To address this question is to "return" to the texts of Freud, in the sense described by Foucault. For if psychoanalytic thinking participates in what it describes, the writings of Freud comprise a privileged, if by no means unique, scenario of that participation. Or rather, of that struggle: for the enterprise of constructing a theory of the unconscious inevitably entails the struggle to wrest meaning from a process that entails the deliberate dislocation of meaning. It is the mark, the stigma of this struggle that I have sought to retrace. In so doing, I have had no choice—though it was also a pleasure!— but to return to the German in which Freud wrote. Not so much because Freud's German is closer to his original intentions, which of course is true, but rather because the *dislocation* of those original intentions is graphically inscribed there, in a manner that must inevitably elude any translation that conceives of itself as a repetition of the same. And this conception never fails to inform the standards of the Standard Edition, which presumes that its "original" text knows what it is talking about, or at least what it wants to say. If such a presumption almost always guides the translation of "theoretical" or "cognitive" writing, it is considerably less self-evident in the case of a discourse concerned above all to demonstrate the ubiquity of forces that compel language to say something different from what the subject consciously means to say.[2] It is this difference that makes the German texts of Freud a privileged theater in which the questions and struggles of psychoanalytical thinking play themselves out. In those texts, explicit propositions and assertions must be read with the same circumspection that Freud applied to discourse represented in dreams, or indeed to all dream-representation: the latter, it will be recalled, furnishes only the material with which the dream constructs its *disfiguration*, its *Entstellung*, and is generally all the more deceptive for its apparent clarity.

That the "figure" of Freud which emerges in this book should seem disfigured, with respect to that of the Standard Edition and the conceptions deriving from it, is hardly surprising. References to the Standard Edition in this text are given precisely to enable the reader to recognize this disfigurement and to reflect upon it. For it is only in remarking the differences between a Freud who has grown all too familiar and another, less comforting, figure that his legend can regain the uncanny force we have "known" all the time, but of which we think less and less.

I. Psychoanalysis Set Apart

If we wish to do justice to the specificity of the psychic, we must not seek to render it through linear contours, as in a drawing or in primitive painting, but rather through blurred fields of color, as in modern painting. After we have separated, we must permit what we have separated to coalesce once again. Do not be too hard on this initial attempt to make the difficult and elusive domain of the psychic intelligible [anschaulich].

Freud, *New Introductory Lectures*

Going My Way

In the year 1920, Freud, hard-pressed financially in the aftermath of the war, considered writing a series of articles for an American magazine. The title he proposed for the first of them was: "Don't use Psychoanalysis in Polemics."[1] The suggestion was indicative of the importance polemics had assumed for psychoanalysis in the years preceding. The resistance aroused by Freud's thought and practice had begun to assume new forms starting in 1910. Before then, opponents of psychoanalysis had preferred to ignore the new movement rather than to confront it directly. Once psychoanalysis had succeeded in establishing itself to an extent, however, such tactics were no longer sufficient. The turning point can be associated with the founding, on Freud's initiative, of the International Psychoanalytic Association (IPA). Four years later, in 1914, Freud described the factors motivating this initiative as "the favorable reception in America . . . the increasing hostility in the German-speaking countries, and . . . the unforeseen acquisition of support from Zurich" (S.E. 14, 42).[2]

The Psychoanalytic Movement was emerging from its isolation. But with its growth, increasing recognition, and interest there came new problems, some of which Freud hoped to counter with the new Association:

I considered it necessary to form an official association because I feared the abuses to which psychoanalysis would be subjected as soon as it became popular. There should be a headquarters whose business it would be to declare: "All that nonsense has nothing to do with analysis, it is not psychoanalysis." (S.E. 14, 43)

3

Designed to serve as a supreme tribunal, as guardian of the purity and unity of psychoanalysis, the Association was directed less against attacks from without than against attempts to blur the very distinction of *without* and *within*. This border was henceforth to be secured, definitively, by the IPA. At the same time, it also had the task of strengthening the movement from within, both by regulating the training of analysts (i.e., the transition from outside to inside), and by encouraging "friendly communication . . . and mutual support" among members of the movement through regular meetings it was to sponsor (S.E. 14, 44).[3]

The communication that ensued, however, proved to be far from friendly. Instead of a source of "mutual support," the IPA became almost at once a battleground, and thereby demonstrated that the most serious threat to psychoanalysis no longer came exclusively from without but from within. The history of the splits and conflicts that dominated the early years of the IPA, effectively paralyzing it and almost destroying the movement that it had been established to defend, is well known. The question of the significance of those struggles, however, has scarcely been raised, much less explored.

Ernest Jones, chronicler of the movement in which he played a leading part, seeks to explain—or to explain away—those early conflicts by portraying them as a kind of infantile malady, the growing-pains of a precocious science, and as such destined to disappear with increasing maturity. Jones points to the then undeveloped state of analytical training, and above all to the absence or inadequacy of training analyses, as a major factor in causing what he considers to be an essentially individaul problem: the neurotic behavior of certain analysts unable to accept the authority of Freud.[4]

This explanation, however, which echoes that given by Freud himself at the time, is not able to account for what Jones himself considers to be a distinctive feature of psychoanalysis: that, by comparison with other "sciences," analysis has had a particularly difficult time coping with its internal conflicts. Jones traces this problem to the specific kind of "data" with which the "investigation of the unconscious" is concerned, and which, he argues, is especially prone to reinterpretation "in terms of some personal prejudice."[5] *Why* this should be so, however, and whether it might not point to structural peculiarities that distinguish psychoanalysis from natural science—or perhaps from "science" as such—is a question that Jones himself does not pursue. Nevertheless, the possibility that the dissensions that arose immediately following the initial attempt to *institutionalize* the psychoanalytic 'movement' might have been a product of this movement itself, rather than merely a result of individual deficiencies and of collective immaturity, is one that demands investigation.[6]

But before we begin to explore this question, let us briefly recapitulate the pertinent events. One year after the founding of the IPA, in 1911, Alfred Adler, who had been Freud's choice to succeed him at the head of the Viennese Group, resigned and established a "Society for Free Psychoanalysis." The next year, Wilhelm Stekel, who had been editor of the *Zentralblatt für Psychoanalyse*, official organ of the IPA, defected from the movement. Finally, 1913 saw the irreparable break with Jung, first president of the Association and designated successor of Freud. The loss of Jung, upon whom Freud had hoped to "transfer" his own authority, can therefore be described as the first critical case of "negative transference" affecting not simply individuals, but the institutions of psychoanalysis.

If, however, the use of such a term can be justified here, "outside" of the analytical situation qua therapy, it is not merely because Freud himself resorts to the word in describing his relation to the defectors, Adler and Jung.[7] Far more significant is that his description situates that conflict squarely within the force-field of transference, inasmuch as it was determined, Freud argued, by unconscious factors. In discussing that process, (in the *History of the Psychoanalytic Movement*, S.E. 14), however, Freud curiously reverses the usual distribution of roles: unlike the situation in analysis, here it is the transferring subject—Freud himself—who is said to act voluntarily and consciously, whereas those who are the 'objects' of the transfer, Adler and Jung, are described as being constrained by unconscious motivations. "Incapable of tolerating the authority of another," Freud writes, Jung was "still less capable of wielding it himself" (S.E. 14, 43). The force of the unconscious, by implication, manifests itself here not in the act of transferring, but in the refusal to accept what is being transferred. The most obvious effect of such a refusal is to call into question both the transferring subject and the subject of the transference: Freud and his authority.[8] The founder of psychoanalysis did not underestimate the seriousness of this challenge, one which no longer could be ascribed to uninformed outsiders. Nonetheless, he hoped to avoid an open confrontation. Shortly before the break with the Zurich group he wrote to Ferenczi:

We possess the truth; I am as sure of it as fifteen years ago. . . . I have never taken part in polemics. My habit is to repudiate in silence and go my own way.[9]

And indeed, had Freud's way been as straightforward as such a statement implies, there would have been no need for him to engage in polemics or otherwise take notice of former adherents who had now strayed from the way. However, in the eyes of the uninitiated at least—and perhaps not only in theirs—the defections of such eminent persons as Adler and Jung suggested that a variety of ways might be possible, each with a claim on the truth. Confronted with this situation, Freud could hardly avoid defending the legitimacy of *his* way, and thus performing the function that the IPA had originally been created to fulfill, that of laying down the law as to what deserved to be called psychoanalysis, and what did not. This task thus fell to Freud, and his *History* was the result:

Although it is a long time now since I was the only psychoanalyst, I consider myself justified in maintaining that even today no one can know better than I do what psychoanalysis is, how it differs from other ways of investigating the life of the mind, and precisely what should be called psychoanalysis and what would better be described by some other name. (S.E. 14, 7)

Where the name of psychoanalysis is at stake, who but its founder and father can decide what merits it and what does not? And yet, Freud's defense of that name is more vulnerable than his position might lead one to suspect. For the good name of psychoanalysis can be defended only to the extent that it permits itself to be defended. It is precisely here that difficulties arise. Psychoanalysis, although a theory of conflict, is according to Freud itself a most unsuitable medium of conflict:

Analysis is not suited, however, to polemical use; it presupposes the consent of the person who is being analyzed and a situation in which there is a superior and a subordinate. Anyone, therefore, who undertakes an analysis for polemical purposes must expect the person analyzed to use analysis against him in turn, so that the discussion will reach a state which entirely excludes the possibility of convincing any impartial third person. (S.E. 14, 49)

Such considerations lead Freud to restrict his objectives in dealing with the renegades: he will, he asserts, seek neither to analyze them as individuals nor to pass judgment upon the inherent quality of their ideas, but instead merely "to show how their theories controvert the fundamental principles of analysis (and on what points they controvert them) and that for this reason they should not be known by the name of analysis" (S.E. 14, 50).

Although Freud makes this assertion at the outset of the polemical third section of his *History*, what he then goes on to do is precisely what he declared he would avoid: personal analysis of his opponents and evaluation of the intrinsic validity of their ideas. In itself, this turnabout is hardly surprising; polemical demarcation inevitably includes devaluation, since the affirmation of difference is rarely separable from the assertion that the other position is inferior to one's own. What distinguishes Freud's polemics, however, is that such affirmations are neither simple nor clear cut, and that they do not have the last word. The arguments that he introduces in order to disqualify the "secessions"--the German word *Abfallsbewegungen* is far more suggestive than this translation would imply—fall back (*fällt ab*, or *zurück*) on what they were intended to set off, elevate, and protect: upon psychoanalysis itself. Psychoanalysis is thereby first tainted, and then drawn into a confrontation it had sought to avoid, one in which the fronts become increasingly blurred, until one begins to wonder what exactly psychoanalysis is—or where it is going.

A Problem of Narcissism

The condemnation of heresy implies the affirmation of orthodoxy. To say what psychoanalysis is *not*, Freud must state what it *is*. He therefore begins his polemics against Adler and Jung by naming the three essential positions of psychoanalytical doctrine, which, he asserts, his former followers have abandoned. The theories Freud mentions are that "of repression, of the sexual motive forces in neurosis, and of the unconscious" (S.E. 14, 50). Having thus established the indispensable foundations of psychoanalysis, Freud then goes on to demonstrate exactly how the two renegades diverge from it. What emerges in the ensuing discussion is that their departure from psychoanalysis is not limited to individual points of doctrine but rather involves something much more fundamental: the very mode of thinking that produces theoretical insight. Psychoanalysis, Freud asserts, has "never claimed to provide a complete theory of human mentality in general" (S.E. 14, 50), and this deliberate, self-imposed limitation distinguishes it profoundly from the theories of its former adherents. The case of Adler being the more straightforward of the two, Freud begins with it:

The Adlerian theory was from the very beginning a 'system'—which psychoanalysis was careful to avoid becoming. It is also a remarkably good example of 'secondary revision,' such as occurs, for instance, in the process to which dream-material is submitted by the action of waking thought. In Adler's case the place of the dream-material is taken by the new material obtained through psychoanalytic studies; this is then viewed purely from the standpoint of the ego, reduced to the categories with which the ego is familiar, translated, twisted and

8

—exactly as happens in dream-formation—misunderstood. Moreover, the Adlerian theory is characterized less by what it asserts than by what it denies. (S.E. 14, 50)

Freud thus invokes the psychoanalytic theory of dreams to criticize, and ultimately to disqualify, Adler, whose thought is equated with the "secondary revision" of the dream, designed to distort its true significance. Adler, despite—or rather because—of his claims to provide a general theory, a system, can be all the more easily incorporated and comprehended by psychoanalysis. The latter, precisely because it seems to "know" its own limits, Freud implies, can absorb and account for the Adlerian "system," assimilating what little it may have of value, and eliminating the rest. Such elimination is no more than befits what Freud constantly refers to as an *Abfallsbewegung*: the word signifies not merely a falling-away, a deviation from the right path of psychoanalysis, but also a movement of waste products. The scatological connotation is, moreover, anticipated by the epigraph, from Goethe's *Faust*, that Freud uses to introduce this third section: "Mach es kurz! Am Jüngsten Tag ist's nur ein Furz!" (roughly translated: "Be short and tart! Come Judgment Day it won't be but a fart!")

But the process of absorption and of elimination proved to be less simple than Freud had anticipated, as can be adduced from a remark he made. In 1932, many years after Adler and psychoanalysis had parted company, Freud noted that Adler's psychology still managed to lead "a kind of parasitic existence . . . at the expense of psychoanalysis" (S.E. 22, 140). That even a parasite cannot thrive without a certain complicity of its "host" was an aspect of the matter Freud preferred not to consider. It is surely significant, however, that in one of his last writings, "Analysis Terminable and Interminable," he concluded not merely with a reference to what he called the "rock of castration," but with an allusion to the Adlerian theory of "masculine protest," which he had condemned so emphatically years earlier.[10]

Such a continuing fascination on Freud's part is all the more remarkable in view of the specific charge he directs at Adler. For to assert that a theory functions in the manner of *secondary revision* is not merely to maintain that it does not know what it is talking about (serious enough for a theoretical discourse), but even worse, that it is designed to keep others from knowing. "Secondary revision" names not merely ignorance, but a strategy of dissimulation and deception; and we need only turn to *The Interpretation of Dreams*, where Freud first discusses the term, to discover how and why.

Freud introduces the notion in the context of his chapter on the "dream-work," as the fourth mechanism of symbolization by which the dream both articulates and conceals conflictual desires. In contrast to the three other procedures, however—condensation, displacement, and considerations of representability (*Rücksicht auf Darstellbarkeit* —a term which would be better rendered as "scenic staging")—secondary elaboration or revision, although essential to the dream, is in no way peculiar to unconscious activity. On the contrary, it involves "a psychic function which is indistinguishable from our waking thoughts" (S.E. 5, 489). It is by virtue of this very familiarity that it can accomplish its task in the dream-work: that of producing a semblance of rationality, a specious intelligibility designed to conceal the dissimulation of the dream, and thus to render it acceptable to consciousness. Through secondary elaboration, the elements of the dream "appear to have a meaning, but that meaning is as far removed as possible from their true significance." (S.E. 5, 490)

Secondary elaboration thus is described as a process of interpretation, essentially unconscious, designed to throw the dreamer off the track by reorganizing and presenting its material in a manner that seems to conform to the logical and rational expectations of the waking mind. The result is that precisely those dreams that seem most coherent and transparent are in reality the most deceptive:

If we analyze them, we can convince ourselves that it is in these dreams that the secondary elaboration has played most freely with the material and has least retained the relations inherent in them. Such dreams might be said to have been already interpreted once, before being submitted to waking interpretation. (*Ibid.*)

If this mechanism is attributed to the "censoring agency, whose influence we have hitherto recognized only in limitations and omissions in the dream-content," here a new, more positive role of the censor becomes apparent. Through secondary elaboration it produces "interpolations and additions," (S.E. 5, 489) and such effects are described by Freud as a continuation of conscious thought:

Our waking (preconscious) thinking behaves toward any perceptual material with which it is confronted in just the same way in which the function we are considering behaves toward the content of dreams. It is the nature of our waking thought to establish order in material of that kind, to set up relations in it and to make it conform to our expectations of an intelligible whole. In fact, we go too far in that direction. An adept in sleight-of-hand can trick us by relying upon this intellectual habit of ours. In our efforts at making an intelligible pattern of the sense-impressions that are offered to us, we often fall into the strangest errors or even falsify the truth about the material before us. (S.E. 5, 499)

The first example that Freud cites of such a tendency involves reading:

In our reading we pass over misprints which destroy the sense, and have the illusion that what we are reading is correct. (*Ibid.*)

It is just this desire to make sense out of what we see that provides the condition of possibility for the trompe-l'oeil of secondary elaboration: our waking mind is so eager to find meaning that it will readily ignore absurdities to get at what seems to be sensible. Such credulousness, Freud insists, is not limited to particularly gullible individuals: it is a characteristic of waking thought as such, which thus opens the way to the "tendentious revision" of secondary elaboration.

Freud's use of the word "tendentious" here anticipates his study of jokes, which he will divide into the two basic categories of "harmless" and "tendentious." But the affinity between secondary elaboration and jokes goes further than the aggressive intent shared by both. What is significant is that such aggression is in both cases linked to the manner in which the unconscious enlists the support of rational thought to impose its own ends. The Witz, like secondary elaboration, is made possible by "expectations of an intelligible whole." I will have occasion to return to this point in more detail later, in discussing Freud's theory of jokes. Here, I want only to call attention to the way in which Freud describes the operation of secondary elaboration as a kind of joke played by the unconscious against, or at the expense of, consciousness:

If I look around for something with which to compare the final form assumed by a dream as it appears after normal thought has made its contribution, I can think of nothing better than the enigmatic inscriptions with which the *Fliegende Blätter* [*Drifting Leaves*, a humoristic magazine] has for so long entertained its readers. They are designed to make the reader believe that a certain sentence — for the sake of contrast, a sentence in dialect and as scurrilous as possible — is a Latin inscription. For this purpose the letters contained in the words are torn out of their contexts, reduced to syllables and arranged in a new order. Here and there a genuine Latin word appears; at other points we seem to see abbreviations of Latin words before us; at still other points in the inscription we may allow ourselves to be deceived into overlooking the senselessness of isolated letters by assuming them to be defaced or fragmentary. If we are to avoid being taken in by the joke [*wenn wir dem Scherze nicht aufsitzen wollen*], we must disregard everything that makes it seem like an inscription, look firmly at the letters, pay no attention to their ostensible arrangement, and so combine them into words belonging to our own mother-tongue. (S.E. 5, 500-1)

To read the dream, we must resist the habit of "making sense" in terms of the given sequence; instead, we must be prepared to analyze, to decompose the apparent units into the individual, component letters, in order then to rearrange them into a language that, though it is less familiar, can nonetheless be compared with "our mother-tongue." Such a process of reading presupposes that the readiness to play with language is strong enough to check the desire to recognize the familiar (the pseudo-Latin of the "inscription"), and thus to accede directly to meaning.

This desire—which presents the major obstacle to dream-interpretation—is, according to Freud, characteristic of a category of persons who are therefore almost by definition destined to "fall" for such jests (*dem Scherze . . . aufsitzen*): *philosophers*. The philosopher, Freud notes, citing Heine, seeks to fill "the holes in the cosmic plan . . . with the bits and bonnets of his pyjamas, just as secondary elaboration fills in "the gaps in the dream-structure." (S.E. 5, 490) In its propensity to become the ideal "fall guy" for the ruse of secondary elaboration, philosophy reveals itself to be less the love of wisdom than the *fear* of it: *phobosophie*.

This characterization of philosophy, or of a certain form of rationalistic thinking, receives renewed attention in *Totem and Taboo*, where Freud once again takes up his discussion of secondary revision. In the context of his description of "animism" as "the first complete theory of the universe" (S.E. 13, 94), Freud uses the notion of secondary revision to explain the implications of such systematic thinking from the perspective of psychoanalysis.

The secondary revision of the product of dream-activity is an admirable example of the nature and pretensions of a system. There is an intellectual function in us which demands unity, connection and intelligibility from any material, whether of perception or thought, that comes within its grasp; and if, as a result of special circumstances, it is unable to establish a true connection, it does not hesitate to fabricate a false one. (S.E. 13, 95)

By comparison with his use of the notion in the *Interpretation of Dreams*, Freud has considerably extended the scope of secondary revision. Its dissimulating function now appears to be no longer restricted to the dream-work, but rather to characterize systematic thinking in general. Such an extension, however, raises a new question: if in the dream secondary revision operates under the influence of the censoring agency, itself a function of the conflicts involved in the dream-wish, what is the equivalent of the censor operating in conscious, systematic thought? "There is an intellectual function in us which demands unity," Freud asserts, but in so doing he only displaces the question. For how can a "function" *demand*? With what resources? Or, more precisely: under what conditions can such an "intellectual function" acquire the *force* to make demands, and the *power* to impose them?

Although this question is never made explicit in *Totem and Taboo*, Freud's discussion of animism is informed by it, and offers a partial response. What makes animism not merely a phylogenetic forerunner of systematic thinking, but rather its paradigm, is its tendency "to grasp the whole universe as a single unity from a single point of view" (S.E. 13, 77), its effort to "explain the essence of the universe entirely." (*Ibid.*) Unity and totality are the categories informing animism, and they make it the model of all systematic thinking: everything must be assimilated, with nothing left over or outside.

This all-embracing, comprehensive quality of animistic thought points to its psychological correlative: narcissism. At the time he wrote *Totem and Taboo*, Freud still construed narcissism largely as a genetic phenomenon, rather than in the more structural terms of his later theory. Freud consequently describes narcissism as a period, in which

The hitherto isolated sexual drives have already come together into a single whole and have also found an object. But this object is not an external one, extraneous to the subject, but is its own ego, which has been constituted at about this same time. (S.E. 13, 89)

The animistic attempt to comprehend the external world in terms of unity and totality corresponds to the newly formed unity within the psyche: the narcissistic ego. The single point of view and the all-embracing comprehension it permits thus reflect the composite unity of the ego. And since "this narcissistic organization is never wholly abandoned"; since "a human being remains to some extent narcissistic even after he has found external objects for his libido," there is no reason to assume that animism, like narcissism, will not persist, in the history of peoples no less than in that of individuals. One of the forms in which this occurs appears to be precisely systematic thought.

If, then, that "intellectual function" which demands "unity, connection, and intelligibility," is able to impose its demands, the energy it requires to do so seems now to have an identifiable source: the libidinally cathected, narcissistic ego. Systematic thought organizes the world in the image of this psychic organization. The intellectual construct we call a "system" reveals itself to be narcissistic, in its origin no less than in its structure: *speculative*, in the etymological sense, as a mirror-image of the ego, and 'phobosophie' as well. If it is driven to fill in the "gaps and cracks" in the edifice of the universe, the fissures it fears are much closer to home. The "expectation of an intelligible whole" described by Freud, the expectation of a coherent meaning, appears thus to denote the reaction of an ego seeking to defend its conflict-ridden cohesion against equally endemic centripetal tendencies. The pursuit of meaning; the activity of construction, synthesis, unification; the incapacity to admit anything irreducibly alien, to leave any residue unexplained—all this indicates the struggle of the ego to establish and to maintain an identity that is all the more precarious and vulnerable to the extent that it depends on what it must exclude. In short, speculative, systematic thinking draws its force from the effort of the ego to appropriate an exteriority of which, as Freud will later put it, it is only the "organized part."[11]

Returning now to Freud's assessment of Adler, we will no longer be puzzled to find what otherwise might be considered a simple contradiction: the characterization of Adler as possessed of "unusual ability, combined with a particularly speculative disposition," on the one hand, and yet as having only a mediocre "gift . . . for judging unconscious material" on the other (*History*, p. 50). For speculation, which Freud associates with narcissism, systematization, and secondary revision, would be a form of thought ill-suited to "judge unconscious material" inasmuch as it is driven precisely to deny the influence of its own unconscious. This, at least, is the essence of the verdict that Freud pronounces on Adler and Jung. The implication of this position is, inescapably, that genuine psychoanalysis stands in the same relation to its Abfallsbewegungen as does the unconscious to secondary revision: the latter is fully controlled by the former, which it serves precisely by obscuring.

But just how far can we take this analogy? Can we conclude that the renegades of psychoanalysis not only conceal their veritable dependency on it—as Freud asserts—but that in so doing they also serve its interests (which Freud would obviously have denied)? This would imply that, as with the unconscious, the interests of psychoanalysis, as an institution, would depend upon a certain kind of self-dissimulation, just as the dream, to fulfill its function, must dissimulate *both* its true nature, and also *that* it so dissimulates. In view of the fact that psychoanalysis entails both a practice and a theory, how are these to be construed if their condition of possibility entails such a double dissimulation?

Such questions—however sophistic they may seem—are difficult to avoid inasmuch as Freud refers to the unconscious in order to establish the authority of psychoanalysis over and against its competitors. It is only by speaking in the name of the unconscious that psychoanalysis can claim such authority, and concomitantly qualify the doctrines of Adler and Jung as theoretical versions of "secondary revision"—that is, as a form of pseudo-rationality that in fact does not really know what it is talking about. But if the theories of Adler and Jung are examples of secondary revision, what about those of Freud himself? Can the theoretical effort of psychoanalysis to conceive and to articulate the unconscious and its effects be free of the narcissistic tendencies Freud attributes to all systematic thought? Is Freud's assertion that psychoanalysis never claimed to be a *Weltanschauung* sufficient to exempt it from the traps that seem to beset all rational explanation and theorization, inasmuch as any theory must rely on systematic comprehension?

One way of pursuing this problem — and it is one that will concern us throughout this book — is to shift our attention for a moment from the general critique under which Freud subsumes both of his adversaries, to the manner in which he distinguishes their two systems. For despite his polemics, Freud insists that there is an important difference between Adler and Jung, and he makes no secret of his preferences.

Of the two movements under discussion, Adler's is indubitably the more important; while radically false, it is marked by consistency and coherence. It is moreover, in spite of everything, founded upon a theory of drives. Jung's modification, on the other hand, loosens the connection . . . with instinctual life [*Triebleben*]; and furthermore . . . is so obscure, unintelligible and confused as to make it difficult to take up any position towards it. Wherever one lays hold of it, one must be prepared to hear that one has misunderstood it; one is thus at a loss to know how it should be properly understood. It presents itself in a peculiarly vacillating manner [*Sie stellt sich selbst in eigentümlich schwankender Weise vor.*] (*Ibid.*, p. 60).[12]

Freud's comparison of the two theories leads him to a curious conclusion: he condemns Adler for being excessively systematic (i.e., narcissistic) but finds Jung even worse for being insufficiently so. Adler, he argues, is at least "radically false," but Jung is not even that: his doctrine is so elusive, so *schwankend*, that it is difficult to pin down at all. If, then, a modicum of coherence, consistency, and systematicity is indispensable to a theory, the question remains: how much? or perhaps, also, of what kind?

That Freud eschewed confronting such questions head-on is well known. After the previous discussion, the reasons for his reluctance may be more understandable. One of the rare occasions when he does address this question occurs in *The Interpretation of Dreams* where — almost parenthetically and in passing — he risks a succinct definition of what a theory should be:

A proposition [*eine Aussage*] concerning dreams, which seeks to explain as many as possible of their observed characteristics from a particular point of view, and which at the same time defines the position occupied by dreams in a wider sphere of phenomena, may be called a dream-theory. (S.E. 4, 75)

To qualify as a theory, an explanation must be inclusive, comprehensive, generalizable: in short, systematic. And the point of departure for such explanation must consist in observations made from a particular "point of view." But can such a point of view avoid becoming just what Freud condemns in others: a standpoint of the ego? To what extent can theory escape the self-deception constitutive of narcissism? These are the questions posed by Freud's polemics, and their addressee is not merely the "Abfallsbewegungen," but psychoanalysis as well.

Observation, Description, Figurative Language

If Freud rejects the Adlerian notion of "masculine protest," it is because he considers the latter to take for granted what in fact can be properly understood only in relation to the context out of which it emerges: the ego. Far from considering the ego to be the basis on which a psychology can be founded, Freud regards it as a "composite entity" (*zusammengesetzte Einheit*), derived from and dependent on processes that transcend its domain and demand intensive investigation. In his essay on Narcissism—which in certain regards develops his critique of Adler—Freud emphasizes that

it is impossible to suppose that a unity comparable to the ego can exist in the individual from the very start; the ego has to develop. (S.E. 14, 77)

The history of this development is inseparable from the dynamics of narcissism, and from the libidinal conflicts to which it responds. Adler's notion of "masculine protest" as the motor of psychic development *presupposes* a sexually differentiated subject already endowed with an identity to be defended. If the Freudian notion of narcissism located the conflict *within* the subject, and ultimately within the ego itself, the idea of "masculine protest" situates it *between* the ego and the other. This presupposition of an originally constituted ego or self is what Freud criticizes in the following passage:

Psychoanalytic research has, from the very beginning, recognized the existence and significance of the "masculine protest" but has always regarded it, in opposition to Adler, as narcissistic in nature and derived from the castration complex.

17

It appertains to the formation of character, into the genesis of which it enters along with many other factors, and it is completely inadequate to explain the problems of the neuroses, in which Adler will take account of nothing but the manner in which they serve the interests of the ego (S.E. 14, 92)

For Freud, what is involved here is not merely a difference in conception, but also a difference in the very mode of theoretical construction. He seeks to elucidate this difference by recourse to a highly significant example:

Let us consider one of the fundamental situations in which desire is felt in infancy: that of a child observing the sexual act between adults. Analysis shows, in the case of persons with whose life-history the physician will later be concerned, that at such moments two impulses take possession of the immature [unmündigen] spectator. Where the latter is a boy, one is the impulse to put himself in the place of the active man, while the other, the opposing tendency, is the impulse to identify with the passive woman. Between them these two impulses exhaust the pleasurable possibilities of the situation. Only the first can be assimilated to the 'masculine protest,' if that concept is to retain any meaning whatsoever. The second . . . Adler disregards . . . he takes account only of those impulses that are agreeable to the ego and are encouraged by it. (S.E. 14, 54)

For Freud, the situation of the subject in the primal scene is characterized by a constitutive disunity: the child is impelled by its desire in two different and mutually exclusive directions. The point of departure is a conflictual position, to which the ego will attempt to respond. But its identity and unity will, for Freud, always be marked and structured by the disunity it seeks to organize.

Adler, Freud argues, will acknowledge only the one striving, the tendency to identify with the "active man." Instead of being defined as the product of a conflictual desire, the Adlerian subject confronts the conflict as a threat from without, against which it protests. That the subject fears what it desires and desires what it fears; that it would seek to be in two places at once, or perhaps in three, is a conception that has no place in Adler's theory, which presupposes an originally unified subject. At the same time, such a unity would also characterize the viewpoint of the theory that situates itself with regard to this subject: the unity implicit in the notion of "masculine protest" would be that of the theory it seeks to found. As theoretical construct and object, the notion of "masculine protest" endows the Adlerian theory with a firm, stable viewpoint. It is this that Freud criticizes as the "standpoint" of the ego: a point on which the subject—ultimately, the theoretical subject—can take its stand.

In this sense, the Adlerian theory implies not simply the abandonment of one or more psychoanalytical notions, but also, perhaps more important, the inability to sustain a mode of thought that seeks to articulate complex, conflictual processes without the aid of an original, founding, and unifying point of reference. Since the identity of a theory is determined by the objects it constructs, that of psychoanalysis must be prepared to recognize the dynamics of conflict it seeks to delineate as part of its own movement as well.

If, for psychoanalysis, the identity of the subject is no longer an original or ultimate point of reference, but rather—as the "ego"—a highly ambivalent, more or less precarious 'compromise formation,' the resultant of a conflict of forces that it seeks to organize but can never fully control, then the theory that endeavors to articulate this state of affairs will itself be no less precarious or ambivalent. For, like the ego itself, it will be unable to define itself in terms of a fixed, undivided and transcendent point of view. To assume such a standpoint, as Adler attempts with his notion of masculine protest, is to condemn oneself to systematic self-deception; deception by virtue of the presupposition of Self and of System. Freud elucidates this deception by referring to another scene, and another spectacle, although one not unrelated to the *Urszene* we have just encountered:

The ego here plays the ludicrous part of the clown in the circus, who, by his gestures, tries to convince the audience that every change in the circus ring is being executed in response to his command. But only the most youthful in the audience are taken in. (S.E. 14, 53)

The clown—in German, "der dumme August"—is Adler's theory, which, like the ego it posits, pretends to control the show in which it in fact plays only a modest role. Yet that role consists precisely in the mimicry Freud describes. Which explains why the ego is the site both of cognition and of illusion, and why the one is difficult to separate from the other. If a distinction is possible—and this is, of course, the necessary premise of any theory, including that of Freud —it can be only by an effort of reflection that takes the topography of the scene into account. The distinctive feature of that topography is that it can never be fully, exhaustively seen: just as the clown is part of the show, so too is the audience. If its most youthful members allow themselves to be taken in by the clown, it is because of their reluctance to be taken in by the spectacle itself. And, as the Urszene demonstrates, the ego of the child has a legitimate interest in keeping its distance.

But that distance can only be specious, since the "circus ring" is merely another figure of that "other scene" as which Freud described the unconscious. And in the theater of the unconscious, there are no simple objects to be seen, as Freud makes clear in regard to the dream, that most "visual" of all unconscious articulations:

The dream-phantasy does not stop at the mere representation of an object; it is intrinsically compelled to involve the dream-ego in what it represents, thus producing an action or plot [*Handlung*]. For instance, a dream caused by a visual stimulus may represent gold coins in the street; the dreamer will pick them up delightedly and carry them off. (S.E. 14, 53)

The dream may represent the dreamer absconding with the loot, but in so doing it has simultaneously represented the basic situation of all dreaming: the loot is a lure to draw the dreamer out and into the dream. The result is that all objects and incidents represented in the dream become "Handlung"—not merely "events," but also and more importantly: stories, scenarios, plot. And if the ego of the dreamer is a participant, an actor, the role it plays is not of its own making. This role is rarely a simple one: the ego may be represented in various figures of the dream. But the ego's performance goes beyond the represented content of the dream to include the process of representation itself: *the narration of the dream*. Contrary to expectations of common sense, the narration does not merely represent a dream that in some sense is already present-to-itself; the dream only comes to be in and through a process of narration that Freud significantly labels not *Darstellung* (presentation), but *Entstellung*: distortion, dislocation, disfigurement. If such distorted articulation can be "true" to the dream, it is only because the latter is already a process of distortion, Entstellung. The distance that separates narration from narrated, like that which separates spectator from spectacle, is not an empty interval, not the space of Darstellung but of Entstellung. It is, in short, a space on the move.

What room does this space leave for theory—for a theory that rejects the specious security of the "standpoint of the ego"? We return to Freud's critique of Adler in search of an answer:

The system is complete; to produce it has cost an enormous amount of labor in the recasting of interpretations, while it has not yielded a single new observation. I fancy I have made it clear that it has nothing to do with psychoanalysis. (*History*, pp. 57-58)

The category that Freud invokes here—as in the passage cited earlier from the *Interpretation of Dreams*—to characterize an authentic theory, is: observation, *Beobachtung*. The narcissism of speculative, systematic theories, Freud insists again and again, is manifest in the poverty of their observations. For Adler, Freud asserts, "observation has served merely as a springboard, to be used for elevation and then foresaken" (*History*, p. 54). Similarly, Jung, "in order to preserve [his] system intact," finds it necessary to turn entirely away from observation and from the technique of psychoanalysis." (*History*, pp. 62-63) "From observation and from the technique of psychoanalysis"—are they then one and the same?

Freud, at least, seemed often to think so. In his essay *On Narcissism*—a text that bears the marks of his polemical separation from Adler and Jung—Freud emphasized the significance of observation for psychoanalysis in a highly programmatic manner:

Conceptions such as that of an ego-libido, ego-drive energy [*Ich-Triebenergie*], etc. are neither particularly clear nor sufficiently differentiated [*inhaltsreich genug*]; a speculative theory of the relations involved would first and foremost want to establish a sharply defined concept as its basis. But in my opinion this is precisely the difference between a speculative theory and a science constructed upon the interpretation of empirical data [*Deutung der Empirie*]. The latter will not envy speculation its privilege of a smooth, logically unassailable foundation, but will gladly settle for nebulously elusive, barely imaginable basic conceptions [*kaum vorstellbaren Grundgedanken*], which it hopes to apprehend more clearly in the course of its development, but which it is also prepared to replace if need be. For it is not these ideas which are the foundation upon which everything rests, but rather observation, and nothing else. [*dies ist allein die Beobachtung*]. (S.E. 14, 77)

The claim that Freud appears to make for observation: that it and it alone provides science with its "foundation" and distinguishes it from speculative forms of thought—seems clear and unequivocal enough. And yet here as elsewhere, an attentive reading of Freud's *text* reveals the assertions it contains to be more complex than they seem at first sight. And indeed, the basic problem circumscribed here is precisely the question of "first sight". For if Freud opposed observation to speculation, it is not in the name of an immediacy of perception, a notion that everything in psychoanalysis would tend to exclude. Thus, whereas Freud insists that "observation alone" must be the foundation of scientific thought, the science he describes is "constructed upon the *interpretation* of empirical data." The problem, then, becomes that of specifying the relation between observation, on the one hand, and interpretation on the other.

In a late text—the *Outline of Psychoanalysis*, written in 1938—Freud returns to this question, while endeavoring to describe the kind of observation peculiar to psychoanalysis:

All sciences are based upon observation and experiences which are medated by our psychic apparatus. Since, however, our science has just this apparatus as its object, the analogy ends there. We form our observations by means of the very same perceptual apparatus, precisely with the help of gaps in the psyche, by supplementing what has been left out with conclusions that lie close at hand, translating the omissions into conscious material. (S.E. 23, 159)

It might seem here, again at first sight, that Freud seeks to derive the specificity of psychoanalytical observation solely from the fact that its object is defined negatively rather than positively, as "gaps in the psyche." This would not be entirely wrong. Yet a closer reading of Freud's text reveals something more: if analytic observation depends on "the very same perceptual apparatus" and on "the help of gaps in the psyche," such gaps (*Lücken*) must be as much a part of the observer as of the observed. And this applies not merely to the observer considered as an individual, but to the process of analytic observation itself. If it is important to stress this difference, it is because what is at stake here is not merely the fallibility of psychoanalysts as individuals, but the possibility of a new conception of "science" in which such fallibility—the effects of the unconscious—would play a constitutive part.

Certain formulations in the passage cited tend to obscure this distinction: Freud writes as though analysts, like the philosophers of Heine's poem, could hope to fill the "gaps" of the universe with "conclusions that lie close at hand" (*durch naheliegende Schlussfolgerungen ergänzen*), and thus to achieve a perfect "translation" of unconscious into conscious "material" (*es in bewusstes Material übersetzen*). But if such conclusions lie "close at hand," the question remains: *whose* hand? Is this hand any less marked by the "gaps" of the unconscious than the perceptual apparatus itself?

In any event the problem Freud describes is more suggestive, more forceful, than the solution he appears to offer. In the absence of further qualification, his allusion to "naheliegende Schlussfolgerungen" can refer only to that most immediate but least reliable of psychic agencies: the (narcissistic) ego. It is this ego, in fact, that is responsible for the production of the very earliest theories, the "infantile sexual theories," in which, for the first time, desire takes the form of the "urge to know," the *Wisstrieb*.

An example: for the child, nothing seems more obvious, *näherliegend*, than the fact that all adults should be endowed with a penis. And hence, nothing is more justified than for the child to reinterpret observed material in the light of this expectation:

The little boy undoubtedly perceives the distinction between men and women, but to begin with he has no occasion to connect it with any difference in the genitals. It is natural for him to assume that all living beings, persons and animals, possess a genital organ like his own . . . This part of the body . . . never ceases to provide new problems for his investigative drive [*Forschertrieb*]. He wants to see the same thing in other people, so as to compare it with his own. . . . We know how such children react to their first perception of the lack of the penis [*Penismangel*]. They deny this lack and believe they see a penis all the same; the contradiction between what they observe and what they expect [*der Widerspruch zwischen Beobachtung und Vorurteil*] is temporized by the notion that the penis is still small and will grow; gradually they come to the conclusion, fraught with emotional consequences, that at least it was there once and then had been removed. The lack of penis is construed to be the result of a castration, and now the child is faced with the task of dealing with the relation of castration to himself [*sich mit der Beziehung der Kastration zu seiner eigenen Person auseinanderzusetzen*]. (S.E. 19, 142-43)

Reading this description of the "castration-complex," one can hardly avoid being struck by what for Freud doubtless seemed an obvious conclusion, so close at hand: that the perception of the female genitals is nothing more or less than that of a Penismangel: that is, an *absence* or *lack* that implicitly installs the penis as the measure of all genitality. "It is natural," Freud asserts, for the boy to make this supposition, and it is no less so for Freud to adjust his terminology accordingly. Indeed, it was only with Melanie Klein that the possibility of other fantasies involving the female body and genitals intruded on Freud's penis-centered perceptual model.[13] Here, then, we have an instance of "conclusions"—those of the child, but also those of Freud, who adopts as it were, the "standpoint" of the male ego— that are ready at hand and yet are nonetheless neither innocent nor unproblematic, for all of their apparent proximity and self-evidence.

But if Freud's account of the development of the castration-complex does little to instill confidence in the notion of "naheliegenden Schlussfolgerungen" as the answer to the epistemological questions raised by psychoanalysis itself, it does allow us to investigate the interaction of observation and interpretation in a situation that is clearly central to the Freudian conception of the subject.

If the child denies the evidence of his observations, this demonstrates the power and primacy of the "expectations" or "prejudices" (*Vorurteile*) that preside over the child's early psychic development. Although Freud designates this Vorurteil as "natural," his description of it anticipates what will later be known as narcissism. The driving impulse of the child is toward *a particular kind of visual experience*: "He wants to see the same thing in other people. . . ." Perceptual recognition, the observation of what is already familiar —"the same thing"—is what the child desires, and this desire is strong enough to bend perceptual "data" to its needs. The development of desire, as Freud describes it in *The Interpretation of Dreams*, is tied not to the perception of objects, but to their hallucination.[14] The decisive modification implied by the "castration complex" is that the deployment of desire implies not merely the production of hallucinations, but their organization into a story. The story of castration attempts to temporize the contradiction between "perception" and "prejudice" by temporalizing it: Once upon a time, there was a penis. . . ."

The "infantile sexual theories" are thus stories the child tells itself to confront the "narcissistic" shock as which Freud always characterizes "castration." the story allows for the Vorurteil that is absolutely constitutive for narcissism, and hence also for the development of the ego: the conviction that the child inhabits a world of "sameness," in which difference and alterity can be regarded merely as privative, negative forms of an original and pervasive identity: as a *Mangel* or *loss* of what once was.[15] But this original identity, which the castration-story seeks to confirm, dialectically as it were, is increasingly subjected to the difference it seeks to deny. The term that Freud uses to designate this process of subjection, which is also the process by which the subject is constituted, is: *Auseinandersetzung*: "and now the child is faced with the task of dealing [*sich auseinandersetzen*] with the relation of castration to himself."

The German verb (*sich*) *auseinandersetzen* is so charged, and so important for Freud's thought, that there seems little choice but to retain it here. In current use it signifies both the act of addressing, dealing with an issue, a problem, or a person (such auseinandersetzen mit . . .) and the kind of polemics Freud practiced in regard to Adler and Jung. Taken more literally, i.e., analyzed into its components (that is, *auseinandergesetzt*), the word designates a process of *decomposition* or analysis that we have already had occasion to encounter at least twice: first, as the kind of reading Freud describes as necessary to decipher the dream (taking apart the speciously meaningful sequence of the dream-text, in order then to recompose it in a different manner); and second, as the *divergent striving* of the child in the Urszene, who literally splits itself apart in order to accomplish the double identification with "active" man and "passive" woman.[16] Between these different meanings a highly complex configuration begins to emerge, in which the postulation (*Setzung*) of identity—be it that of the subject, the object, or of meaning itself—appears increasingly to be the effect of a process of reduplication or of reciprocal separation (*aus-ein-ander*). Such a process seems to necessitate a form of articulation that is inevitably narrative: the "story" that "begins" with the primal scene, and which continues in the denials of difference that constitute "castration," culminates in the Auseinandersetzung with the relation of castration to the developing subject. What seems characteristic of this Auseinandersetzung is precisely its tendency to shift from the hallucination of objects (penis absent or present), to the problem of relations, in which the subject itself is inextricably engaged and set apart. The setting apart of the subject, its Auseinandersetzung, culminates in the relation between ego and superego. This relation marks a turning-point in the "story" or history that leads from the primal scene to castration. For if castration can be considered to embody the ego's narcissistic effort to maintain the fiction of an undivided identity by constructing a narrative in which its heterogeneity assumes the form of a *loss*, the institution of the superego transforms the space in which—or rather, *with* which—the ego has hitherto sought to delimit its relation to alterity. The space of Freud's second topology (of id, ego, and superego) is no longer neutral, empty, or continuous; it is no longer a space in which the ego can confront its nonidentity in the form of an object or a perception, or temporalize that other in the form of a loss. For this space is not one of extension, in which discrete and self-identical entites all occupy fixed and determinable places. Rather, it is a space marked by *overlapping*: the ego only comes to be by setting itself *apart* from the id, as the latter's "organized portion," yet it remains *a part* of the id; similarly, the identity of the ego is no longer merely a function of its own "organization" but rather of its (ambivalent) relation to the superego, which in turn is both heir to the ego's narcissism and product of the id. The ego thus sets itself apart not merely in *opposing* itself to what it is not, but in *dispersing* its Self in conflictual relations to other "agencies" that it can never either fully assimilate or entirely exclude.[17]

If, then, the ego articulates itself by setting its Self apart, the space of this Auseinandersetzung cannot be construed in terms of observation; that is, it can never be observed as such, nor is it compatible with observation conceived as the act of a subject confronting and apprehending an object. Observation, as Freud is well aware, is a function of conflictual desires, and not merely the response or reaction to an object. But if Freud "knows" this, he often "forgets" it, for the simple but compelling reason that such knowledge cannot but affect the status of psychoanalytic cognition itself. If the latter is not grounded in observable data, then Freud's effort to set psychoanalysis apart from the narcissistic theories of Adler and Jung, for instance, becomes immeasurably more complicated and more difficult.

A significant instance of this "forgetting" is provided by the most speculative of Freud's essays, *Beyond the Pleasure Principle*. In that text Freud is constrained to defend his own speculative hypotheses of the repetition-compulsion and the death-drive by distinguishing them from *mere*, that is, merely narcissistic, speculation. This defense takes the form of contrasting his new hypotheses with the earlier ones:

I do not ignore the fact that the third step in the theory of drives, which I take here, cannot lay claim to the same degree of certainty as the two previous ones: the extension of the concept of sexuality and the hypothesis [Aufstellung] of narcissism. These two innovations were *direct translations of observation into theory*, and were no more open to sources of error than is unavoidable in such cases. It is true that my assertion of the regressive character of the drives also rests upon observed material, namely, on the facts of the repetition-compulsion. It may be, however, that I have overestimated their significance. (*Beyond the Pleasure Principle*. New York, Norton Library, 1975, p. 53; my italics.)

If the "third step" that Freud here takes is indeed more speculative and conjectural than the first two, none of the three can be adequately described as "direct translations of observation into theory"; rather, even the first two "translations" entail constructions and concepts that are in no way simply derived from observed data. The description of hysteria as the conversion of conflictual desire into physical symptoms, or the analysis of the dream as dissimulation both involve the *interpretation* of "gaps" in consciousness in which discontinuities are bridged by the construction of concepts designed to explain them (such as "primary" and "secondary" process). However, where the context of his argument is *proleptic*—that is, designed to meet and answer anticipated objections—Freud adopts the convenient strategy of appealing to a conception of observation that his entire approach to the psyche otherwise undermines. For what distinguishes psychoanalysis from science in its more familiar forms is precisely the non-observability of the "phenomena" it addresses:

We need not feel greatly disturbed in judging our speculation upon the life and death drives by the fact that so many bewildering and obscure processes [*befremdende und unanschauliche Vorgänge*] occur in it—such as one drive being driven out by another, or a drive turning from the ego to an object and so on. This is merely due to our being obliged to operate with the scientific terms, that is to say with the figurative language [*Bildersprache*] peculiar to psychology (or more precisely, to depth-psychology). We could not otherwise describe the processes in question at all, and *indeed we could not even have perceived them*. (*Beyond*, p. 54, my italics)

Given the *Unanschaulichkeit* of the processes with which psycho-analysis is concerned, perception—and hence a fortiori "observation"—cannot provide a ground for the "direct translation" of data into theory." Moreover, those processes themselves are invariably described by Freud as consisting in a kind of translation, be it in the sense of an *Übertragung* (transfer) of energy or in that of a displacement of representations. Far from translating observed data into the language of theory, what psychoanalysis actually does, according to Freud, is to transcribe a translation that itself is rendered perceptible, observable, cognizable only through the Bildersprache that repeats and replaces it.

It is inevitable that this characterization of psychoanalytic discourse as a process of Übertragung—transference—cannot but affect the nature of the cognitive insights that are thereby produced:

> The indeterminancy of all our discussions that we call 'metapsychological' is of course due to the fact that we know nothing of the nature of the excitatory process that takes place in the elements of the psychic systems, and that we do not feel justified in framing any hypothesis on the subject. We are consequently operating all the time with a large unknown factor—a capital X—that we are obliged to carry over into every new formula. (*Beyond*, pp. 24-25).

At the heart of psychoanalytical theory, then, is not, as Freud would have us believe, a privileged proximity to observed data, but rather a singular relation of cognition to the unknown, figured and disfigured —*entstellt*—in that "capital X," that here emerges as the *chiasmatic cipher* of the metapsychological Auseinandersetzung itself. For psychoanalytic theory sets itself apart in an ambivalent movement that both disperses itself in categories that overlap and converge with each other, and at the same time projects its constitutive dislocation as an outward movement of heretical divergences, as a "falling away" (Abfallsbewegung) it can then appear to confront and condemn. As we shall see, this is precisely the movement that Freud describes as being that of the ego in repression, symptom-formation, anxiety, and its other defensive strategems. Nor should this surprise us, since description, as we have just read, is a function not so much of the object described as of the Bildersprache that describes it.

Does this not condemn the theoretical discourse of psychoanalysis as tautological? As narcissistic and speculative, in much the same way that Freud criticized in Adler and Jung? The response would be easy to give if the Auseinandersetzung of psychoanalytic metapsychology could be identified as a closed, and self-identical circle. But as we shall try to demonstrate, the movement disfigured by Freud's "capital X" is precisely not circular and hence, impossible to identify, once and for all. The trajectory it follows is also that which it describes: one of *Ent-stellung*, a dislocation that can be retraced and retold, but never comprehended as such. For every effort to determine it—i.e., to recognize it—is inevitably caught up in that ambivalent movement in which "economic," "topical," and "dynamic" perspectives converge, overlap, and set themselves apart in the chiasmatic, noncircular, elliptical Bildersprache of Freud's metapsychology.

To demonstrate the noncircular, nontautological character of this Bildersprache we must turn away from it, for a moment—away from its immediate manifestations, from its formulas and formulations, to one of those "descriptions" that Freud refers to as the "direct translation" of observation into theory. This detour is inevitable for at least two reasons. First, Freud scrupulously avoided developing a systematic and extended reflection upon the language he employed, and he was surely justified in so doing. For such a *reflection* would, by its very nature, have entailed the premise that the figurative language of metapsychology could give way to a metalanguage capable of recognizing its basic rules and procedures. To make this assumption, however, would imply nothing less than the possibility of determining the Bildersprache of metapsychology from the fixed and immovable "standpoint of the ego"—from the vantage-point, that is, of one of its elements or effects. To thematize or objectify metapsychological discourse as such would therefore be to fall prey to the pretensions and pretenses of the ego. By not making this gesture, Freud—at the risk of seeming epistemologically naive—refuses to submit metapsychological discourse to the authority of a reflexive metalanguage. Second and more important, Freud practiced what he did not (want to) preach. He used that Bildersprache to describe a phenomenon that almost looks like its mirror-image. I am referring to his description of the language of the dream as a *Bilderschrift*: a pictorial script, an ideogrammatic text. This script, of course, is precisely *not* a theoretical discourse, in any traditional sense, for rather than seeking to disclose and discover, it is epistemophobic, striving to dissimulate and, moreover, as we have seen, to dissimulate its own dissimulation. In describing this Bilderschrift, Freud was inevitably led to touch on the manner in which that script must be read:

The dream-thoughts are immediately comprehensible, as soon as we have learnt them. The dream-content, on the other hand, is as it were given in a pictographic script [*Bilderschrift*], whose characters [*Zeichen*] must be transposed individually into the language of the dream-thought. If we attempted to read these characters according to their pictorial value instead of according to their semiotic relations [*Zeichenbeziehung*], we should clearly be led into error. . . . A dream is a picture-puzzle. (S.E. 4, 277)

Freud's conception of the dream-language seems structuralist *avant la lettre*: it is not the representational, thematic, "pictorial" content of the dream-signs that determines their "value," but rather their relations to other signs. These "other" signs are, first of all, those represented "in" the dream. But this limit—and in general, the distinction between an *inside* and an *outside* of the dream—will be progressively undermined in the course of Freud's discussion. Before we arrive at this distinctive and decisive aspect of Freud's conception, however, let us first note that the "logic of relations" here described is identical with that already encountered in our discussion of secondary elaboration. To read the dream properly, its manifest sequence must be disregarded, or rather, it must be intensely regarded, but not from the standpoint of its apparent meaning. The meanings represented in the individual ideograms are themselves signifying elements, subordinated to a logic—or rather, a "graphics"—in which the spatial, syntactic relations of the individual signifiers is often determining. The dream, Freud observes,

renders logical connections as simultaneity. . . . Whenever (the dream) shows us two elements close together, one can be certain that there is a particularly intimate [*innigen*] connection in the dream-thoughts that correspond to them. This resembles a system of writing: "ab" means that the two letters are to be pronounced in a single syllable. (S.E. 4, 314)

What characterizes the mode of articulation of the dream is that particularly "intimate" or "inward"—innigen—semantic relations are transcribed into and as "outward" relations of signifiers or graphemes. Meanings, generally regarded as inhering in objects (the objects of consciousness), are literally and graphically *spaced out*, with the result that in the script of the dream it is the syntactic arrangement itself that becomes the bearer of meaning. This applies to the relation of individual signifiers within a single dream no less than to the relation of dreams to each other. But perhaps most important, it also applies to the relation of the dream "itself" to its narration. For, if the dream is itself the result of a retranscription of "thoughts" and wishes existing prior to it, this process continues and culminates in the process of repetition and of dissimulation by which the dream is articulated: the process of its *narration*.

Freud's emphasis on the *synchronic* character of dream-articulation —another striking parallel with structuralist, and above all Saussurean semiotics—includes, however, the very *diachronic* dimension that the Geneva linguist sought to banish from his conception of "la langue." Dream-articulation for Freud is diachronic in two senses: first, the dream reproduces preexisting wish-conflicts by transcribing them into the apparently static synchrony of its Bilderschrift; second, this script only comes to be post facto, as it were, in the narrative discourse of the dreamer recalling and recounting the dream.

The term that Freud uses to describe this process is: Entstellung, signifying, as already mentioned, both *distortion* and *dislocation*. If these two terms generally imply their opposites—that is, an undistorted original, and a proper place—Freud's use of the word explicitly excludes such an implication. It is surely no accident that the passage in which he makes this clear is once again marked by a proleptic anticipation of the Auseinandersetzung his conception is bound to provoke. At the beginning of Chapter Seven of *The Interpretation of Dreams*, Freud addresses possible objections that might be made to his analysis of dreams as elaborated in the first six chapters of the book. One of these is the contention that all of Freud's previous discussion might well be nothing but mere projection of the author, since it is based not on direct contact with the dream itself, but only on testimony after the fact, which is neither reliable nor verifiable. Freud's response is, as it were, to up the ante:

It is true that we distort [entstellen] dreams in attempting to reproduce them; here again we find at work the process that we have described as the secondary (and often misleading) elaboration of the dream by the agency of normal thought. But this distortion [Entstellung] is itself nothing but a part of the elaboration to which the dream-thoughts are regularly subjected as a result of the dream-censorship. (S.E. 5, 514)

By conceding the objection, Freud seeks to deprive it of its critical power. Yes, he admits, the dream-narration is a reproduction, one which inevitably distorts—entstellt—the dream itself. But that dream "itself" is already a distortion, and this is precisely what legitimates the subsequent distortions it undergoes. They are all part of a general process of Entstellung, in which the narrating subject is as much implicated as the dreamer during the dream.

The apparent synchrony of the dream thus tends to become unraveled in the dissimulating diachrony of its narration. In the process, the standpoint of the dreamer as spectator is revealed to be an element of the scene, or rather of the scenario, just as the child is progressively compelled to abandon his position of observer (of the primal scene) and to assume that of story-teller, in "castration." Thus, like the child, the dreamer participates in the story told, but this participation encompasses the telling itself. Narration therefore emerges as the theater in which the dream is both situated and dislocated. In this sense, the synchronic aspect of the dream—which, taken by itself, would like all synchrony, imply the reference to a transcendent standpoint—is caught up and displaced by the narrative that retells it.

When Freud thus replaces the category of Darstellung by that of Entstellung to characterize the dream; when he stresses that it is neither the manifest nor the latent content that constitutes its specificity "as a particular *form* of thinking," but rather the "dreamwork" (i.e., the work of Entstellung) (S.E. 5), he is not merely replacing a false determination of the dream by a true one. For if the dream is constituted by and as Entstellung, this is tantamount to asserting that its limits are determined by a process that itself cannot be free of the very distortion it seeks to define. And a "theory" that seeks to assume this position, it is clear, does not merely provoke Auseinandersetzung from without: it carries it "within," by depriving itself of the traditional basis of theoretical legitimation: the recourse to a given, self-identical, generalizable object.

Short of calling this notion of the object into question, and of elaborating other forms of "legitimation," Freudian thought is indeed caught in a double-bind: its Bildersprache can be successful only by reproducing and continuing the distortions it seeks to describe, as in the case of the Bilderschrift of the dream. Its individual propositions and assertions can function only by the distortions and dislocations they trace, not by what they represent (darstellen). Or rather, the descriptive, cognitive value of its figures depends on the movement of their inscriptions, the style and sequence of their arrangement, and the relations they establish with each other, rather than on the referents they seem to denote. This in turn requires a readiness to read, not in terms of Setzungen (positions or propositions) but in those of an Auseinandersetzung, a movement of conflictual decomposition and recomposition in which that which is posited (*gesetzt*) sets itself apart: that is, both demarcates itself from an other to which it is opposed; and *de-marks* itself by prescribing yet another, third term, which inexorably replaces and displaces the other two.[18] It is the story of this other Auseinandersetzung that must now be retold.

Metapsychology Set Apart

That Freud's "metapsychological" speculations might bear any kind of structural relationship to his polemics against Adler and Jung would at first glance seem itself to be far-fetched speculation. The effort to integrate his observations and descriptions into a larger, theoretical framework—the motivation and purpose of the metapsychology—can be traced back to Freud's earliest analytical writings. The *Project* of 1895 and the seventh chapter of *The Interpretation of Dreams* are elaborate, if preliminary, essays in metapsychology. Moreover, the project of composing a coherent body of theoretical texts under the general title, "Prolegomena to a Metapsychology" (*Zur Vorbereitung einer Metapsychologie*) is first mentioned by Freud in 1915, a year and a half after the break with Jung.

Freud himself certainly would have denied any such connection. Indeed, his overall conception of intellectual and literary endeavor leaves little place for the influence of others:

No one writes to achieve fame, which anyhow is of a very transitory nature, nor for the illusion of immortality. Surely we write first of all to satisfy something within ourselves, not for other people. Of course, when others recognize one's efforts, it increases the inner gratification, but nevertheless we write in the first place for ourselves, following an inner impulse. (Cited in Ernest Jones, Vol. II, p. 397.)

And yet, Freud's entire theoretical effort to articulate the importance of the unconscious belies the clear-cut distinction between "inner impulse" or gratification, and "other people." If the unconscious means anything whatsoever, it is that the relation of self and others, inner and outer, cannot be grasped as an *interval between polar opposites* but rather as an irreducible dislocation of the subject in which the other inhabits the self as its condition of possibility.

Such dislocation is perhaps most evident in Freud's final "topology" of the psyche, and in particular in the relation of ego to superego. The superego defines the aporetic identity of the subject: it represents both the ideal toward which the ego strives, and the interdictory limit it can never attain. As such, the superego embodies the indispensable and irreducible element of alterity, in which both intrapsychic and metapsychic moments converge. "Inner gratification" thus depends on recognition by this instance, which combines both the history of the individual subject and that of the society and culture to which it belongs. If the "something within ourselves" that comprises the addressee of writing is bound up with the superego—and according to this last conception of Freud, it must be—this is tantamount to acknowledging that in writing for "ourselves," we inevitably write for an other that can never be identified with the self, since the latter defines its identity in relation to that other.

If the subject can thus articulate itself only in and through an ambivalent relation to an other that it can neither fully assimilate nor totally exclude, the same holds for the psychoanalytic project itself. To define itself, it must simultaneously set itself apart from what it is not. That such a *setting-apart* is ineluctably haunted by what it seeks to exclude, is particularly striking in regard to Freud's metapsychology, which, he writes, is intended "to clarify and deepen the theoretical assumptions upon which a psychoanalytic system could be based" (S.E.15, 219). Written in 1916, this assertion comes a scant two years after Freud had definitively condemned and excommunicated Adler and Jung from the psychoanalytic movement precisely because their thought was too *systematic*, speculative, and narcissistic. But if the metapsychology is to provide the theoretical foundations for "a psychoanalytic system," will it be any less speculative and narcissistic? If psychoanalysis itself cannot avoid a certain systematicity, it can also not disregard the problems raised by its critique of Adler and Jung. It must therefore demonstrate that its own "translation" of unconscious "material" does not succumb to the same falsifications and reductions it attributes to its competitors. Freud's attempt to establish a basis for this distinction, in the essay intended to inaugurate the series of metapsychological texts, *Drives and their Vicissitudes*, indicates some of the difficulties this entails:

The true beginning of scientific activity consists rather in describing phenomena and then proceeding to group, classify and correlate them. Even at the stage of description it is not possible to avoid applying certain abstract ideas to the materials at hand, ideas derived from various sources and certainly not the fruit of the new experience only. Still more indispensable are such ideas—which will later become the fundamental concepts of the science—as the material is further elaborated. They must at first necessarily possess some measure of uncertainty; there can be no question of any clear delimitation of their contents. So long as they remain in this condition, we come to an understanding about their meaning by repeated references to the material of observation, from which we seem to have drawn our abstract ideas, but which is in point of fact subject to them. (S.E. 14, 117)

This passage, which also serves as a general methodological introduction to the Metapsychology, exemplifies Freud's mode of *thinking* and of *writing*. For the passage is remarkable not simply for what it asserts but perhaps even more so, for the manner in which those assertions are inscribed: read in relation to one another, the individual statements undermine and displace the propositions they advance. Thus, if Freud begins by designating "description" as "the true beginning of scientific activity," he then proceeds to argue that description is never simply a beginning at all, inasmuch as it presupposes always and inevitably, "certain abstract ideas," which themselves derive not solely from experience—from individual experience, that is—but from "various sources."

Far from establishing the "true beginning of scientific activity," then, Freud's text demonstrates that there is no such "true beginning." Instead of a reassuring answer to a familiar question, we are left with a problem: how do those "abstract ideas," drawn from "various sources" and not from individual experience alone, operate? The answer is not to be found in explicit discussions but in Freud's metapsychological "practice" itself: that is, in a style of writing that ineluctably diverges from the propositional content of its individual assertions. The term most apt to designate this dynamic divergence, by which Freud's concepts articulate and disarticulate themselves, is: *Auseinandersetzung.* I shall retrace it at work in three of the most important metapyschological notions: primary and secondary process, repression, and anxiety.

A. Primary and Secondary Process

Freud's effort to articulate the psyche in terms of a *primary* and a *secondary process* is as old as psychoanalytic thought itself. In the *Project* of 1895 Freud distinguishes "primary psychic processes," in which "the wish-cathexis tends towards hallucination, which in turn entails the full development of displeasure and of defense," from "secondary processes," which involve "moderation of the former . . . through correct evaluation of reality-signs," and which "are only possible by virtue of an inhibition of the ego" (*Origins of Psychoanalysis*, New York, 1977, pp. 388-89).

It was not until the seventh chapter of the *Interpretation of Dreams*, however, that Freud attempted to give a comprehensive account of these two psychic processes. This elaboration was inscribed in the train of reasoning that led Freud to the conclusion that "the most complicated achievements of thought are possible without the assistance of consciousness." (S.E.5,593). The theory of primary and secondary processes emerges as an attempt to account for this possibility. The point of departure is Freud's analysis of the dream-work:

It will be seen that the chief characteristic of these processes is that the whole stress is laid upon making the cathecting energy mobile and capable of discharge; the content and the proper meaning of the psychic elements to which the cathexes are attached are treated as being of little consequence (S.E. 5, 597).

Freud's earlier-quoted warning against interpreting the dream-images in terms of their pictorial (or representational) content, rather than by virtue of their relations to one another, finds its objective correlative and explanation in what he designates as the "primary process," that mode of articulation in which "the content and the proper meaning of psychic elements" count less than their capacity to render energy-cathexes "mobile and capable of discharge." Mental energy is tenuously "attached" to a representation, while remaining ready to detach itself if and when tension rises above a certain threshold.

To understand the implications and consequences of the *mobility* of energy-cathexes, which is the distinctive feature of the primary process, it is helpful to recall the manner in which Freud derives this process from what he calls "the exigencies of life" (*die Not des Lebens*). Such exigencies first make themselves felt as the child's "major somatic needs," which—given the helplessness of the infant—only "outside help" can fulfill. Such needs and the alleviation of the tension they produce constitute the first "experiences of satisfaction," when the "internal stimulus" and the unpleasant tensions it engenders have been reduced by external intervention (most often on the part of mother or nurse).

However much Freud begins by stressing the quantitative, energetic, "economic" aspect of this experience of satisfaction, he does not fail to underscore its equally important qualitative side. For it is precisely through this qualitative element that the process ceases to be merely organic or physiological and becomes psychological. Freud links this qualitative side to the operation of perception and of memory:

An essential component of this experience of satisfaction [*Befriedigungserlebnis*] is a particular perception (that of nourishment, in our example), the memory image of which remains associated thenceforward with the memory-trace of the excitation produced by the need. (S.E. 5, 565)

The next time the excitation occurs, the same memory image is produced automatically, through a kind of reflex:

An impulse of this kind [i.e., one that seeks to reproduce the previous perception] is what we call a wish; the reappearance of the perception is the fulfillment of the wish, and the shortest path to the fulfillment of the wish is one leading directly from the excitation produced by the need to a complete cathexis of the perception. Nothing prevents us from assuming that there was a primitive state of the psychic apparatus in which this path was actually traversed, that is, in which wishing ended in hallucination. Thus, the aim of this first psychic activity was to produce a "perceptual identity" [*eine Wahrnehmungsidentität*] —a repetition of the perception linked to the satisfaction of the need. (S.E. 5,566)

This offers a dynamic explanation of why the figurative writing of the dream does not operate with simple, straightfoward images. What Freud here calls the "perceptual identity" is formed from the material of perception, but that material does not function by virtue of what it represents. For its representational, or ideational content— its *Vorstellungsinhalt*—functions only as a sign of something radically different, something that is unrepresentable as such, since it consists of a change in tension, a quantitative, differential alteration in the distribution of energy, producing a qualitative effect: the transition from pain to pleasure. What is decisive in the notion of perceptual identity is that the identity involved is the result of a repetition in which the qualitative content functions simply as a formal support for the unpresentable experience of satisfaction it is meant to conjure.

As long as the cathexis of representations—i.e. of memory-images —occurs under the direct domination of the pleasure-principle; as long, that is, as the psychic stability and accessibility of such cathexes remain a function of their proximity to pleasurable experiences (which, for Freud, means the avoidance of tension rather than the search for pleasure), it is the primary process that characterizes psychic operation. Under the pressures of the "exigencies of life," however, the psyche is constrained to develop another mode of operation, the secondary process:

The bitter experience of life must have changed this primitive thought-activity into a more expedient secondary one. The establishment of a perceptual identity along the short path of regression within the apparatus does not have the same result elsewhere in the mind as does the cathexis of the same perception from without. Satisfaction does not follow; the need persists. . . . In order to arrive at a more efficient expenditure of psychical energy, it is necessary to bring the regression to a halt before it becomes complete, so that it does not proceed beyond the memory image, and is able to seek out other paths which lead eventually to the desired perceptual identity being established from the direction of the external world. This inhibition of regression and the subsequent diversion of the excitation become the task of a second system. (S.E. 5, 566)

In other words, once it is clear that the impulses of the primary process are not only nonproductive but counterproductive, allowing tensions to mount rather than eliminating them, the psyche is forced to develop a mode of influencing the external causes of tension in order to change them in the desired manner. This, however, presupposes an activity other than hallucination; reality must be apprehended, inspected, even and especially where it has become a source of pain and of discomfort (*Unlust*). The psyche must develop the capacity of forming representations (perceptions, memory-images, concepts), even if these are associated with unpleasant experiences. The mobile cathexes of the primary process must therefore yield progressively to the more stable ones of the secondary process. Or, as Freud puts it, the "regressive" tendencies to hallucinate must be "inhibited."

The problem, of course, is to provide an adequate account of how such inhibition takes place. At this relatively early stage in his thinking, in the *Interpretation of Dreams*, Freud tends to construe the process in terms of a quasi-automatic reflex-reaction of a self-identical subject to the external "exigencies of life." But this binary model leaves him unable to explain the manner in which such a subject passes from a "primary" to a "secondary" process, which, if it is obviously necessary to its survival, is not therefore intelligible. To argue that such a development *must* happen, if the child is to survive, is not to explain *how* it happens.

However, if the author of the *Interpretation of Dreams* is not yet in a position to account for the inhibition of regression in emphatically psychoanalytical terms, he is able to *indicate* the decisive element of such an account: the process of "binding," by which mental energy is "attached" to representations. The quality of this attachment is what distinguishes the mobile cathexes of the primary process from the more stable ones of the secondary process. But to evaluate the nature of the two different types of "binding," we must reflect for a moment on the very distinction Freud makes between "primary" and "secondary" processes, a distinction that prefigures subsequent oppositions such as primary and secondary narcissism, masochism, and repression. The relationship "primary/secondary" is described by Freud as being both structural and chronological; at the same time, however, he acknowledges that it is a "theoretical fiction":

When I described one of the psychical processes occurring in the mental apparatus as the "primary" one, what I had in mind was not merely considerations of relative importance and efficiency; I also intended to choose a name which would give an indication of its chronological priority. It is true that, so far as we know, no psychical apparatus exists which possesses a primary process only and that such an apparatus is to that extent a theoretical fiction. But this much is a fact: the primary processes are present in the mental apparatus from the first, while it is only during the course of life that the secondary processes unfold and come to inhibit the primary ones; it may even be that their complete domination is not attained until the prime of life. In consequence of the belated appearance of the secondary processes, the core of our being, consisting of unconscious wishful impulses, remains inaccessible to the understanding and inhibition of the preconscious (S.E. 5, 603)

If Freud designates the primary process as a theoretical fiction, it is only by virtue of its nonobservability; the "fact" that such a process is present in the psyche "from the first" is not affected by this admission. And yet, Freud's own description suggests that the "fictionality" of the notion of primary process may be far more radical in scope. For there is another aspect of the primary process that renders its primacy highly questionable: for any cathexis whatsoever to be formed, even the highly mobile cathexes of the primary process, energy must be *bound* to representations so as to insure a minimal reproducibility of those representations, for instance as "perceptual identities." Yet in describing the primary process as a reflex-action of hallucinatory reproduction, Freud is unable to offer any explanation of *how* such reproduction effectively occurs. "Inhibition," necessary for the stability of a cathexis, is associated exclusively with the secondary process. If this is so, than either the primary process is not a process of cathexis, or, if it is—as indeed it *must* be for it to be distinguishable from a mere reflex—then it must already entail, from the first, the inhibition of the secondary process in order to constitute itself at all. The "fictionality" of the primary process would then relate not merely to the empirical unverifiability of what it seeks to designate, but to *its own structure as a theoretical concept*. For the condition of the primary process, entailing the binding of energy to representations (cathexis), would be the inhibitory force of the secondary process Freud seeks to oppose to it.[19]

The result of this "theoretical fiction," then, is by no means simply negative: if the primary process is unthinkable except as an effect of the secondary process, what *is* primary—in the sense of being theoretically, and practically, irreducible—is the notion of inhibition as the necessary condition for cathexis.

This "primacy" of inhibition is even more the inhibition of the Primary. As such, however, it marks much more than a mere paradox in Freud's thinking. Rather, it indicates the necessity of a shift in conceptualization, from terms that designate self-identical objects, to those that signal irreducible conflict.

B. Repression

Freud's differentiation of the psychic apparatus into primary and secondary processes culminates in the question: how is libidinal energy bound to representations? The problem of *binding*, involving the "inhibition" of the tendency for energy to distribute itself in accordance with the "pleasure principle," is at the heart of Freud's theory of repression:

Let us bear this firmly in mind, for it is the key to the whole theory of repression: the second system can only cathect an idea if it is in a position to inhibit any development of unpleasure that may proceed from it. (S.E. 5, 601)

Repression is thus situated at the juncture of primary and secondary processes, which are separated and distinguished from one another by the degree of "inhibition" they admit. At first, Freud tends to describe repression as an immediate effect and element of the primary process:

This effortless and regular avoidance by the psychical process of the memory of anything that had once been distressing affords us the prototype and first example of *psychical repression*. (S.E. 5, 600)

The "prototype and first example" of repression is described here, in accordance with the general character of the primary process, as operating in an "effortless and regular" manner, thus bringing about the quasi-automatic avoidance of the distressing memory-image or trace. But if we scrutinize Freud's use of the term, we discover that this "prototype" (in German: *Vorbild*, literally: prefiguration)—the primary, original form out of which the more observable, secondary phenomena are said to develop—distinguishes itself from the latter by lacking what is precisely their essential characteristic. In the case of repression, what the prototype lacks is the element of conflict. The "first example" of repression is described as a movement of "avoidance," *Abwendung* (literally: turning away from). This notion of repression as a kind of *flight* will provide Freud with a major point of reference in seeking to conceptualize the term. However, if the comparison is useful, it is ultimately by virtue of the dissimilarity it engenders. For what distinguishes repression from flight in general is that it can never escape from what it is fleeing, since the latter, as Freud repeatedly insists, is endopsychic. And the psyche cannot simply flee from what it in some sense "contains."

In short, if repression is the response to, and articulation of, an endopsychic conflict, it must involve not merely an action, "flight," but an *interaction* constituting a reciprocal alteration of the agents concerned. Such a process of interaction, although not discussed explicitly by Freud in his first attempts to come to grips with the notion, is nevertheless implied in the term he uses: Abwendung, which might best be translated not as "avoidance," but as "aversion." For the German word signifies both a turning away of the subject, in the sense of avoiding an unpleasant perception or memory, and also a warding off of the undesirable object ("eine Gefahr abwenden" = to avert a danger). If, in the passage cited, the syntax makes it clear that Abwendung is being used to describe only the evasive movement of consciousness, in subsequent discussions Freud will acknowledge that the process of repression must be considered as a double movement that affects not merely the repressing instance but also that which is being repressed (the originally cathected representation).

But to construe repression in this manner, as simply a redistribution of energy from one representation to another, fails to resolve the problem posed by the notion of primary and secondary process. For if their distinction presupposes the efficacy of "inhibition" to bridle the volatile energy of the primary process, the manner in which this operation is to be conceived remains a mystery. In introducing and elaborating the notion of repression, however, Freud takes a decisive step toward conceptualizing the irreducibly conflictual nature of the psychic processes he seeks to describe. The two terms in which this conceptualization of conflict[20] articulates itself are "anticathexis" (*Gegenbesetzung*) and hypercathexis (*Überbesetzung*).

These terms—the transcription of that "capital X" into the apparently more familiar figural language of the metapsychological Bildersprache—stand in very different relation to the process of repression. Since that of anticathexis is far more explicit, I will discuss it first. If a representation can be shunted aside, excluded from consciousness, this can occur only by means of another representation *taking its place*. The representation that replaces that which is repressed Freud designates as an "anticathexis." the latter functions as a kind of counterweight, absorbing some of the energy hitherto attached to the representation that is now excluded from consciousness. Gegenbesetzung thus designates both the substitute-representation, and the process of cathexis by which such substitution is effected. Such a process is not accomplished in a single act, once and for all; it must be constantly renewed, demanding an incessant expense of energy and a series of reiterated events. These reiterations are by no means simple repetitions of the same, since they often involve shifts, both in the relation of the conflicting cathexes to one another, and in the individual representations employed.

Although the relation of anticathexis to repression is thus clear and explicit in Freud's work, that of hypercathexis is not. Freud used the term primarily to designate the economic process by which a particular representation becomes conscious by drawing attention to itself. Since hypercathexis is thus related to consciousness, it would seem to have little significance for repression, which designates the process by which representations are barred from consciousness.

The conflictual dynamics of repression entails, however, not merely the exclusion of ideas from consciousness, but concomitantly and necessarily their replacement by other ideas—anticathexes—which in turn *are* conscious. A durable repression, therefore, entails the formation not merely of anticathexes, but of hypercathexes as well. Indeed, it could be argued that anticathexis and hypercathexis name the same process, the former from a dynamic (conflictual) perspective, the latter from an economic one.

The problem that thereby emerges for the metapsychology is to articulate the precise relation between these two perspectives, or aspects, of repression. The question thus posed by the relation of anti- and hypercathexis is, in short, none other than that of the mechanism of inhibition, as the following passage from *The Interpretation of Dreams* makes clear:

> The tendency of thinking must therefore move in the direction of acquiring ever greater freedom from the exclusive regulation by the unpleasure principle, and of keeping, through intellectual effort, the development of affects to a minimum, which can be exploited as a signal. This more sophisticated achievement is to be attained through a new hypercathexis effectuated by consciousness. (S.E. 5, 602)

Inasmuch as repression entails the substitution of one representation by another, which is accessible to consciousness, repression depends on a process of hypercathexis that Freud, in this passage, associates with the formation of what he calls a "signal." In regard to repression, then, hypercathexis designates the process by which the repressed representation is replaced by another representation, which gains access to consciousness as a "signal" of the unpleasurable, repressed idea.

Since repression, in Freud's work, ultimately designates the conflictual process by which the psyche articulates and differentiates itself, the importance of his notion of *signal* can hardly be overestimated. For it marks the manner in which consciousness develops its organization under the sway of the unpleasure principle.

The significance of this conception of signal is demonstrated, negatively as it were, by Freud's efforts to provide an account of the mechanism of repression without including the signal in his explanation, as for instance in the following passage, also from *The Interpretation of Dreams*:

The memories, on the basis of which the unconscious wish brings about the release of affect, were never accessible to the Pcs (Preconscious); hence, this release cannot be inhibited either. Precisely by virtue of this development of affect, the representations remain inaccessible even by way of the preconscious thoughts to which they have transferred their wishful force. Instead, the unpleasure-principle takes over and causes the preconscious to turn away [*sich abwendet*] from these transference-thoughts. They are left to themselves, "repressed," and thus it is that the presence of a store of infantile memories, inaccessible to the Pcs from the very first, becomes the precondition of repression. (S.E. 5, 604)

Instead of describing "inhibition" as the active force, intervening to curtail the "release of affect" (*Affektentbindung*), Freud introduces the notion of "repression" to designate the more passive move of the preconscious, turning away from the unpleasant thoughts, which, "left to themselves," somehow constitute an original nucleus of "infantile memories . . . the precondition of repression."

The tautology of this account is unmistakable: to explain repression, Freud posits (*setzt*) an origin in which it has already taken place: the constitution of a "store" of memories, excluded from consciousness "from the very first." Such circularity haunts all of Freud's repeated attempts to explain the conflictual workings of the psyche in genetic terms, by going back to an origin—a "primary" state—from which the more observable phenomena can be derived. This is why the perspective he adopts toward the problem fifteen years later, in his essay on "Repression," represents a significant and productive shift:

Psychoanalytic experience . . . forces us to the conclusion that repression is not a defense-mehanism present from the very beginning, and that it cannot occur until a sharp distinction has been established between conscious and unconscious activities. (S.E. 14, 147)

In thus restating the problem, Freud begins to move away from a genetic model toward a more structural one: "Until we have learnt more about . . . what differentiates consciousness from the unconscious . . . all we can do is to assemble in purely descriptive fashion" material gleaned from clinical observation, Freud concludes. His next move, however, is not to "assemble" clinical observations, but rather to offer a highly speculative hypothesis that appears to be a relapse into the genetic mode of explanation already discussed:

We have reason therefore to assume a primal repression [*Urverdrängung*], an initial phase of repression which consists in denying [*versagt*] mental representations [*Vorstellungs-Repräsentanz*] access to consciousness. This is accompanied by a fixation; from this moment on, the representation concerned remains unchanged together with the drive that is attached to it. (S.E. 14, 140)

Despite appearances, the hypothesis of an Urverdrängung does not merely repeat the previous distinction of primary and secondary processes: it *combines* the two by associating them with what Freud calls "fixation." The point of departure is no longer described as a pure state of unbound energy, but rather as a particular combination of binding (*Bindung*) and release (*Entbindung*). Freud's thinking thus shifts from a binary scheme, based on the original priority of *one* of its terms, to a ternary model in which no one term is conceivable apart from its relation to the others. Bindung and Entbindung thus emerge, not as the poles of an opposition, but as aspects of a process of *Verbindung* (combination, connection):

We are inclined . . . to forget too readily that repression does not hinder the drive-representative from continuing to exist in the unconscious, from organizing itself further, forming offshoots and developing connections [*Verbindungen anzuknüpfen*]. (S.E. 14, 149)

What now appears to characterize unconscious cathexes is neither their mobility nor their stability, but the particular manner in which the two are combined.

The (repressed drive-representative) develops in a more unchecked and luxuriant fashion if it is withdrawn by repression from conscious influence. It proliferates [*wuchert*] in the dark, so to speak, finding extreme forms of expression which, when they are translated and presented to the neurotic, seem not only alien to him, but also . . . terrifying. (S.E. 14, 141).

Freud's figural description of repression thus implies a nucleus of representation—the *Triebrepräsentanz*—which is by no means stable, self-identical, or static, but rather *metastatic*, weaving a terrifying tissue of relationships that only becomes accessible to consciousness in its outlying reaches.

But if "fixation," and hence repression, can no longer be conceived in terms of the simple polarity of bound and unbound energy, we still have no account of the factors involved in the establishment of such fixity. We know only that it entails both the proliferation of Verbindungen, and the exclusion of such Verbindungen from consciousness. If, however, we reread the formulation in which Freud describes this exclusion, we find, barely legible, the hint of a possible explanation. In the passage already cited, Freud writes that repression "denies mental representations access to consciousness." But the English translation eliminates a connotation of the German text. The word translated into English as "denies" is *versagt*: "*Die Übernahme ins Bewusste [wird] versagt.*" *Versagen* literally signifies *interdict*, and the linguistic reference it contains is bound up (*verknüpft*) with another linguistic figure, used to designate the "passage" or transition from the unconscious to consciousness, and which, precisely, appears to be interdicted by repression: the term, "*Übersetzung*," translation. One of Freud's earliest descriptions of repression, in a letter to Fliess, speaks of it as "the interdiction of translation," "*die Versagung der Übersetzung*" (*Origins*, p. 175). All of the questions we have been addressing—the nature of cathexis (*Besetzung*), its relation to hypercathexis and countercathexis (Überbesetzung, Gegenbesetzung), the operations of binding, unbinding, and combining (Bindung, Entbindung, Verbindung)—converge in the essay, "The Unconscious," in which Freud "discovers" what in a certain sense he "knew" all along: that the "sharp distinction" he has been searching for, between conscious and unconscious, involves nothing other than a particular form of translation and of interdiction (*Versagung*):

It strikes us all at once that now we know what the difference is between a conscious and an unconscious representation . . . The conscious representation comprises the thing-representation [*Sachvorstellung*] plus the corresponding word-representation [*plus der zugehörigen Wortvorstellung*], the unconscious one consists in the thing-representation alone. . . . The system Ucs contains the thing-cathexes of the objects, the first and authentic object-cathexes; the system Pcs originates in a hypercathexis of this thing-representation through its being linked [*durch die Verknüpfung*] with the word-representations that correspond to it [*mit den ihr entsprechenden Wortvorstellungen überbesetzt wird*]. It is such hypercathexes [*Überbesetzungen*], we may suppose, that bring about a higher psychic organization and make it possible for the primary process to be succeeded by the secondary process which dominates the Pcs. We can now also formulate precisely what it is that repression denies to the rejected representation in the transference neurosis: the translation into words capable of remaining attached to the object [*die Übersetzung in Worte, welche mit dem Objekt verknüpft bleiben sollen*]. The non-verbalized representation, or the non-cathected act, then remains repressed in the Ucs. (S.E. 14, 201-2)

The difference between conscious and unconscious thought Freud declares, with an inhabitual enthusiasm (to which we shall return shortly), is nothing more nor less than the possibility of verbalization; that is, of a certain translation. In the case of conscious thought, the hypercathexis (Überbesetzung) of the "corresponding word-representation" permits the "object-representation" to be translated appropriately; in the case of unconscious thought, we are left with "the thing-representation alone." The seductive simplicity of this account, however, does not resist a moment's reflection. For it presupposes just what Freud's general conception of the primary process excludes: that "the first" cathexes were also "authentic" representations of the objects they cathect. Nothing could be further from Freud's notion of mental development, as we have had occasion to discuss in regard to the concept of "perceptual identities." The latter, it will be recalled, are in fact the most "inauthentic" representations of objects, with which they are linked metonymically, as it were, by the concomitance of an experience of satisfaction that itself bears no intrinsic relation to the objects cathected. Such qualitative nonidentity is precisely what characterizes the cathexes of the primary process, as opposed to the more stable cathexes of the secondary process. To describe those "first" object-cathexes as "authentic" is once again to presuppose identity instead of explaining how it comes about. And yet, Freud's entire "discovery" here is based on just such a presupposition. The notion of "translation" that he employs to distinguish conscious from unconscious thought requires the existence of stable, self-identical "object-representations" prior to their verbalization. What Freud is trying to argue is that repression denies the translation of one kind of identity (object-cathexes) into another (word-cathexes); that, in short, repression is merely a *privative* process, contributing nothing of its own to the articulation of the psyche but only depriving the latter of self-consciousness.

Read in this light, one can interpret the enthusiastic tone with which Freud announces this discovery as itself the symptom of a repression, or, as Nietzsche would have put it, of a very "active forgetting." For, taken at face value, Freud's assertion does little more than repeat the observations he had made some twenty years earlier, in the *Project* of 1895, where he had conjectured that "speech associations" were responsible for the emergence of "conscious, observant thought," as well as of "memory."[21] The problem, then as later, remains that of explaining just *how* this linguistic function is to be conceived within the context of the mental operations being described. In the earlier text, Freud touches on one aspect of "word-images" that seems relevant to this question, without elaborating upon it: the peculiar advantage of such associations, he suggests, relates to the fact that words are "closed (few in number) and exclusive." If Freud does not take up this remark later, it is probably because his work on dreams demonstrated that word-*associations* need not necessarily be "closed," even if the words themselves are "few in number"; on the contrary, he discovered that words lend themselves to the condensations and displacements of the dream-work precisely because they are open and overdetermined. In short, words need not function to establish stable "correspondences," but on the contrary, to dissolve them.

When Freud therefore contends, in the passage cited, that repression denies the translation of thing-representations into the "corresponding" word-representations, he is in fact not presenting a solution as much as indicating, implicitly, a problem: that of how such verbal correspondences are constituted for the psyche. It is in reponse to this question that the relation of repression to translation must be rethought. For Freud's assertion notwithstanding, our previous discussion has demonstrated that repression itself entails a certain form of translation: an objectionable representation is repressed only insofar as it is replaced by—i.e., *translated* into—an anticathexis, which is simultaneously hypercathected as the conscious surrogate of the repressed thought. The difference between the translation of repression, in this sense, and the translation that repression is said by Freud to impede thus emerges as the difference between two different kinds of translation. What distinguishes the translation of consciousness from that of the unconscious, is not, as a rapid reading of Freud might suggest, verbalization as such, but rather a specific kind of verbalization. Consciousness entails a translation into words that correspond to an object in an enduring manner.

But this notion of correspondence—upon which Freud's entire differentiation of consciousness from the unconscious here ultimately depends—again raises more questions than it answers. First, as we have seen, there is the question of just how object-cathexes themselves come to be stabilized. Second, there is the question of the relation of the psychic to the social order, inasmuch as enduring and corresponding verbal associations imply the relation of the individual subject to a preexisting language-system, and hence to a social and cultural context. Third, in view of the overdetermined nature of words, manifest in dreams, jokes, and other articulations of the unconscious, the notion of "correspondence" raises the question of the intrapsychic mechanism that establishes verbal identity. If the verbal discourse of consciousness tends to be "closed and exclusive," how does this closure and exclusion come about?

This last question impels us toward a response that runs counter to the explicit assertion of Freud in the passage cited above, and yet one that, I believe, is alone compatible with his general account of repression: repression, far from simply blocking the verbalization of conscious discourse, is also its indispensable precondition. By excluding certain representations from consciousness, and by simultaneously replacing them with others, repression arrests what would otherwise be the interminable and indeterminable play of the primary process under the rule of the pleasure principle, and thereby allows *all cathexis* to take place. In short, the hypercathexis of verbal-representations can operate only by virtue of the exclusions operated by repression, through the mechanism of anticathexis. Or again: only through being anticathected do words acquire the quality of closure and exclusivity that render them the privileged and distinctive medium of consciousness.

Repression, then, emerges as nothing less than the condition of identity in the psychic order; but if this is so, we can begin to understand the difficulties faced in trying to identify repression itself. For although it is the *condition* of identity, whether that of the "thing-representation" or of the "word-representation," repression is not identical-to-itself, and this for two reasons. First, because it produces the conditions of identity, that is of a certain *closure*, only by *excluding*: that is, by installing a relation to exteriority at the core of all that is enclosed. This is why every cathexis, and in particular the hypercathexes of consciousness, is also inevitably an anticathexis.

But if this is so, then the same must hold of "repression itself": the hypercathexis of the *word*, "repression," designating the conflictual operation of the psyche, is itself an anticathexis. Just *what* it counters we have already touched on; the *intrapsychic* mechanism of repression, as word and as object, is in turn dependent on interdictions that antedate and transcend the realm of the purely psychic: *repression depends on systems of social constraints and sanctions*. Its power to exclude and hence to enclose—which is nothing short of its power to allow cathexes and, hence, the psychic, to take place—depends on a *place* that it does not constitute, but that is already structured by metapsychic forces and traditions. The nature of this dependency is suggested by the two words that Freud uses to designate what in English we have had to translate as "correspondence": *zugehörig* and *entsprechend*. The first term is formed from the root, *hören*, to hear or listen; the second, from *sprechen*, to speak. If the "word-representations" of conscious discourse can hope to "correspond" to "object-representations," it is by virtue of "listening" and "addressing," two processes about which we will have more to say in connection with Freud's theory of jokes. Here it will perhaps be sufficient to note that such *listening* and *addressing* reinscribes the problem of consciousness and of the unconscious in a discursive process that can no longer be construed dyadically as the relations of "words" to "things," nor as being purely "psychic" in character.

Repression, in short, consists not merely in the denial of translation, but in its *interdiction*. This Versagung, however, is not merely the absence or negation of language, since it itself constitutes a mode of translation. But the translation of *Versagung* is ambiguous and ambivalent: it effectuates both the exclusion necessary for the cathexis of a "closed and limited" number of word-representations, and at the same time, by determining those cathexes as anticathexes, it places them in relation to what they exclude. In this sense, the Versagung of repression is nothing other than the "saying" of an Other, or, as Freud will call it, a *signal*. For the significance of the signal is always elsewhere, different from and deferring that which it represents, designates, reproduces. This is why the "object" of the signal is inevitably a *danger*, and its subject: *anxiety*.

C. Anxiety

The position of anxiety in Freud's thought is a curious one. On the one hand, it is closely related to his conceptions of the primary and secondary processes, and of repression, and as such is situated close to the center of his concerns. Indeed, for many years Freud considered anxiety to be the direct product of repression, before he then reversed this view, declaring anxiety to be not the effect but the cause of repression.[22] On the other hand, notwithstanding Freud's lifelong interest in the problem, anxiety stands apart among the phenomena with which he dealt. Unlike the other major categories we have discussed, "anxiety" was not a term introduced by psychoanalysis, nor did it designate a phenomenon whose significance was so decisively transformed by Freud's work that it could be said to have been rediscovered by him—as was the case, for instance, with sexuality or hysteria. There has, therefore, been little tendency among students or followers of Freud to assign anxiety that signal importance for psychoanalysis that Freud himself never doubted it possessed.[23] "The problem of anxiety," he wrote in the *Introductory Lectures,*

is a nodal point in which the most diverse and most important questions converge, an enigma, the solution of which would doubtless shed considerable light upon our entire psychic life. (S.E. 16, 373)

Given the importance Freud attributed to the problem, it is not surprising that anxiety drew his attention from his earliest attempts to articulate a systematic account of the psyche. The "enigma" it posed also constituted a major challenge to the science psychoanalysis sought to become: could it succeed in giving a more satisfactory account of the problem than had hitherto existed, its claims to scientific credibility would be difficult to dismiss. Freud's various efforts to explore and explain anxiety in psychoanalytic terms invariably provide us with a demonstration of their theoretical fecundity as well as of their limitations.

In his initial writings on the subject (1893-1895),[24] Freud seeks to explain anxiety by reference to sexuality, and along much the same lines as hysteria. In this account, anxiety results when sexual tension has accumulated to a point where the psyche is incapable of dealing with it; the excess excitation is thereby "converted" into the physical manifestations characteristic of anxiety, such as heart palpitation, sweating, shortness of breath, etc. Such manifestations, Freud argued, were to be understood as "surrogates of . . . the specific action" toward which "sexual excitation" tends: discharge, which had been blocked. What distinguishes anxiety from hysteria, therefore, is the specific kind of blockage at work; in the case of anxiety, the blockage consists in a purely somatic process, which, as opposed to hysteria, is not susceptible of any further *psychological* analysis. Thus, if hysteria derives from a conflict of desire, anxiety was to be considered as the product of an obstacle standing in the way of the fulfillment of a purely physical striving: that of sexual energy to attain discharge. Unable to reach discharge, such energy becomes "free-floating" and is discharged through the surrogate symptoms that provide the physical accompaniment to the "anxious expectation" in which Freud discerned the "core-symptom of (anxiety) neurosis," and which consists in the tendency of the free-floating energy to "attach itself to any suitable representation at any time." (S.E. 3, 93)

Thus described, anxiety is located on the periphery both of the psyche and of psychoanalysis itself. As the result of the interruption of what Freud construed as a self-contained, physical process, anxiety excludes any further psychological analysis: that is, any further *psychoanalysis*. At the same time, it represents virtually a prototype of the kind of conflict psychoanalysis came to declare as its privileged domain: inhibited or conflictual sexuality.

The peculiar position of anxiety, marginal and central at once, is particularly manifest in Freud's identification of its primary or characteristic cause: *coitus interruptus*. This term designates the blockage of sexual discharge that Freud conceived to be at the source of anxiety. But in another, more figurative sense, the term also can be seen to describe not merely the cause, but the effect of anxiety. For if the latter consists in the accumulation of energy in a "free-floating" state, then what has been interrupted is the "coming-together"—the *coitus*—of such energy with mental representations. What characterizes anxiety, then, is precisely what characterizes the "primary process": the absence of stable, enduring cathexes as the precondition of pleasurable discharge.

It is no wonder, then, that Freud soon came to identify anxiety with the manifestation of the "unpleasure principle," and hence also with *repression*. In *The Interpretation of Dreams*, he describes anxiety as resulting when repression breaks down and the repressed begins to reimpose itself upon consciousness. Freud thus conceives repression as the condition or cause of anxiety, which is associated with the return of the repressed. Nevertheless, his subsequent reversal of this conception is already implicit in his "economic" theory of anxiety. For if repression presupposes the existence of "cathexis," *anxiety calls the very process of cathexis itself into question*. To employ Freud's later characterization of repression: if repression consists in the *nontranslation* of a "thing-representation" into its corresponding "word-representation," anxiety entails an even more radical nontranslation, that of energy ("excitation") into representations.

The specific problem posed by anxiety, then, is that of *the relation of the psychic to the nonpsychic*, or in other words, *the delimitation of the psychic as such*. But if anxiety poses this problem, its examination and solution are complicated by the fact that anxiety itself both simulates and dissimulates the relation of psychic to nonpsychic, of "internal" to "external":

The psyche arrives at the affect of anxiety when it feels itself incapable of fulfilling, through the appropriate reaction, a task (danger) *emanating from without*; it develops anxiety-neurosis when it notes [*merkt*] its incapacity of alleviating (sexual) excitation that has arisen endogenically. *It acts, therefore, as though it had projected this excitation outwards*. (S.E. 3, 112, emphasis Freud's)

It would not be an exaggeration to assert that this passage, from Freud's first published essay on the subject ("On the Grounds for Detaching a Particular Syndrome from Neurasthenia as 'Anxiety-Neurosis,'" 1895) condenses both his later approach to the problem and the difficulties he will encounter in attempting to resolve it. On the one hand, anxiety is described as a reaction of the psyche to an external danger; on the other, that reaction entails the "projection" of the dangerous "excitation" outwards. Such a projection thereby creates a *second exteriority*, which in a certain sense takes the place of the first. As we shall see, it is not always easy to tell the two apart, whether for the anxious psyche, or for the theory that seeks to comprehend it.

All of Freud's efforts to render anxiety intelligible, therefore, will hinge upon the manner in which he determines the external danger to which anxiety reacts, the process, that is, in which the extrapsychic imposes itself upon the intrapsychic. The ambiguity of the problem is already clearly inscribed in the passage cited: the danger that the psyche confronts *approaches it from without* ("eine *von aussen nahende* . . . Gefahr"); but the "excitation" that constitutes the immediate form of that danger, *arises from within*, "endogenically." The difficulty of reconciling these two assertions will be to explain just how the psyche can "note" (merkt) a danger that is both exogenic in origin and endogenic in operation.

This difficulty in turn relates to what Freud from the very first recognized to be the double character of anxiety: on the one hand, it entails a psychic reaction that is often expedient and functional in the face of "real" danger; on the other, it can become a reaction that reproduces, as it were, the very danger it strives to react against. An adequate theory of anxiety must therefore be able to explain the phenomenon both as a normal, necessary, and useful defense, *and* as a neurotic, dysfunctional threat.

If Freud's initial approach to the question focused primarily on the latter aspect, he came increasingly to see neurotic or pathological anxiety as an offshoot of its realistic or expedient form. The text in which he finally sought to articulate this position most fully is, of course, *Inhibition, Symptom, and Anxiety*, the last of the great metapsychological essays, published in 1926.

This study was written in response to the most serious challenge posed to Freud's thought since that of Adler and Jung: Rank's theory of the birth trauma. This theory posed a danger to Freud not merely because of the renown of its author, who had been one of his closest collaborators, but because it in substance appropriated many of Freud's own conceptions concerning anxiety. The idea of the birth trauma, as Freud put it, not without malice, "was originally my own" (*Inhibition*, p. 87).[25] Had Freud sought to describe anxiety as the reaction of the psyche to an external, ultimately nonpsychic, *real* danger, then Rank's hypothesis of the birth trauma carried that approach to its logical conclusion. For what danger could be both more "real" and more original than that of birth? "I was obliged," Freud writes, "to go back from the anxiety reaction to the *situation of danger* that lay behind it" (*Ibid*.) The manner in which Freud does this constitutes the essence of his effort to rearticulate the problem of anxiety. It is, therefore, of some importance to note that his treatment of anxiety is itself provoked by the challenge—or should we say "danger"?—posed to psychoanalysis by the development of one of its followers. In readdressing the question of "danger," then, Freud is also striving to defend psychoanalysis itself from a threat that, although originating "internally", is now *projected* as *emanating from without*. What is at stake, in short, both for the conception of the psyche and for psychoanalysis itself, is the integrity and coherence of a certain "within" in its relations to the "outside"; and that integrity can only be defended by redrawing and reinforcing the lines that set apart inside from outside, psychoanalysis from birth-trauma, Freud from Rank.

The problem, however, is that those dividing-lines converge and blur in the notion of danger. Freud thus attacks the problem by seeking to unravel this knot and "nodal point":

But what is a 'danger'? In the act of birth there is an objective danger to life. We know what this means in reality. But psychologically speaking this tells us nothing. The danger of birth has as yet no psychical content. (*Inhibition*, p. 6)

"Reality," in short, is not sufficient to establish the psychological significance or intelligibility of a danger. And yet, Freud himself will not cease to stress the "real" nature of the danger from which anxiety ultimately arises. And indeed, he must do so if his explanation of anxiety in terms of the danger to which it reacts is to be plausible: if that danger is not determined so as to be independent of the reaction it produces, it will not provide the explanatory basis of the theory Freud is seeking to construct and to defend.

Thus, it is not the "reality" of danger as such that Freud will criticize in Rank, but rather the latter's specific *conception* of this reality. Rank's effort to retrace all forms of anxiety to the trauma of birth, Freud objects, is based on the assumption

that the infant has received certain sensory impressions, in particular of a visual kind, at the time of birth, the renewal of which can recall to its memory the trauma of birth and thus evoke a reaction of anxiety. This assumption is quite unfounded. . . . It is not credible that a child should retain any but tactile and general sensations relating to the process of birth. (*Ibid.*)

The hypothesis of Rank, Freud therefore implies, errs in much the same way as did that of Adler (to whom he compares him): by hypostasizing the ego. In declaring the birth trauma to be the origin of anxiety, Rank must attribute to the infant mental capacities that in reality are acquired only gradually, with the development of the ego. If birth is a trauma, Freud suggests, it is not one that leaves perceptual, visual traces, but only "tactile and general sensations."

Thus, although Freud will agree that anxiety entails the reproduction of a previously experienced "trauma," the manner in which he determines that trauma will diverge radically from that of Rank. Trauma, for Freud, cannot designate any particular, determinate objective reality, for what it entails is precisely the inability of the psyche—or more specifically, of the ego—to determine, its inability to bind or to cathect an excess of energy that therefore tends to overwhelm it. This is why Freud's definition of the trauma is inevitably vague: it derives from a "situation of helplessness." Thus, if the trauma constitutes the point of departure for the development of anxiety,

what is decisive is the first displacement of the anxiety-reaction from its origin in the situation of helplessness to an expectation of that situation—that is, to the danger-situation. (*Inhibition*, p. 93)

This first displacement is decisive because it marks the emergence of a subject-object relationship. In marking the shift of energy from an unbound to a bound state, it provides the indispensable condition for the constitution of stable, object-cathexes. The reality of an object, as Freud had written in his essay on "Negation" (*Verneinung*), is not something that is "discovered" but rather that is "rediscovered,"[26] a cathexis that entails the repetition of the same. The possibility of such a repetition hinges on an inhibition or deflection of the unpleasure principle that dominates the primary process, which otherwise would tend to produce ever-changing cathexes as an effort to reduce tension. Thus, what Freud here calls the "first displacement" is, strictly considered, not first at all but rather the displacement of the displacements of the primary process, which in turn have culminated in the "situation of helplessness." Through a process of repetition, then, the psyche displaces the displacement of "helplessness" and thus alters the incessant alteration implied by the primary process. It does so by the production of what Freud calls a *signal*:

The signal announces: "I am expecting a situation of helplessness to set in," or "The present situation reminds me of one of the traumatic experiences I have had before. . . . Anxiety is therefore on the one hand an expectation of a trauma, and on the other, a repetition of it in a mitigated form (*Inhibition*, p. 92)

Through this production of the danger-signal, itself the reproduction of a trauma, what Freud is in fact describing is nothing less than the manner in which the ego constitutes itself by setting itself apart from the indifferentiation of the primary process. If the latter can be said to consist in the incessant alteration of ever-different cathexes—that is, in an indeterminable alterity—anxiety entails the alteration of that alterity through a process of repetition that organizes space and time in terms of a dyadic opposition: that of inner/outer and past/future. In so organizing space and time, anxiety situates the ego as the dividing-line between the two opposing poles.

In a double, ambiguous but also ambivalent sense, then, anxiety sets the ego apart: it repeats the trauma, but in an altered form, as something recognizable: "A danger-situation is a recognized, remembered, expected situation of helplessness" (*Ibid.*). But it also, more literally, sets the ego apart by virtue of the fact that the trauma it repeats, recognizes, and remembers is "itself" both unrecognizable and immemorial. It is unrecognizable because it consists of ever-changing cathexes that can be "recognized" only by being displaced, dislocated, disfigured (*ent-stellt*). And it is immemorial, because the "actual" situation of helplessness resists the bifurcation into past and future that is the condition of memory and of anticipation.

This is why the peculiar kind of apprehension that characterizes anxiety and distinguishes it from "fear" is marked by a certain "indeterminacy and objectlessness" (*Inhibition*, p. 92); for the "danger" that it recognizes and anticipates—that it represents—is in fact as trauma never present as such. The trauma is always in excess of its recognition or representation, and hence danger is only present, or presentable, as the approach of something else.

Anxiety thus emerges as the conflictual, contradictory process by which the ego seeks to represent the unrepresentable, to alter alteration and thereby to *organize* itself: for, as Freud insists,

the ego is an organization . . . [whose] desexualized energy betrays its origins in its striving for binding and unification, and this compulsion to synthesize increases in proportion to the strength of the ego. (*Inhibition*, p. 24)

In signaling the approach of a danger, the ego does not merely react to a given state of affairs that constitutes a potential menace to its organization—although this is how Freud explicitly attempts to present anxiety; rather, it seeks to consolidate its identity by projecting the trauma as an event it can then con-front. In short, it seeks to appropriate the "economic" disturbance of incessant displacement by displacing it outwards and forwards, by making it into a *Vorstellung*: a re-presentation, to be sure, but also, literally, something that is *placed-out-in-front*, spatially as well as temporally.

Through this process of Vor-stellung, what the ego pre-sents or introduces (again: vor-stellt) is the disfigurement of itself: itself as Entstellung. And it does this by the cathexis of perceptions. If the ego is able to set itself apart from the id, Freud reminds us, it is "in virtue of its intimate connections with the perceptual system — connections which, as we know, constitute its essence and provide the basis of its differentiation from the id" (*Inhibition*, p. 18). To be more precise, the ego develops its organization through the formation or cathexis of perceptual objects. These are precisely *not* the "perceptual identities" of the primary process, which, as we have argued, are not identities at all but rather constantly shifting alterations. But if the question of *how* such perceptual identities could in fact become identical — the question of the possible "inhibition" of the "unpleasure principle" has hitherto remained unanswered — and as such, the driving force of Freud's Auseinandersetzung, first of the primary and secondary processes, and then of repression — a possible response now begins to emerge. For in developing the capacity of indicating the presence of danger, and thereby of temporalizing and temporizing the trauma, the psyche can be seen as striking a compromise with the unpleasure-principle that would allow the repetition of difference, the mobile cathexes of the primary process, to be repeated as more of the same, a movement of identity. A perception that functions as danger-signal signifies not merely the object it represents but the unrepresentable loss of perception itself. The disruptive force of the trauma is thus temporalized, as potential (future) loss, and thereby temporized, since it remains cathected to an object or situation, albeit an ambiguous one. Moreover, the dyadic or dialectical notion of loss implies both that what is perceived as lost was once possessed, and that such possession can be regained through the avoidance of the danger that impends. Thus, if "what is decisive is the first displacement . . . from . . . the situation of helplessness to an expectation of that situation," the form this expectation assumes (for the ego) is that of a loss of perception:

The first condition of anxiety that the ego introduces is therefore that of the loss of perception, which is equated with the loss of object. (*Inhibition*, p. 96)

With this introduction — Vorstellung — of the loss-of-perception, the ego is able to install its organization in face of the id, and give itself a history.[27] This history recounts the ego's loss and its effort to reappropriate what it strives to consider its original property. This, of course, is the story of castration—a story that the narcissistic ego tells itself in order to organize and to appropriate the alterity on which it (id) depends. The ego perceives the anatomical sexual difference as the loss of the phallus; it "recognizes" the female genitals as "castrated," and thus conserves the belief in the ubiquity of the phallus; that is, in its own ability to recognize and to repeat difference as identity. The "danger" that it thereby signals is thus interpreted as one that is external to its organization, and hence, as one that in principle at least, can be avoided.

Freud, in seeking to establish the ego as the "site" and the "source" of anxiety, is invariably led to retell this story, as evidence of the reality both of the ego and of the danger to which it reacts. Just as the ego seeks to master the indifferent alterity of the trauma by temporalizing and temporizing it through the construction of a narrative, with beginning, middle, and end, Freud too seeks to master the elusive, ambiguous, and ambivalent phenomenon of anxiety by *isolating* and *dividing* it into two distinct forms: neurotic and "real" or "realistic" anxiety. This division is in turn dependent on an anterior distinction of danger:

Real danger is a danger that is known, and realistic anxiety is anxiety about a known danger of this sort. Neurotic anxiety is anxiety about an unknown danger. Neurotic danger is thus a danger that has still to be discovered. Analysis has shown that it is a danger deriving from drives. (*Inhibition*, p. 91)

"Analysis," which shows that "neurotic anxiety" derives from a danger produced by the drives, also seeks to show that the danger entailed by the latter is ultimately a real danger. This, at least, is what Freud seeks to argue when he contends that castration, the paradigm of neurotic anxiety, is ultimately derived from a *real*, external sexual danger.

We should not be threatened with castration if we did not entertain certain feelings and intentions within us. Thus, such drive-impulses are determinants of external dangers and so become dangerous in themselves. (*Ibid.*, p. 71)

However, Freud's effort to insist upon the ultimately realistic nature of the danger from which anxiety—even in its neurotic, purely psychic form—derives; his effort, in short, to replace his economic theory of anxiety by a topical explanation that would explain it as an essentially functional, purposive, and expedient response, founders upon the very "historical" character that Freud attributes to the phenomenon, as the reproduction of a previous experience. For what anxiety repeats, above and beyond all the particular and determinate dangers that the ego has experienced, is the economic turmoil of a trauma that can never be repeated *as such*. Freud implicity concedes as much, when he acknowledges that

the external (real) danger must also have managed to become internalized if it is to be significant for the ego. It must have been recognized as related to some situation of helplessness that has been experienced. (*Inhibition*, p. 94)

But the "experience" of that "situation of helplessness" is, in itself, incognizable, for it has no "self." It is a process of displacement that makes place for the ego by being displaced, in and as anxiety. If the ego is therefore the "seat" of anxiety, anxiety is equally the site of the ego. And in this site, the ego is never comfortably set. Nor is the theory, that seeks to "grasp" anxiety by deriving it from the ego:

The time has come to pause and consider. What we clearly are seeking is an insight that will make the essence of anxiety accessible to us, an either/or that will separate truth about it from error. But that is difficult to obtain, anxiety is not simple [*einfach*] to grasp. Up to now we have reached nothing but contradictions, among which it was impossible to choose without prejudice. I now propose to proceed in a different way: we will try to collect everything that can be said about anxiety impartially, and thereby renounce the expectation of a new synthesis. (*Inhibition*, p. 58)

But the "renunciation" of the "expectation of a new synthesis"—like all renunciation—is easier said than done. For even the apparently modest and prudent project of "collecting everything that can be said about anxiety impartially," presupposes that one can know what cannot be said about it; that is, that one possesses precisely that "either/or" that will enable one to "separate truth about it from error."

This difficult renunciation marks the ambivalence of Freud's arguments in this essay: on the one hand, he seeks to reject his earlier, "economic" explanation of anxiety as the automatic transformation of libido and to replace it with the more "realistic" topical explanation of anxiety as a function of the ego. Such an attempt is entirely informed by the very "either/or" alternative that Freud wishes to renounce. On the other hand, however, he is constrained to acknowledge the ambivalent nature of anxiety, as *both* "automatic transformation" of energy *and* as the intentional, purposive, expedient reaction of the ego to danger. Since he cannot simply ignore or deny these two aspects of anxiety, Freud simply seeks to keep them apart, and then to declare his disinterest in the former:

Our former hypothesis of a direct transformation of libido into anxiety possesses less interest for us now than it did. (*Inhibition*, p. 88)

In so arguing, Freud reproduces a mode of thinking that he has described, earlier in his paper, as one of the defensive strategies the ego uses to avoid danger. It is the mechanism of "isolating," in which an event or idea is not repressed, but rather separated "from its affect" and from "its associative relation . . . so that it stands as though isolated."[28] Although this defensive mechanism is most manifest in cases of obsessional neurosis, Freud is quick to point out its affinity to more "normal" forms of thought:

> The normal phenomenon of concentration provides a pretext for this kind of neurotic procedure: what seems to us important in the way of an impression or a piece of work must not be *interfered with* by the simultaneous claims of any other mental processes or activities. But even a normal person uses concentration to keep away not only what is irrelevant or unimportant, but above all, *what is unsuitable because it is contradictory.* He is most *disturbed* by *what once belonged together but has been torn apart in the course of his development.* . . . Thus, in the normal course of things, the ego has a great deal of isolating work to do in its function of directing the current of thought. (*Inhibition*, p. 47, my italics)

In separating "automatic" anxiety from ego-anxiety, Freud repeats precisely what he describes the ego as having to do to constitute itself; keeping apart "what once belonged together" but what "is unsuitable because it is contradictory." And yet, what is unsuitable here is nothing but anxiety itself, or rather: anxiety as affect. For as an affect, anxiety "disturbs" and "interferes" with the theoretical effort to identify it, to explain it in terms of cause and effect. What Freud is therefore constrained to do is to separate anxiety from its affect, which is also its effect. For that effect cannot be limited to or determined exclusively as the ego's response to a danger, since anxiety can itself become the danger to which it reacts. Freud's attempt, in seeking to replace his earlier "economic" theory by a "topical" one, is intended to put anxiety in its proper place. But his own discussion demonstrates that anxiety *has no proper place*: it marks the impossible attempt of the ego to construct or delimit such a place, but this place is inevitably displaced, dislocated, entstellt.[29]

Freud seeks, in short, to situate and "grasp" anxiety in the dyadic, dichotomized space and time that anxiety itself engenders and disrupts at once. He seeks to ground anxiety in a danger that would be "real" in the sense of external, objective, and self-identical. But in determining anxiety as the reproduction of a trauma, he is inevitably compelled to return to the "economic" factor he sought to exclude. For if the "danger" to which anxiety reacts is real—that is, distinct from the ego, the "organized part" of the "id,"—it is not therefore self-identical. It is, Freud acknowledges, "the economic disturbance caused by an accumulation of amounts of stimulation which require to be disposed of . . . [and] which is the *real essence* of 'danger'" (*Inhibition*, p. 63). But such a *reality* can never be fully grasped by theoretical "insight," since it can never be seen, named or recognized as such.[30] This is why "reality" consists in precisely that "capital X," the unknown variable that "we are obliged to carry over into every new formula." This "X" marks the spot to which psychoanalytic thinking is constrained, often against its will, to return, a spot that is impossible to occupy (besetzen) because it is impossible to locate. Any attempt to identify it, situate it, name it—for instance, as "trauma"—must be regarded as the signal of a danger that can be apprehended, but never recognized as such.[31] The "capital X" of Freud's metapsychology can therefore be designated as *the signal of psychoanalytical thinking.*

But if Freud's effort to replace the economic with the topical, and thereby to put anxiety in its place, proves unsuccessful, it is not insignificant: for the result of his displacement is to underscore the only "explanation" that psychoanalytic thinking has to offer, and that is neither simply "economic," in the sense of dealing with pure quantity, nor simply "topical," in the sense of dealing with pure place; rather, what emerges from the Auseinandersetzung of the two points-of-view is *the ineluctable imposition of the dynamic, conflictual factor as that which characterizes the psychoanalytic conception of the psychic.* The latter can neither be *opposed* to the nonspychic, nor *derived* from it; it cannot be explained in terms of cause and effect, outer and inner, reality and unreality, or any other of the opposing pairs to which Freud inevitably recurs. But if conflict characterizes the psyche, it is also inscribed in psychoanalytic thinking itself. And nowhere, perhaps, is this more striking than in the assertion with which Freud seeks to counter the theory of Rank:

It is unnecessary to suppose that the child carries anything more with it from the time of its birth than this way of indicating the presence of danger. (*Inhibition*, p. 63)

But if the child must be conceived as possessing the capacity to indicate danger *from the very first*, this is tantamount to acknowledging what no causal explanation can admit: that there is no "very first," since from the first there is repetition, i.e., indication. There is, therefore, no possibility for a theoretical discourse to accede to a time or place "beyond" or "before" the operation of such indication and repetition. But if there is no such Beyond, there is also no simple Here either: and the psychoanalytic articulation of anxiety is thus suspended, as is anxiety itself. Anxiety, Freud writes, is always "Angst vor etwas" — a phrase that is impossible to render in English, as the Standard Edition notes (p. 91). For the "vor" that positions anxiety means both "before" and "in front of." If we keep this ambiguity in mind, the English translation "about" ("it is anxiety *about* something") can be suggestive, especially in its spatial indetermination: anxiety is *about* and *around* that which it seeks to recognize. And psychoanalysis, for which "thought" was always a matter of "signals," thinks no differently: it *repeats* the anxiety it *describes*.

In so doing, psychoanalytic thinking sets itself apart.

II. The Other Part

Here it is. It is only with great reluctance that I could bring myself to let it out of my hands. Personal intimacy alone would not have sufficed, had there not been our intellectual candor to support it. It is written entirely following the dictates of the unconscious, in accordance with the celebrated principle of Itzig, the Sunday horseman. "Itzig, where are you riding?" "Don't ask me, ask the horse." I never knew at the beginning of a paragraph where I would land.

S. Freud, Letter to W. Fliess

The Meaning of the Thallus

Every science is informed by a notion of meaning, which serves to legitimize the knowledge it seeks to produce. That such a notion presided over the emergence of psychoanalysis is clearly indicated by the programmatic statement with which Freud begins *The Interpretation of Dreams*:

In the pages that follow I shall bring forward proof that there is a psychological technique which makes it possible to interpret dreams, and that, if that procedure is employed, *every dream reveals itself to be a meaningful structure [ein sinnvolles Gebilde]* which can be inserted at an assignable point in the mental activities of waking life. (S.E. 4, 1, my italics)

The condition that Freud here mentions, the "procedure" or "technique" (*Technik*) to be used, is of course the specific kind of interpretation elaborated in his study of dreams. From the very first, then, Freudian psychoanalysis was bent upon demonstrating both the ubiquity of "meaning" in the realm of mental activity and the peculiar interpretive techniques required to get at such meaning. One of the primary obstacles that Freud faced in this context was the traditional conception of meaning, which construed it either as the implementation of conscious, volitional intention, or as the expression of organic, physiological processes. It is this alternative — conscious intentionality and/or physiology — and above all, its first term, that Freud attacked from the start. Throughout *The Interpretation of Dreams* he insisted again and again that "the most complicated mental achievements are possible without the collaboration of consciousness (S.E. 5, 593), and hence that meaning, in respect to mental activity, could not be restrictively identified with conscious intentionality or thought. "Psychiatrists have been far too ready . . . to abandon their belief in the connectedness of psychical processes" (S.E. 5, 528-29), he argued, precisely because they have construed such connectedness and purposivity exclusively in terms of conscious thought.

The method of interpretation developed in Freud's study of dreams is presented as the mirror-image of the dream-itself: reversing the path traveled by the psyche in composing the dream, interpretation seeks to travel the same road but in reverse, proceeding from the "manifest" content to the dream's hidden, "latent" meaning. No wonder, then, that the essence of the Freudian conception of dreams came to be identified with this dualistic structure of manifest/latent content. Such identification entails a basic misconception that Freud, in a long note appended in 1925 to the sixth chapter of his book (dealing with the dream-work), sought to set straight:

> I used at one time to find it extraordinarily difficult to accustom readers to the distinction between the manifest content of dreams and the latent dream-thoughts. . . . But now that analysts at least have become reconciled to replacing the manifest dream by the meaning revealed by interpretation, many of them have become guilty of falling into another confusion to which they cling with equal obstinacy. They seek to find the essence of dreams in their latent content and in so doing they overlook the distinction between the latent dream-thoughts and the dream-work. At bottom, dreams are nothing other than a particular *form* of thinking. . . . It is the dream-work that creates the form, and it alone is the essence of dreaming—the explanation of its peculiar nature." (S.E. 5, 506-7)

All dreams, like mental phenomena in general, are, Freud insists, meaningful, but it is not their *meaning* as such that constitutes their "essence." The distinctive structure of the dream resides not in the semantic content of the "latent" dream-thoughts, but rather in the particular *form* that the dream-work impresses on those thoughts. The characteristics of that "particular form of thinking" are summed up in Freud's term, Entstellung, a term that can be understood properly only when placed in contrast to the notion of Darstellung. To identify the essence of the dream with its hidden, "latent" content would be acceptable only if the dream were in fact a Darstellung, a form of representation in which one set of thoughts was simply and directly replaced by another, corresponding set. But this, Freud insists, is not the case. Although in dreams there is, of course, substitution and replacement of "latent" dream-thoughts by "manifest" dream-content, such processes cannot be considered as instruments of the representation of one (self-identical) set of thoughts by another. The dream is motivated not by the goal of representing, but rather — if a neologism may be permitted — *de-presenting*, and this despite the fact, to which Freud alludes, that the dream depicts its images in the present. For the presentation of (predominantly visual) images in a dream is governed by the syntax of a scenario, the defining relations of which cannot be comprehended in the present tense. The operative mechanisms of that syntax — the language of the unconscious — coincides with the four kinds of dream-work: condensation, displacement, representability,[1] and secondary elaboration. These operations are what make the dream a "particular form of thinking" distinct from our waking conscious thought. If the latter articulates itself through predications, propositions, and assertions, in conformity with the law of identity and noncontradiction, the language of the dream is one in which identity and noncontradiction are strategic, calculated, and misleading after-effects of differential relationships, transformations, and displacements. If the language of the dream is that of the "unconscious," it is not primarily because certain "wishes" cannot be consciously "fulfilled," but rather because the dream works in and through a medium that is structurally irreducible to the predicative grammar of conscious thought. Consciousness requires identical terms: subjects, objects, predicates, in order to *be* or *become* conscious (i.e., conscious of some-*thing*); as *Ent-stellung* (disfiguration, but also dislocation), however, what the dream does is to operate changes of place, and through such changes, alterations of identity. Moreover, as we have seen in our discussion of "secondary elaboration," the dream does this in a characteristic way: not only does it disfigure, distort, dislocate, (the dream-thoughts, or wishes), but it also dissimulates this very process of distortion. The logic of identity takes its place in the dream's strategy of displacement as that which dissimulates the distortions that have taken place, have taken *the* place of the conscious mind precisely by seeming to yield to it.

The effects of this peculiar and distinctive dream-operation are more obvious and easier to deal with in regard to the dream considered as an *object* than in respect to the *subjects* who interpret, or theorize, dreams. That the dreamer is necessarily deluded is easy enough to assert and to accept, as long as such delusion serves to establish the insight and authority of those who make such assertions. That psychoanalytically schooled dream-interpreters may themselves be deluded, in equating the dream with the meaning their interpretation reveals, is less comfortable but still tolerable as long as there is something, or someone, to which the delusion does *not* extend; the theory of the dream-work, "Freud." But what if that is no longer the case? What if the analysis of the dream as Entstellung points to the fact that the interpretation of meaning, at least as traditionally construed and practiced, is itself only part and parcel of a larger process, one of *verstellenden Entstellung (dissimulating dislocation)*? Where would this leave the interpreter of dreams, or the theorist of dream-interpretation?

Such questions are at work in the first pages of the seventh and final chapter of *The Interpretation of Dreams*. The chapter begins as follows:

Among the dreams which have been reported to me by other people, there is one which has special claims upon our attention at this point [*der jetzt einen ganz besonderen Anspruch auf unsere Beachtung erhebt*]. (S.E. 5, 509)

That "point" in time (jetzt) at which the dream Freud is about to recount makes its special claim upon our attention is a decisive one. It follows the long, elaborate and central chapter in which the dreamwork, "essence" of the dream, has been discussed and described. And it both precedes and introduces an entirely new dimension of investigation, in which the "psychological"—or as Freud will later say, the "metapsychological"—implications of phenomena, such as the dream, are to be studied. These introductory pages, and above all the particular dream they deal with, have the function of effectuating and motivating the transition from the descriptive-analytical account of dreams to their synthetic-theoretical conceptualization; in other words, the task of preparing a certain *speculation*, toward which, as we have seen, Freud is irresistibly drawn. This speculation manifests its ambivalent attraction here—"jetzt"—with strange clarity. Freud continues his introduction of the dream:

It was told to me by a woman patient who had herself heard it in a lecture on dreams: its actual source is still unknown to me. Its content made an impression on the lady, however, and she did not miss the chance of "redreaming" it, that is, of repeating elements of the dream in her own dream, in order through this transfer [*Übertragung*] to express agreement [*Übereinstimmung*] in one particular point. (S.E. 5, 509)

What this particular point is, we are never told. All the more striking, however, is the distinct description of the network by which the dream has been *transmitted* (in German, another meaning of Übertragung). Inscribed in a sequence of repetitions and recountings, its "actual source still unknown," this scene recalls, or anticipates, another scenario, with which we will deal in the following section: Plato's

Symposium and the use Freud makes of it in *Beyond the Pleasure Principle*. As in Plato's text, it is a woman who serves as the agent of the immemorial recounting, but here, in *The Interpretation of Dreams*, the woman remains nameless, described and situated only as "a woman patient," impressed by what Freud himself will call a *"vorbildlichen"* dream: a "model dream", exemplary, but also, perhaps, one which is premonitory, prefigurative:

The preliminaries to this vorbildlichen dream are as follows:

A father has been watching beside his child's sick-bed day and night on end. After the child has died, he goes into an adjoining room to rest, leaves the door open, however, so that from his bed chamber [*Schlafraum*: literally, *sleeping-space*] he can look into the room where the corpse of the child lies in state, surrounded by tall candles. An old man has been hired to keep watch and sits next to the corpse, murmuring prayers. After a few hours' sleep, the father dreams that the child is standing at his bedside, grasps him by the arm and whispers reproachfully to him, "Father, don't you see that I'm burning?" He wakes up, notices a bright glare coming from the next room [*Leichenzimmer*], hurries there, finds the old watchman dozed off, the coverings [*die Hüllen*] and one arm of the cherished body burned by a lighted candle that had fallen on them.[2] (S.E. 5, 509)

The dream itself, we see, continues the series of repetitions that marks its transmission: the father, watching over his son's sickbed, is replaced by "an old man" who watches over the deathbed. The father falls asleep, the old man dozes off. The son "awakes," and wakes the father, who sees the light that the old man cannot see. And, as we shall "see," the repetitions by no means stop here. But let us follow Freud, as he proceeds to interpret the dream—or rather, to recount the interpretation of a dream that, he will contend, is so simple that it indeed needs no interpretation:

The explanation of this moving dream is simple enough and, so my patient told me, was correctly given by the lecturer. The glare of light shone through the open door into the sleeping man's eyes and led him to the conclusion he would have arrived at if he had been awake, namely that a candle had fallen over and set something alight in the neighbourhood of the body. It is even possible that he had felt some concern when he went to sleep as to whether the old man might not be incompetent to carry out his task. (S.E. 5, 509-10)

Dead son, slumbering old man, and, in between the two, a father whose vigilance falters after the death of his son, to revive just in time to save the mortal remains of the child, with only a singed arm and "wrappings"—Hüllen—as marks of the near-catastrophe. This "moving" dream, Freud asserts, presents absolutely no difficulties to its interpreters: be it "the lecturer," the woman patient, or the author of *The Interpretation of Dreams*. The dream, according to Freud, "is simple enough" and it is precisely this simplicity that will be of interest. But first, in what does this alleged simplicity consist? First, in the effect of the glare, and of the other "day-residues" in producing the dream; such residues include, apparently, the father's possible "concern" with the "incompetency" of the old man to perform the task assigned to him. Second, there is "the fulfillment of a wish" residing in the desire of the father to see his child live once again.

Having thus asserted the simplicity of this dream, Freud goes on to explain why he has introduced it at this very point in his text:

There can be no doubt as to which peculiarity of this little dream has captivated [*fesselt*] our interest. Hitherto we have been predominantly concerned with the secret meaning of dreams, the ways in which it can be discovered and the means employed by the dream-work in order to conceal it. And now we stumble upon a dream which poses no problem of interpretation, whose meaning is obvious and unveiled [*dessen Sinn unverhüllt gegeben ist*], and yet we observe that this dream still retains the essential characteristics through which dreams diverge so conspicuously from our waking thought and provoke our need for explanation (S.E. 5, 510)

And the conclusion that Freud draws from this appreciation of this model-dream is nothing less than the radical *mise-en-question* of everything he has hitherto written on the subject of dreams:

It is only after doing away [*nach der Beseitigung*] with everything that concerns the work of interpretation that we can notice how incomplete our psychology of dreams has remained. (S.E. 5, 510-11)

Freud's conclusion calls to mind the jingle that occurs to Leopold Bloom at various points in *Ulysses*:

> What is home without
> Plumtree's Potted Meat?
> Incomplete.
> With it an abode of bliss.

What is a dream-theory without a metapsychology? Incomplete, writes Freud. With it, an abode of bliss, to be sure. But the path to this abode is as dark and uncertain as it is unavoidable:

Hitherto, unless I am greatly mistaken, all the paths along which we have travelled have led us toward the light—toward elucidation and fuller understanding. But as soon as we endeavour to penetrate more deeply into the mental processes involved in dreaming, every path will end in darkness. (S.E. 5, 511)

The way to speculation is obscure because it leads away from the known toward the unknown, away from elucidation (*Aufklärung*) and into the murky realm of hypothesis and supposition (*Annahmen*). Even in the best of cases, Freud concludes, where errors in the calculation and combination of such hypothetical constructs are kept to a minimum, no definitive insight will be attainable through the study of dreams alone:

The psychological hypotheses drawn from our analysis of dream-processes will have to wait at the station until the transfer comes along [*an einer Haltestelle warten müssen, bis sie den Anschluss . . . gefunden haben*], linking them with the results of other investigations that seek to penetrate the nucleus of the same problem by other points of attack. (S.E. 5, 511)

That the description of metapsychological speculation here slides into the language of warfare and transport should, after our discussion of Auseinandersetzung, no longer come as a total surprise. Indeed, the remainder of this introductory section of the metapsychological seventh chapter of *The Interpretation of Dreams* stands entirely under the sign of a proleptic Auseinandersetzung with possible objections that might be addressed at the previous discussion of dreams.

What captivates our interest here, however, is the manner in which Freud introduces and prepares that Auseinandersetzung, by himself seeming to pull the rug out from under his preceding theory. The "little dream" is exemplary, vorbildlich, he claims, in that it demonstrates how little questions of meaning and interpretation suffice to account for the specificity of the dream. This, Freud asserts, must convince us of the incompleteness of the previous study. Were we, however, to take Freud's interpretation of this dream at face value: namely, as a dream which neither needs nor suffers any further interpretation, since it presents its meaning without veils, *unverhüllt* —the consequence would not simply be the "incompleteness" of Freud's first six chapters, but their fundamental inadequacy. For the result of those chapters is, as we have already suggested, nothing more or less than the conclusion that the dream is—essentially and structurally—a dissimulating distortion, *eine verstellende Enstellung,* and hence, that it always and inevitably requires interpretation to be understood. *Either* the very notion of a fully transparent dream, one whose meaning is *unverhüllt gegeben*, is a non sequitur; *or* the theory of the dream as a particular form of unconscious thought characterized by the dissimulating activity of the dream-work must be drastically revised.

But does Freud really claim that the meaning of this dream is "obvious," transparent, "unverhüllt gegeben"? He does, inasmuch as the assertion stands explicitly in the text. But, in accordance with the graphics of Auseinandersetzung, he also undermines the simplicity of that assertion with a discreet but indelible remark, one that I have hitherto omitted from my previous discussion of this passage since its obvious discrepancy with the main thrust of Freud's argument would have rendered any summary impossible and incoherent. That incoherence, of course, is just what demands that we return to it now. Having *apparently* endorsed the "simple" explanation of the dream as given by the lecturer and relayed by the woman patient—that it was the glare from the neighboring room that alerted the father to the fire—Freud adds the following, seemingly innocuous qualification:

> Nor have we any changes to suggest in this interpretation, except perhaps to add the requirement that the content of the dream must be overdetermined and the words uttered by the child composed of words really uttered while alive, in connection with events possessing importance for the father (S.E. 5, 510)

This modest addition does nothing less than to dislocate the interpretation of the dream as one whose meaning is given "without veils." The "requirement" (*Forderung*) that this dream, like all others previously analyzed, "must be overdetermined" reintroduces the necessity and centrality of interpretation that Freud is at pains here to call into question. For if the model dream is overdetermined, the interpretation that Freud seeks to privilege by no means suffices to demonstrate the limitations of interpretation as such in accounting for the peculiarities of dreams. Above all, the little dream ceases to operate as Freud would like it to: to demarcate a clear-cut border separating the previously explored realm of light and meaning, the interpretation of dreams, from the hypothetical speculation that will seek to map out the obscure context of the phenomenon.

Freud's dream here is of a sphere beyond—*jenseits*—interpretation, an uncharted field shrouded in darkness, waiting to be discovered, a virgin land. It is the desire to mark out the necessity and the integrity of this promised land that leads him to attempt the sacrifice of the "child" he has just spawned, by pointing up all of its inadequacies. This gesture—which will recur frequently throughout Freud's writings —is, of course, always made with a view toward subsequent reappropriation and gain: if the dream-theory is still incomplete, what is to come will insert it in a larger and more powerful whole, provided that one has the necessary courage, intelligence, and above all, patience to wait at the station (*Haltestelle*) until the right connection (*Anschluss*) comes along.

The question that persists here concerns the itinerary of this trip and the space that it traverses. Looking back on the distance hitherto covered, Freud seeks to divide that space into a neat opposition of light and dark, black and white; but his daydream is disrupted by the night-dream that is summoned to confirm it. Instead of demonstrating the transparency of meaning and thus pointing toward the necessity of a theoretical speculation beyond all interpretation, jenseits, this model dream suggests that interpretation has not yet really begun, even while going on all the time. If this little dream can be regarded as exemplary, it is because it indicates precisely what Freud here seeks to deny: that interpretation and speculation cannot simply be *opposed* to one another, since a certain form of speculation is already at work within the interpretation of dreams, even and especially in what may seem to be its most obvious instances. "Don't you see?" The child's admonition to the father is, in the context of *The Interpretation of Dreams*, also a reproach directed by the text at its "father." For although the father of the "little dream" will discover that both the child's "arm" and his "veils" (Hüllen) have been burned, the father of *The Interpretation of Dreams* wants to separate the two: his child from the veils in which he has been clothed.

"Father, don't you see?" And yet, in a certain sense Freud *does* see here, he sees without seeing. By mentioning, and be it in passing, that these words of the child must relate to "events of importance to the father," he points directly to what his interpretation seeks to obscure: the conflictual ambivalence that characterizes desire in general and infantile desire in particular, and which is responsible for the inevitable (and structural) overdetermination of dreams. Freud "sees" all this but seeks to avoid its consequences by the use of a mechanism discussed earlier in this book, that of *isolation*: the fact of overdetermination is noted, but its implication: that the meaning of this dream cannot be simply unveiled, "unverhüllt gegeben," is ignored.

It would, no doubt, be interesting to speculate about the desire that produces Freud's interpretation-to-end-all-interpretation: the desire for a dream that would simply mirror a reality and *speak for itself*, for a meaning given without veils, for a world neatly divided into light (the past) and dark (the future). One would doubtless come back to an insight that psychoanalysis will articulate again and again, in different forms: that there are times and spaces where light can be more threatening than dark, especially when the two can no longer be simply opposed to one another as discrete entities, but *cohabit the same space*; when, for instance, a Leichenzimmer can no longer be opposed to a Schlafraum (as reality to a dream) or clearly separated from it. The dream of the burning child, together with the interpretive discourse it elicits, stages this cohabitation or convergence in what might be called an *Urszenario*, where narrator and narrated come strangely to resemble one another.

Less speculatively, it may be noted that the immediate effect of this model dream within the economy of Freud's text is quite the opposite of what it is explicitly intended to bring about: instead of moving beyond interpretation, the dream is followed by some of the most extensive and probing discussions of interpretation and meaning that Freud will ever undertake. These discussions suggest that what this "moving" dream in fact *moves* us toward is less the necessity to transcend hermeneutic questions as such, but rather that of widening and transforming their scope. Here, Freud's argumentation progresses with the lack of logicality that he has previously ascertained to be one of the distinguishing characteristics of dreams. Having identified the model dream as one that speaks simply, clearly, and univocally, Freud goes on to discuss

a number of further, somewhat disconnected points on the subject of interpreting dreams. . . . It is only with the greatest difficulty that the beginner in the business of interpreting dreams can be persuaded that his task is not at an end when he has a complete interpretation in his hands—an interpretation which makes sense, is coherent and throws light upon every element of the dream's content. For the same dream may perhaps have another interpretation as well, an "over-interpretation," which has escaped him. . . . The reader will always be inclined to accuse the Author [*dem Autor vorzuwerfen*] of squandering his wit unnecessarily; whoever has acquired this experience for himself will know better. (S.E. 5, 523)

The child's reproach to the father ("Don't you see?") is here repeated as the anticipated reproach that the reader will direct at the author. Could the attempt to find a dream that requires no further interpretation be the effort of Freud to elude this reproach? If such is the case, however, it is bound to fail, since there is always the possibility —and indeed, usually the necessity—of an "over-interpreation," not in the sense of an excessive, overingenious, and superfluous exercise of "wit," but rather as one demanded by the structural tendency of the dream to be overdetermined. Interpretation, we sense, begins to become a problem, not because there is too little meaning in dreams, bur rather because there is *too much*: confronted by "the abundance of the unconscious trains of thought, striving to find expression (and) active in our minds," how can the interpreter know for certain which train he should take, which connection is the "right" one? To refer the skeptical reader to "experience" can hardly be sufficient, since the latter is nothing but the conscious residue of the same conflicts that produce the uncertainty in the first place.

If there is no simple answer to the question of certainty, what does emerge is that the position of the interpreter, and the activity in which he is engaged, can no longer be construed on the model of contemplation: the interpreter is no longer, as traditionally construed, essentially a spectator or an observer, he is also and at the same time a protagonist, and the results of his actions are determined by a relation of forces in which he is inscribed:

The question whether it is possible to interpret *every* dream must be answered in the negative. It must not be forgotten that in interpreting a dream we are opposed by the psychic forces which were responsible for its distortion [Entstellung]. It is thus a question of relative strength whether our intellectual interest, our capacity for self-discipline, our psychological knowledge and our practice in interpreting dreams enable us to master our internal resistance. (S.E. 5, 525)

In short, the very forces that make interpretation possible—by forming the dream in the first place—also render its results uncertain, incalculable, and impossible to verify (or to falsify) definitively. For there can be no such "definitive" instance precisely because there is no Archimedean or transcendental point from which such a definition or delineation could be established. The topographical structure of the dream seems designed in a way that renders such demarcations impossible. This, at least, is what emerges from what is surely the most celebrated passage in this entire section—and perhaps in the book as a whole—where Freud attempts to describe what he calls "the navel of the dream":

Even in the best interpreted dreams, there is often a place [*eine Stelle*] that must be left in the dark, because in the process of interpreting one notices a tangle of dream-thoughts arising [*anhebt*] which resists unravelling but has also made no further contributions [*keine weiteren Beiträge*] to the dream-content. This, then, is the navel of the dream, the place where it straddles the unknown [*dem Unerkannten aufsitzt*]. The dream-thoughts, to which interpretation leads one, are necessarily interminable [*ohne Abschluss*] and branch out on all sides into the netlike entanglement [*in die netzartige Verstrickung*] of our world of thought. Out of one of the denser places in this meshwork, the dream-wish rises [*erhebt sich*] like a mushroom out of its mycelium. (S.E. 5, 530)

Here, perched on the threshold of metapsychology, on the border that ostensibly divides the transparent realm of dream-interpretation from the obscurities of speculation, Freud looks back, only to discover, or describe, a shadowy place in the midst of the light. And yet, there is no tone of anxiety, no sense of shock, no cause for concern, for the "place that must be left in the dark," "even in the best interpreted dreams," can still be put squarely in its place, despite—or rather *because* of its obscurity. It is as if its shadowy contours are all the more readily identifiable, localizable, by virtue of the clarity against which they are silhouetted. However impenetrable this "tangle" may be, however much it resists unraveling, there is no question —for Freud, at least—that these dream-thoughts have "made no further contributions to the dream content." No *further* contribution? Just enough to put us on the track, to guide us to this curious place, nothing more, or so Freud implies. But if the tangle of thought eludes further analysis and interpretation, how can we be so certain that it has made no further contribution to the dream?

Freud, in any case, seems content to leave it at that. Having "isolated" the tangle, he proceeds to name and describe it, in a figure that has caught, indeed captivated the imagination of his readers. The figure he thus creates is so striking and graphic that it appears to resolve all obscurities in a single illuminating stroke: *the navel of the dream*. What could be more reassuring and familiar, more primordial and powerful than this reference to the place where the body was last joined to its maternal origins. That this place is also the site of a *trace* and of a *separation*, but also of a *knot*, is a reflection that carries little force next to the reassuring sense of continuity, generation, and originality connoted by the figure.

Transposed or transcribed into the text at this point, the navel of the dream thus appears doubly consoling: its impenetrable obscurities mark the identifiable site and sight of the dream-wish, source of the dream's meaning. Out of its shadowy tangle, this dream-wish surges into view, thus providing elucidating interpretation with its ultimate object and confirmation.

Or so it might seem to the reader of the Standard Edition who lacks access to the German text. Such a reader is liable to read quickly over Freud's description of the interminable nature of the dream-thoughts without stopping to consider its ramifications, since the Strachey translation renders them far less striking than they are in the German. For Strachey, the dream-thoughts "branch out in every direction into *the intricate network* of our world of thought." But Freud's "net" is not merely intricate, in the sense of being infinitely complex: it is also, and perhaps above all, a *trap*. Traps, particularly those of the unconscious, are rarely less effective for being ignored.

The words of Freud's German, which the Standard Edition translates as "intricate network," are "netzartige Verstrickung." The inversion of the terms emphasizes the alteration: the "net" at work in Freud's text is not a stable or distinct *object* but a *movement* in which one becomes entangled, *verstrickt*. Or rather, the tangle (*Knäuel*) of dream-thoughts does not stay in its place, it begins to invade the thoughts that constitute the light of day, of our waking, conscious life.

But with this movement, the dream-navel branches out not so much into the reassuring solidity of a tree, as the Standard Edition would suggest, but rather into the more disquieting snares of a trap. The consoling inexhaustibility of infinite ramification is overshadowed in Freud's text by the unsettling entanglement in a familiarity that is no longer quite as familiar as it seemed. Above all, the clear-cut difference between dream-thoughts and waking thought begins to be blurred; the fact that the one expands into the other, "ohne Abschluss," as Freud writes, leaves us unable to distinguish the two as clearly as before.

Since our first reading of this passage is "ohne Abschluss," "inconclusive," let us retrace our steps and start again. If, in even the "best interpreted" of dreams, we must nonetheless leave one area shrouded in darkness, it is first of all because we see or notice—"man . . . merkt"—that place in a certain way. The "tangle of "dream-thoughts" is unmistakable not merely as a spot of darkness in a sea of light, but also as something that rises (anhebt) above the rest. Although we cannot disentangle the strands of the figure, its position seems strikingly clear: it "straddles the unknown" (dem Unerkannten aufsitzt). Its site, therefore, marks the point where interpretation reaches its enabling limit, but also threatens to get out of hand. Hence, the implicit injunction in Freud's description of the dream-navel: "this far and no further," since were we to continue, we would doubtless lose track of the dream, of the wish it fulfills, and begin to lose ourselves in the labyrinth of our everyday thoughts. Since those strands make "no further contributions" to the dream, there is no need to go any further. We can, must, and indeed *should* stop right here, contemplating the navel.

But just where is this "here"? This dense and shadowy place where "the dream-wish rises (erhebt sich) like a mushroom out of its mycelium"? The figure of the navel would suggest a position towards the center of the dream, a point from which the dream is generated. Such a place, at the originating center of the dream, is that usually ascribed to the dream-wish. And yet, as we have already seen, the dream-wish as such does not comprise the "essence" of the dream: it antedates the dream and moreover is formulated in the language and logic of conscious thought. The "essence" of the dream is the movement of *dislocation* to which that thought, that wish, is submitted in and through the dream-work. The specificity of the dream is thus constituted by the transcription of dream-wish into dream-facade: by the tissue or "meshwork" (*Geflecht*) woven by the different chains of dream-thoughts.

As we follow the movement of these chains or trains of thought, we move away from the manifest form of the dream and toward its latent content, the dream-wish. But we also move away from the dream as such and toward its ramifications in our overall world of thought (*Gedankenwelt*). This is why, if we did not know precisely where to stop, we might lose track of precisely what we are seeking: the dream "itself."

Fortunately, Freud assures us, we *do* know where to stop: there (*dort*), where the different strands come together to form a positively impenetrable but unmistakable knot: a knot composed of we know not what. The question that remains, indeed insists, is: how can we know just when and where we have reached this crucial place in our interpretation of dreams? Is our inability to continue our interpretation a sufficient sign that we have reached the impenetrable core of the dream? And can we even be certain that this curious navel is in fact at the *center* of the dream, since our interpretation moves us ever further from the dream's manifest form, and ever closer to "our world-of-thought"?

What we need is a guide, to orient us in this confusing space and place.

Indeed, in recent years, just such a guide has presented himself, in the person of Jacques Lacan. At the beginning of his lectures of 1964, now published as *The Four Basic Concepts of Psychoanalysis*, Lacan announced to his listeners (and future readers): "When you read the texts of Freud, you can rely upon the terms I have introduced to guide you."[3] There can be no doubt that the terms introduced by Lacan have guided many of those who heeded his appeal for a "return to Freud." All the more significant, therefore, that the discourse of Lacan, within which these terms are inscribed, leads directly to the place with which we are here concerned:

No discourse can, in this respect, be inoffensive, and the very discourse that I have been able to conduct during the past ten years derives at least some of its effects from this fact. It is never without consequences when, even in a public discourse, one aims at subjects, touching what Freud called the navel—the *navel of dreams*, he writes, thus designating, in the final analysis (*au dernier terme*), the center of the unknown—which, like the anatomical navel itself, its representative, is nothing but the abyss (*béance*) of which we speak.[4]

Whatever else may be unclear in Lacan's discourse, there seems little doubt that, "in the final analysis"—*au dernier terme*—its terms lead us to the "center of the unknown," and to derniers termes such as *béance*. Lacan here repeats the gesture that we have retraced in Freud: the gesture of the final analysis itself, of a certain termination and determination: that of the dernier terme designed to put an end to the indetermination of an interminable proliferation. The final term, here *béance* (there *manque*), designates the place where one can stop and get off the train, having finally arrived at the desired destination. It is the final station, the Terminus or Terminal, where every voyage begins and ends; very different from the obscure, out-of-the-way Haltestelle, where, according to Freud, one must be prepared to wait patiently for a connection (Anschluss).

The certitude with which Lacan designates the precise site of the dream-navel, first placing it at the "center of the unknown," and then identifying this center with the "*béance* of which we speak," reposes upon a certain conception of the Freudian Bildersprache that allows Lacan to declare that the dream-navel and "the anatomical navel" stand in a relation of representation to one another, and that this relation in turn is derived from a property common to (present in) both: that of the béance, the gap or abyss that both are said to entail.

Paradoxically enough, then, it is this very absence, split, or void, that of the béance, that gives the reader, guided by the terms of Lacan, something firm enough to hold on to:

If you keep this initial structure in hand, you will not run the risk of losing yourself in this or that partial aspect of the unconscious . . . you will see, more radically, that the unconscious must be situated in a dimension of synchrony . . . a dimension where the uttering subject [*sujet de l'énonciation*] both loses and finds itself again in both its phrases and its modes . . . in short, at a level where everything in the unconscious that unfolds, is diffused like a mycelium — as Freud says in regard to the dream — *around a central point*. (my italics)[5]

Were it only a question of what Freud said, or wished to say, we might indeed go along with Lacan here and follow him toward a place that in the final analysis is as central as it is empty: the site of what Lacan calls "the subject qua indeterminate."[6] Were it a question of what Lacan and Freud might have wished to see: for instance, the meaning of the dream *rising* majestically out of its mycelium, the meaning of the phallus, Lacan's Baedeker might suffice. But, quite apart from Freud's proclaimed distate for such Baedekers,[7] his texts resist the mappings of such guides. In the case at hand, for instance, nothing in them permits us to conclude that the navel of the dream is either central or empty. On the contrary, it seems curiously full, oversaturated, and if it presents difficulties to our understanding, it is because it contains too much rather than too little. In short, whatever else it may be, a Knäuel is not simply a béance (or an *Abgrund*). And, above all, nothing permits us to assert that the chains and trains, strands and snares that compose the meshwork of the "navel" are neatly "diffused" *around* a center. If Freud's description of this navel differs from Lacan's, it is precisely because it brings into movement just what Lacan seeks to arrest: the very notion and place of a *center*. Freud's navel neither contains a center, nor comprises one. It does something very different: it straddles the unknown, "dem Unerkannten aufsitzt." Let us therefore reflect for a moment upon the peculiar posture or position of the dream-navel, perched on, straddling the unknown. And let us begin by examining—clinically, as it were—some of the meanings of the word "straddle." According to the Oxford English Dictionary, the word derives from the verb, *to stride*; but the meanings that the dictionary lists underscore the transformation that the word has undergone. From a verb designating forward movement, progression, *straddle* has come to signify various kinds of arrested movement, and hence, the assumption of a certain kind of position. Among the meanings given by the O.E.D. we find the following:

"1. *intr.* To spread the legs wide apart in walking, standing, or sitting. b. of the legs: To stand wide apart. c. Of a thing, esp. of a thing having legs; also, to sprawl. 2. To walk with the legs wide apart. 3. To set (the legs) wide apart (in standing or walking). 4. To sit, stand, or walk with one leg on either side of; to stride over; to bestride. b. To stand or lie across or on both sides of (something). 5. *U.S. colloq.* To occupy or take up an equivocal position in regard to; to appear to favour both sides of. 6. *Poker.* To double (a stake, bet). 7. *Gunnery.* To find the range of (an object) by placing shots first to one side of it and then on the other." And, at the end of the article, a synonym: "Bot. divaricate."

Just when we think that we have arrived at the conclusion, au dernier terme, we come upon a final, puzzling reference. And so, to make absolutely certain that nothing important has escaped us, we turn to:

Divaricate: (fr. Dis- + *varicare*, f. *various*, straddling). 1. *intr.* To stretch or spread apart; to branch off or diverge; in *Bot.* and *Zool.* to diverge widely. 2. trans. To stretch or open wide apart or asunder. 3. To cause or spread out in different directions.

The English rendition of Freud's "Aufsitzen" thus as "straddling" thus appears to condense the very movement we have traced in the first part of this study, that of an Aus-einander-setzung, both transitive and intransitive, a process of divergence. Only here, this movement is not one of ideas or concepts, but of a body: in particular, of legs:

standing, sprawling, walking with one's legs stretched far apart. "To occupy or take up an equivocal position . . . to favour both sides," also reminds us of the "occupation"—the "Besetzung" or "cathexis" of "representations" by unconscious drives (*Triebe*), for is not every such posture deceptive, an imposture designed to "*impose*" an impossible *compromise*? Does not such a compromise also imply a kind of poker in which you inevitably have to up the ante to stay in the game?

Freud's "legs" are thus planted squarely on both sides of an untenable alternative, which he "straddles" in all of the meanings suggested so provocatively by the O.E.D., and of which the so-called primal scene is perhaps only the most graphic figuration. But we are not yet done with the ramifications of Freud's Bildersprache, a language that does not so much re-present as it de-presents, "ent-stellt." For Freud does not simply stop at the designation of the dream-navel as the "place where (the dream) straddles the unknown;" he *describes* that unknown, or rather, what emerges from it: the dream-wish, surging forth "like the mushroom out of its mycelium." The dream-wish, which both emerges from the navel of the dream and also renders its "unknown" aspects knowable, is thus inseparable from something called a "mycelium." What, then, is there to be said about a mycelium? Once again, we turn to the O.E.D. for a response, and once again we are not disappointed:

Mycelium. (f. Gr. *mýkes* mushroom, after *epithelium*.) Bot. The vegetative part of the thallus of fungi, consisting of white filamentous tubes (hyphae); the spawn of mushrooms.

If the dream-wish erects itself, phallic-like, out of the mycelium, the latter serves to remind us of what the Lacanian reading would like to forget: that the dream-navel cannot be reduced to a question of the phallus, of the béance, split or absent center of a subject, for one simple reason: the thallus. The dream-navel, as it is inscribed and described in Freud's text, points us in another direction, less visible, but not invisible either. The question raised here concerns the *site* of the navel, the place on which the dream-wish rises. The question, in short, is that of the "signification du thallus." For one last time, we consult the O.E.D., to discover a curious definition: one which consists almost entirely of *negations*:

Thallus, (Gr. *thallos*, green shoot, f. *thállein* to bloom.) Bot. A vegetable structure without vascular tissue, in which there is no differentiation into stem and leaves, and from which true roots are absent.

No wonder that it is so difficult here to "see more *radically*," as Lacan promises ("You will see, more radically, that . . ."). For the essence of this curious figure can, it would appear, be articulated only in *ne-gations*, that is, in precisely that form of language that the unconsious employs to render itself accessible to consciousness while avoiding repression.[8]

We begin to understand why Freud stopped his description at the mushroom and its mycelium, without mentioning the thallus. For what could he have told us about it, except what we now know, and don't know: that it is a structure "without vascular tissue," lacking "differentiation into stem and leaves," and above all, "from which true roots are absent." The "root" of the dream-wish, its foundation, is defined by this absence of *true* roots. Does this mean that there are *false* ones contained within its tissue?

Compared with the thallus, Lacan's "signification du phallus" appears to be child's play: *manque d'un manque*, béance, signifier of the effects of the signifier—all such formulae move easily within the stable, homogeneous spatial continuum that the thallus distorts and distends, dislocates and disfigures.

Perhaps this indicates the limits of a reading of Freud that takes his Bildersprache as the representation of something that can be grasped, named, once and for all, au dernier terme. Perhaps a different kind of reading is called for, one prepared to straddle Freud's text in another manner. For, if at the limits of interpretation we discover, not the abyss of an absent center, but a navel and a thallus, the very notion of *meaning* has begun to change before our eyes—particularly if our eyes are directed at Freud's text. For the word we have been translating as "straddle" has yet another meaning in German: *jemanden* or *etwas aufsitzen* can also signify "to be duped or deluded by someone or something." By the unknown (das Unerkannte), for instance. Or by the terms introduced by Lacan: for instance, that of the *Nom-du Père* (Name-of-the-Father), which, he suggested, must also be read as: *les non-dupes errent* (the non-dupes err). Yet if this error must be understood as constitutive of the very gesture of denomination itself, then this cannot be without consequences for every form of discourse that seeks to articulate truth by means of naming: be it that of Freud, of Lacan, or of this text itself.

From this vantage-point, the meaning of the thallus begins to appear to be—or rather *to play*—a very bad joke on all attempts to articulate meaning. For the ramifications of Freud's description of the dream-navel suggest that interpretation originates and ends in a kind of calculated deception: in a posture necessarily, and structurally, an imposture, and perhaps also an imposition.

In any case, it is beyond doubt that such questions were what impelled Freud to move—walking, striding, straddling—from his interpretation of dreams, the royal road to the unconscious, to the less regal realm of jokes. As we shall see, this was, and is, no laughing matter.

The Joke: Child's Play

One of the earliest criticisms that Freud encountered in regard to *The Interpretation of Dreams* came from his "first reader and critic," Wilhelm Fliess, to whom Freud sent portions of the manuscript. Fliess, "representative of the others,"[9] as Freud called him, was the first to formulate an objection that psychoanalysis was to elicit again and again, in a variety of forms, the most general of which was surely that made famous by Karl Kraus, who contended that "psychoanalysis is the illness it claims to cure." Fliess's version of this suspicion was directed at the surprising ingenuity demonstrated by the dreams that Freud purported to interpret. How, in effect he asked, could a mental activity so far removed from conscious volition display a characteristic hitherto associated exclusively with consciousness? Perhaps, he suggested, what Freud took to be characteristic of dreams as such was in reality only the product of his own interpretation. Freud's response to this objection was twofold. On the one hand, he defended the ingenious, witty aspect of his interpretation as a quality of the dream itself:

It is certainly true that the dreamer is too ingenious and witty [*zu witzig*], but this is neither my fault nor does it justify a reproach [*einen Vorwurf*]. All dreamers are just as insufferably witty, and they have to be, because they are under pressure, the direct way is barred to them. . . . The apparent wit of all unconscious processes is intimately connected with the theory of wit and of the comic.[10]

To his first reader's murmured reproach, the father of psychoanalysis replies in an ostensibly straightforward manner: it's not my fault, he

84

declares, if the dream is witty, even insufferably so—it cannot help being so; it has no other choice, since it cannot be as straightforward as I am, here and now, in my response to you. But Freud's response is itself less straightforward than it might seem. For, while appearing to exculpate himself from the charge of overingenuity and falsification—ultimately, the rebuke of Entstellung—Freud undercuts this argument with his concluding conjecture. The semblance of wit displayed by all unconscious processes, he writes, "is intimately connected with the *theory* of wit and of the comic." *Theory*, however, is not written by the unconscious itself—not directly, at least—but by a conscious subject. The appeal to the object, to "all dreamers" or "all unconscious processes," cannot therefore simply exempt theoretical interpretation from all suspicion.

The question thus shifts: if the witty character of dreams can be attributed to the conflictual situation which they articulate and to which they respond with their characteristic Entstellungen, to what extent is this also a characteristic of the *theory* that seeks to comprehend these processes? In short, to what extent is the theory of Entstellung itself an Entstellung?

The tenacity of this problem determines Freud's second response. Having first denied all personal responsibility for the ingenuity of dreams, Freud then acknowledges a certain dissatisfaction with his previous attempts to formulate the matter adequately:

The dream business itself [*die Traumsachen selbst*] I consider to be unassailable; what I dislike about it is the style, which was incapable of finding the simple, elegant expression and which lapses into overwitty, image-searching circumlocutions [*in witzelnde, bildersuchende Umschreibungen verfallen ist*]. I know that, but the part in me that knows it, and knows how to appreciate it, unfortunately does not produce.[11]

The "I" that "knows" all about the problem is, "unfortunately," unproductive: it is only a part "in me," and it is another part that produces the style which so displeases Freud. In other words, like the dreamers he studied, Freud had no choice but to lapse into those "witzelnde, bildersuchende Umschreibungen" that cast such grave doubts over the scientific objectivity of his investigations, because the "direct way" was barred to the author of *The Interpretation of Dreams*. Like the dreamers, he had to search out images that could not but seem contrived, "witzelnd." In his Auseinandersetzung of dreams and of the unconscious processes they entail, Freud's language is, by his own admission, contaminated by its "object." And this is no laughing matter, since such contamination places the very integrity and reliability of his analyses in question. For the authority of a scientific discourse that treats of distortion, deception, and deformation depends on its keeping itself free of the phenomena it seeks to comprehend. Yet, just this freedom and distance is at stake here, and Freud admits as much in his next letter to Fliess, when he concedes that the latter's objections are not without foundation:

Somewhere inside me there is a feeling for form, an appreciation of beauty as a kind of perfection; and the tortuous sentences of my dream-text, vaunting their indirect words, squinting after thoughts [*die gewundenen, auf indirekten Worten stolzierenden, nach dem Gedanken schielenden Sätze meiner Traumschrift*], have sorely offended an ideal in me. I am therefore hardly unjust in deeming this lack to be the sign of deficient command of the material. You must have sensed the same thing.[12]

The sense of regret, the acknowledgement of his "deficient command" of the material, is the index of a serious problem: to interpret dreams at all, the interpreter must allow himself to participate in the very movement of Entstellung that produces and reproduces the dream. Indeed, the dream—as we have noted—only comes to be in and through such Entstellung and repetition. And yet, if the interpretation hopes to be taken seriously, the logical, chronological, and structural series, the sequence, must not be fully disrupted. The interpretation *of* something other than itself, something that precedes it in principle if not in fact—such at least is the presumption under which Freud operated, and under which most scientific discourse even today continues to work.

What is at stake, implicitly, in the reproach of the "representative of the others," is nothing less than the authority of Freud's theoretical discourse. From this vantage-point, Freud's contention that "the apparent ingenuity (*der scheinbare Witz*) of all unconscious processes is intimately *connected* with the theory of the witty and of the comic," takes on an additional connotation: the "connection" (*Zusammenhang*) marks precisely the problem. The status of Freud's theory depends on its connection to the scheinbare Witz: either it is able to pierce that *Schein* and penetrate to the essence it conceals, that of the unconscious as a serious, substantial entity; or the scheinbare Witz will end up by making a laughingstock out of the theory.

Freud's decision to make the Witz an object of investigation thus responds to a dilemma in which nothing less than the authority and autonomy of his entire theoretical undertaking is at stake. The precautions taken at the outset of his study are indicative of his effort to establish a context in which these stakes will be barely obvious. The very title of his book—*The Joke and its Relation to the Unconscious*[13]—tends to suggest what readers have taken for granted ever since: that the investigation of jokes is nothing more than a case of applied psychoanalysis, in which the latter's theoretical acquisitions demonstrate their fecundity by illuminating a question with which psychoanalysis as such is only marginally concerned. Jokes, the title tells us, are to be studied "in their relation to the Unconscious"—that is, in relation to the major theoretical discovery of psychoanalysis. Throughout Freud's book, psychoanalytic theory appears to serve as the foundation, the point of reference from which the phenomenon of wit is approached, analyzed, and elucidated. One would hardly suspect that in this study, perhaps more than in all others, it is psychoanalytical theory itself that is in question.

That question, of course, is never posed directly. It emerges only gradually, but following a pattern with which we are slowly becoming familiar: Here, as with the dream, the sign or symptom of this pattern crystallizes in the difficulty of delimiting the object of study. The problem appears in the very first pages of Freud's "Joke-Book": in order to place the Witz in relation to the Unconscious, it must first be localized, identified. And it is here that a major obstacle arises: that of determining authentic and reliable examples on which an analysis of jokes as such can be based. Freud remarks upon the curious way in which his predecessors have confined themselves to a small number of canonical jokes in their investigations:

It is striking with what a small number of examples of jokes, recognized as such, the authors are satisfied in their enquiries, and how each takes over the same ones from his predecessors. (*Joke*, p. 15)

Although Freud is prepared to accept this traditional canon, treating his predecessors with more respect than was the case in *The Interpretation of Dreams*, he nevertheless insists on both the necessity and the obligation of widening it through the inclusion of new examples of jokes, which, although lacking the authority of a long tradition of inquiry, have "most struck (us) in the course of our life and have made us laugh the most" (*Joke*, p. 15). In the first section of the book, Freud thus proceeds to accumulate a variety of such jokes; but as their number increases, the increase is accompanied by a growing sense of doubt as to the precise status of these examples, drawn largely from personal experience. Exemplary of the difficulties involved in the accumulation of such examples is the case of jokes utilizing the technique of "analogy" (*Gleichnis*):

We have already admitted that in some of the examples examined we have not been able to banish a doubt as to whether they ought to be regarded as jokes at all; and in this uncertainty we have recognized that the foundations of our enquiry have been severely shaken. But in no other material do I feel this uncertainty as strongly and as frequently as in jokes of analogy [*Gleichniswitze*]. The sensation, which . . . tells me "this is a joke, this can be presented as a joke," even before the concealed character of the joke has been discovered—this sensation leaves me in the lurch most readily with such joking analogies [*witzigen Vergleiche*]. (*Joke*, p. 114)

It is as if Freud had begun to doubt whether the joking analogy is a valid species of joke, or the illusory analogy (Gleichnis) of one. And it seems to be of particular significance that the problem of identifying the joke in its essential authenticity is posed precisely with reference to the use of analogy. Analogy, it will be recalled, was the point of departure for the modern reflection on the Witz in the eighteenth century. For Kant, the function of wit was to "bring together (assimilate) heterogeneous representations," and he defined it as the "faculty of producing resemblances" (*Verähnlichungsvermögen*).[14] That Freud's uncertainty about the status of wit should be provoked by just this aspect of its activity is indicative of what distinguishes his approach from that of his predecessors. For analogy or resemblance is a property of representations, and it is precisely this function of representation, traditionally used to define the Witz, that Freud rejects. For him, the specificity of *Witz* cannot be tied to representations alone, or more generally, to the operation of a cognitive faculty, as Kant, for instance, had argued ("Wit . . . pertains to the Understanding . . . insofar as it subsumes objects under genres"[15]). Rather, the distinguishing property of wit, for Freud, resides in the peculiar effect it produces, an effect that both gives us the certitude that something is indeed a joke, and at the same time renders everything else uncertain. This effect is laughter, and laughter seems just what is usually lacking in jokes using analogy:

If to begin with I unhesitatingly pronounce an analogy to be a joke, a moment later I seem to notice that the enjoyment it gives me is of a quality different from what I am accustomed to derive from a joke. And the circumstance that joking analogies are very seldom able to provoke the explosive laughter which signalizes a good joke makes it impossible for me to resolve the doubt in my usual way—by limiting myself to the best and most effective examples of a species. (*Joke*, p. 82)

A joke that does not produce "explosive laughter," Freud will argue, cannot be considered effective or successful, and perhaps not even a joke at all. The essence of the joke is thus inseparable from the effect of laughter that it produces. This feature, however, raises particular difficulties for any theoretical discussion of jokes. For the property of laughter is not merely one among others; if it allows us a measure of certainty in identifying jokes, it simultaneously poses an obstacle to their analysis and comprehension. It does this by introducing what might be called a *discontinuous temporality* into the structure of the Witz. For, as Freud stresses repeatedly, in order for laughter to "break out" or "explode"—and these are the metaphors used to describe the result produced by the joke—it is necessary that the person who laughs not know what he is laughing at. The constitutive condition of laughter is that one be ignorant of its object. In contrast to all forms of comparison, in which recognition of the similar plays a decisive role, the process of laughter can never be directly related to an object or a representation as such. This, at least, is the conclusion that Freud draws from his accumulation of "examples" and his categorization of them in terms of the "techniques" they use:

(A) joke may be of great substance [*gehaltvoll*], it may assert something of value. But the substance of a joke is independent of the joke and is the substance of the thought, which is here, by special means, expressed as a joke. No doubt, just as watchmakers usually provide a particularly good movement [*Werk*] with a similarly valuable case [*Gehäuse*], so it may happen with jokes that the best performances [*Witzleistungen*] may use the most substantial thoughts as their guise [*Einkleidung*]. (*Joke*, p. 92)

Freud's witty comparison of the joke with the watchmaker confirms in practice what he has been affirming in theory: that witty comparisons alone do not necessarily produce vigorous, explosive laughter. Except, perhaps, if one adds another comparison to those we have been working with: comparing, for instance, the translation of the Standard Edition, which symptomatically *inverts* what Freud has written in the German text (and what I have translated above). Dedicated above all to the production of a clear and meaningful text, the Standard Edition simply reverses the admittedly unusual but also decisive relation that Freud is at pains to articulate. For Strachey, meaning must be the essence and nucleus of any comparison, including those of Freud; and so we read in his translation of the passage just cited that "the best achievements in the way of jokes *are used as an envelope for thoughts* of the greatest substance" (my italics). What Strachey has difficulty in accepting is precisely the point Freud, in his study of jokes (and indeed, in his entire psychoanalytic theory) is striving to make: that "the most substantial thoughts," products of conscious intentionality, are used by the unconscious as a foil, "envelope," or guise (Einkleidung), to disguise and conceal its operations.

This lapsus of the Standard Edition, by pointing up the chasm that separates "the most substantial thoughts" of Freud from those of his most celebrated English translator, serves to underscore the specific peculiarity of that "substance": thoughts, in the articulations of the unconscious, serve as foils, lures, and snares for something else, far more difficult to articulate. And this holds as much for Freud's own language, his Bildersprache, as for that which it seeks to describe—in this instance, jokes and their relation to the thoughts they "express."

If the essence of the joke is precisely *not* to be found in those thoughts—in its contents (*Gehalt*)—this is tied to the peculiar nature of laughter as a specific form of ignorance. And yet, it is just this ignorance that makes it particularly difficult to develop a *theory* of jokes. For such a theory must rely upon the identification—that is, upon the recognition—of authentic examples of jokes in order to arrive at generalizable insights concerning the structure of jokes in general. But if the specificity of the joke is inseparable from the momentary effect of a laughter that precisely excludes knowledge, then how can one be certain that the jokes that one remembers are in fact authentic specimens? How can one know that one's examples are in truth exemplary? The discontinuous temporality of the joke excludes, in principle, its indefinite repetition; and yet, the reflecting recollection of jokes is the indispensable condition for the accumulation of "data" on which any theoretical study must be based. If all that we can retain and repeat in a joke is its Gehalt, but not the laughter it evokes, are we not left with the mere Ekleidung?

This dilemma notwithstanding, the would-be theoretician of jokes has no choice but to collect such guises, and disguises, since there is no other access to what he is seeking. At the very beginning of his book, Freud describes this desideratum by criticizing the deficiencies of his predecessors in the field. Their studies, he asserts, have tended to identify partial aspects of the joke but failed to bring them together into an organic whole:

> They are *disjecta membra*, which we should like to see combined into an organic whole. Ultimately they contribute to our knowledge of jokes no more than would a series of anecdotes to the characterization of a personality about which we have the right to ask for a biography. (*Joke*, p. 14)

But is it certain that we do have the right to ask for the "biography" of a "personality"? Does psychoanalysis have this right? Can the various "case studies" to be found in the writings of Freud be assimilated (wittily or otherwise) to "biographies," in the sense of the "organic whole" that Freud finds wanting in his predecessors? Such questions are even more difficult to answer in the affirmative in the case at hand, where it is not "personalities" that are to be "characterized," but a phenomenon whose essence is not merely hidden behind a guise of meaning, but situated elsewhere, in a burst of laughter, the convulsive singularity of which seems to resist all objectification and even description.

Read with these questions in mind, the first section of Freud's Joke-Book appears as an enormous and ultimately futile effort to determine the essential characteristics of a phenomenon that, by essence, eludes characterization for the simple reason that, confronted with theory, the joke inevitably has the last laugh. Or rather, because that laugh does not *last*: it erupts, passes, and recurs as the silent accompaniment of each of Freud's efforts to track and capture the "hidden, essential character of the joke." (*Joke*, p. 82) Thus, after he has isolated all of the various "techniques" employed in the examples of jokes he has collected, Freud must still admit that the essence has escaped him: "It can no longer be doubted that technique alone is insufficient to characterize the nature of jokes. Something further is needed which we have not yet discovered." (*Joke*, p. 73)

The search therefore continues. Following his description of the joke's techniques—reducible to the two mechanisms already analyzed in his study of the dream-work, displacement and condensation—Freud proceeds to investigate jokes in terms of their function or strategy: what he calls their "tendentiousness" (a word whose agressive connotations the Standard Edition neutralizes to mere "purpose"). Having distinguished four major types of "tendencies": obscene, hostile, sophisticated, and skeptical, Freud once again sees himself confronted by the question of the character of jokes, of their organic unity.

If it is correct to say that the pleasure provided by jokes depends on the one hand on their technique, and on the other on their tendency, what common point of view will enable such different sources of pleasure to be brought together? (*Joke*, p. 116)

And, we might ask further, will that "bringing together," that "*Vereinigung*" be merely witty, or based on true understanding? Will it be good theory, or merely a good joke? The theory of the joke, or a joke (on) theory?

Freud's initial effort, at the beginning of the "synthetic part" of his joke-book, to uncover the essential, hidden character of the joke, culminates in his assertion that it is "the principle of economy" that unifies the various aspects of the Witz and endows it with its essential character:

All these techniques are dominated by a tendency to compress, or rather to *save*. It all seems to be a matter of economy. In Hamlet's words: "Thrift, thrift, Horatio!" (*Joke*, p. 42)

According to this thesis, what the joke "saves" is "having to express a criticism or give shape to a judgment" (43). Were this hypothesis to hold, the joke would also "save" the theory that seeks to comprehend its diverse manifestations, its "examples," by bringing them together under a single tendency or characteristic.

But no sooner has this conjecture been formulated than the author —or should we say, narrator—of the joke-book is overcome by doubt, not entirely unlike the Shakespearean to whom he here appeals. "It all *seems* to be a matter of economy," he asserts, but is that semblance to be trusted?

It may be that every joke-technique shows the tendency to save something in expression, but . . . not every economy of expression . . . is on that account a joke as well. There must therefore be some peculiar kind of abbreviation and economy on which the characteristic of being a joke depends. And let us, further, have the courage to admit that the economies made by the joke-technique do not greatly impress us. . . . What does a joke save by its technique? . . . Is not the economy in words uttered more than balanced by the expenditure of intellectual effort? And who saves by that? Who gains by it? (*Joke*, p. 44)

The notion of "economy" is thus unsatisfactory, since it leaves both the subject and the object of the "saving" unaccounted for. A more complex explanation is required, one that Freud attempts to develop in the "Synthetic Part" of his book. If jokes produce a "saving," this cannot be construed in purely quantitative terms. The pleasure that it affords, Freud argues, consists of two elements: first, in the temporary lifting (*Aufhebung*) of existing inhibitions (*Hemmungen*), and hence of the energy-expenditure required to maintain them; and second, in the (verbal) reduction of what would normally be a complex train of thought. These two forms of economy are described by Freud as constituting the envelope (*Hülle*) and the nucleus (*Kern*) of the joke, respectively:

Accordingly it can be said that the pleasure of jokes exhibits a nucleus of original pleasure in play and an envelope of pleasure consisting in the lifting of inhibitions. (*Joke*, p. 138)

Although these two facets of the joke-pleasure are equally indispensable to its workings, they do not share the same structural or psychological status. The pleasure in play—*Spiellust*—is "original" and archaic, and Freud therefore seeks to retrace the development of the joke by elaborating what he calls its "psychogenesis." This leads him into a discussion of the nature of play in its earliest manifestations in children, a discussion that touches upon some of the same questions that we have come across before. Indeed, one can already discern what will subsequently be his critique of Adler in Freud's treatment of the theory of Gross, who seeks to derive play from an impulse to dominate. Freud rejects such an explanation, while at the same time accepting Gross's description of play as a rediscovery of the familiar, as re-cognition. Play is pleasurable, he asserts, not because it involves a "joy in power . . . in the overcoming of a difficulty," but simply because "recognition is pleasurable in itself—i.e. through relieving psychical expenditure." (*Joke*, pp. 121-22)

Freud's effort to develop a genetic explanation of the joke, by tracing it back to an original tendency to reduce psychic expenditure, merely transposes the problem of economy onto a different, apparently more fundamental ground: that of the play of the child, construed as the effort to avoid the more onerous activity of discrimination by means of analogization. Wit develops out of play, because play, in the child, is witty to begin with. But—and here Freud seeks to account for the conflictual aspects associated with all manifestations of the unconscious, including jokes—the childish pleasure in play is made inaccessible to the adult by the claims of reason (and ultimately by the reality principle). There comes a time when the pleasure in recognizing the same can no longer be readily indulged in, when "one does not venture to say anything absurd" (*Joke*, p. 126), when "the meaningless combination of words or the absurd putting together of thoughts must nevertheless have a meaning" (*Joke*, p. 129). And it is this development that ushers in the phenomenon of the joke, by making the pleasure of play no longer directly accessible as such. The joke, Freud now asserts, arises out of the conflict between play and meaning, *Spiel* and *Sinn*. If play is thus the "origin" of the joke, it is only through its negation or inhibition, imposed by the demands of meaning and of the critical intellect, that the joke proper is forced to emerge. Its initial form is that of the "jest" (*Scherz*). Although the jest represents a lowly and rudimentary form of the joke (a distinction somewhat obliterated by the English word, "joke," which overlaps with the German Scherz), Freud emphasizes that this evaluation does not affect its structural status as a joke, for the jest already contains and fulfills all the essential conditions of the joke. What distinguishes jest from joke, and creates what might be called their qualitative difference, is precisely the *inessential* aspect of wit: the particular meaning articulated. For if the meaning of the joke (Witz) is important, whereas that of the jest is usually trivial, this does not in any way affect the latter's standing as wit, since meaning only operates wittily inasmuch as it functions to distract and immobilize the inhibitory force of critical reason. Meaning, in short, has for the Witz no intrinsic value; it is only instrumental, serving to eliminate temporarily the barriers to play. The result of this determination of meaning is not without a certain paradoxical element: if the "jest" relates to the "joke" as does the "bad" to the "good," Freud is nevertheless constrained to conclude that "'bad' jokes are by no means bad as jokes, that is, unsuitable for producing pleasure" (*Joke*, p. 121).

But there is another paradoxical aspect of Freud's treatment of meaning in the joke: by determining it to be the external facade, the instrumental envelope of the joke, as opposed to its original core of play, Freud seeks to construct the joke as a proper, i.e., meaningful, object of theory. The essence of joke, his theory contends, resides in the manner in which meaning is placed in the service of play. Freud's "psychogenesis" of the joke, seeking to retrace it to an origin of pure and simple play, is the theoretical strategy by which this conception is articulated. To work, however, the play that Freud places at the origin of the joke—and of the pleasure it entails—must indeed be *pure and simple*. This is why he criticizes Gross's effort to derive play from power: "I see no reason to depart from the simpler view that recognition is pleasurable in itself," Freud contends. One can, of course, relate this critique to Freud's refusal to hypostasize the kind of constitutive subject that every such notion of an original will-to-power inevitably implies. But in stressing the simplicity of play and of the pleasure it affords, and in asserting that "recognition is pleasurable *in itself*" because it entails a reduction in "psychical expenditure," Freud also presupposes the existence of an originary, constitutive subject, in terms of whose unity such "expenditure" can be calculated.

If one asks, as Freud himself does, who benefits from the economies of play, and how, the response must be: the ego, and this in the emphatic sense of the term that Freud will theorize only many years after the writing of his joke-book. If processes of repetition, rediscovery, and recognition, as the recurrence of the same, afford pleasure, it is not because of an intrinsic property (which is both tautological as explanation and incompatible with the Freudian conception of the psyche), but rather because of a process he will come to describe as that of narcissistic identification, through which the ego is cathected and constituted as a libidinal object. The ego takes its place by taking the place of the other, by replacing that other within itself and by seeking to deprive it of its alterity. One of the most powerful forms this process can take is precisely the desire to rediscover the same, to repeat, to recognize, and thus to transform a movement of difference into one of identity.

In 1905, as Freud wrote his text on jokes, he had yet to work out his theory of narcissism and his second topology of the psyche. In

1920, however, both of these developments had already taken place, and taken their place within the corpus of psychoanalytical theory. It is therefore all the more conspicuous that when Freud returns to this question of the play of the child for the last time, in *Beyond the Pleasure Principle*, his discussion of it seems little influenced by the theoretical acquisitions made since the earlier study of jokes. Nevertheless, however implicit the influence of such theories may be, it is nonetheless profound and transforms the very framework in which Freud approaches the phenomenon of play. This transformation, it is true, is inscribed in a place that easily eludes observation: on the margins of his text, as it were, on the borders of a scene that has captivated all eyes from the very first. Let us recount that celebrated scene once again, to call attention to its less famous reflection, situated unobtrusively off in the wings, as it were. But first, to the center stage:

> The child had a wooden reel with a piece of string tied round it. It never occurred to him to pull it along the floor behind him, for instance, and play at its being a carriage. What he did was to hold the reel by the string and very skillfully throw it over the edge of his curtained cot, so that it disappeared into it, at the same time uttering his expressive "o-o-o-o." He then pulled the reel out of the cot again by the string and hailed its reappearance with a joyful "*da*" ("there"). This, then, was the complete game—disappearance and return. (*Beyond*, p. 9)

In his discussion of this scene of "child's play," Freud collects a variety of possible interpretations of the motivating force behind it. By comparison to his analysis in the joke book, however, what is striking is the total absence of any reference to any economy or saving of energy. Instead, we discover what might be called a return of the theoretically repressed: the reference to *power* that Freud was so eager to dismiss in his critique of Gross:

> At the outset [the child] was in a *passive* situation—he was overpowered by the experience; but, by repeating it, unpleasurable as it was, as a game, he took on an *active* part. These efforts might be put down to an instinct for mastery. (*Beyond*, p. 10)

A further motive, Freud continues, could be the desire of the child "to revenge himself on his mother for going away from him" (*Beyond*, p. 10). Active control, revenge, rivalry, and the desire to "make themselves master of the situation" dominates Freud's conjectures as to the impulses behind the playing of children, even and especially where it is evident that the experiences thus repeated could not, in and of themselves, be sources of pleasure. If such game-playing nevertheless does not contradict the pleasure principle—and this is of course the perspective from which Freud approaches the phenomenon in *Beyond the Pleasure Principle*—it is "because the repetition carried along with it a yield of pleasure of another sort but none the less a direct one" (*Beyond*, p. 10)

What this other kind of pleasure might be, Freud does not explicitly tell us, not at least in the body of his text. But it is this open question that should alert us to the subsidiary scene inscribed on the margins of the main text, more precisely, in a footnote, where yet another recurrence of the *Fort-Da* game plays itself out. This time, however, the future that disappears is neither the mother, the father, or any other relative, but rather the child himself:

One day the child's mother had been away for several hours and on her return was met with the words "Baby o-o-o-o!" which was at first incomprehensible. It soon turned out, however, that during this long period of solitude the child had found a method of making *himself* disappear. He had discovered his reflection in a full-length mirror which did not quite reach to the ground, so that by crouching down he could make his mirror-image "gone." (*Beyond*, p. 9)

If, then, the activity of producing a disappearance is the more pleasurably intense of the two moments that comprise the game of *Fort-Da*, as Freud suggests; and if this activity is linked to the establishment of control, of mastery, then it is this marginal scene, itself a repetition of the "primary" game, that indicates unmistakably what the "subject" of this power-game must be: the narcissistic ego, in the process of consolidating itself in what Lacan has taught us to recognize as the "mirror-stage." According to Lacan, a certain attempt at identification with the mirror-image serves, genetically and structurally, as the prototype for the narcissistic formation of the ego, which can only establish its identity by engaging in the Sisyphean task of taking the place of another that, qua image, appears to possess the unity that the subject itself lacks. Such an aporetic project in turn determines the narcissistic identity of the ego as one that is inherently ambivalent, since it is constantly engaged in a relation of rivalry with that other whose unity it both postulates and simultaneously denies (by the very effort to appropriate it.)[16]

The Lacanian theory of the mirror-stage, with its stress on the ambivalent identity of the narcissistic ego, could be taken as a direct commentary on this marginal scene. And yet, the footnote plays no major part in Lacan's discussions of *Beyond the Pleasure Principle*, for reasons that are as illuminating in regard to Freud as to Lacan. For Lacan, *Beyond the Pleasure Principle* is above all the text that describes the entry of the subject into the realm of the Symbolic, that is, of language structured by the Signifier. As such, the move it is held to describe is one precisely away from the ambivalent dimension of the Imaginary, associated with the mirror-stage and the narcissistic ego that emerged from it. What Freud's footnote demonstrates, on the contrary, is that there is an *other scene* of the Symbolic, of the Fort-Da game, and it is precisely: the Imaginary, in all of its aggressive, narcissistic ambivalence. Far from relating to one another as an alternative, or as a simple opposition—itself a highly "imaginary" form of relation—symbolic and imaginary, language and mirror-image, signifier and signified are inscribed in a scene that repeats itself, marginally, in a movement, or scenario, from which a certain narcissism seems to be inseparable. And this applies not merely to the scene being described, but also to the theoretical mise-en-scène that reinscribes it. For both theoretical description and the game it describes participate in a similar game, a kind of child's play, but one which is by no means limited to children. For both seek to assign *names* to the elusive phenomena or activity they perform. For Freud, these names are: pleasure principle, mastery, repetition, and finally, death drive. For Freud's nephew, the child playing the game of Fort-Da, the names are precisely: *Fort* and *Da*. But this aspect of the game Lacan's theory of the Symbolic cannot accommodate and must therefore overlook: for if this game marks an "entry" into the Symbolic order of language, the latter is not characterized, as Lacan asserts, by pure Signifiers, in the sense of differential elements. "Fort" and "Da" are not primarily signifiers, but rather words, semantically determined marks used to designate determinate "signifieds." And if the signified states designated by those words entail the important activity of departing and returning, what Freud's description of the child's game suggests is that the subject who articulates the absence of the other—the mother, but also of itself—is one that seeks to *remain* (itself), in spite of the other. In short, the narcissistic ambivalence toward the image of (and as) the other seeks to affirm its self-identity precisely in and as (what Lacan would call) the symbolic subject of the utterance, *sujet de l'énonciation*, dialectical subject par excellence.

Freud, read through the categories of Lacan, thus disrupts the latter's authoritative-authorizing hierarchy based on the primacy of the Symbolic, a primacy that is no longer tenable. The Symbolic emerges as yet another lure of the Imaginary, particularly powerful in the realm of conceptualization peculiar to theoretical discourse. But Lacan also disrupts and displaces the explicit assertions of Freud by pointing to the implicit instance that underwrites the "pleasure of play": *the narcissistic ego*.

Returning to Freud's joke-book, we can conclude that the play with language, which is presented as intrinsically pleasurable, original, and innocent, is in fact pleasurable only for the narcissistic ego, and hence, neither original nor innocent. The diverse forms of repetition, such as the use of rhythmic patterns or rhyme, peculiar both to children's language and to certain joke-techniques (but also to poetry), produces a pleasure not merely because the identification of the same is "easier" than the discrimination of difference, but rather because it serves the interests of the narcissistic ego bent upon reducing alterity to a variation of identity. Seen in this perspective, Freud's effort to construe the relation of play and meaning in terms of an opposition between two, essentially unrelated terms loses much of its force. For *play* and *meaning* now appear not as oppositional activities, but as complementary ones, both deriving from the effort of the narcissistic ego to appropriate the other upon which it depends and in the image of which it constitutes its identity. If the pleasure of play is thus replaced and "inhibited" by critical reason, it is only better to serve the goal that both play and meaning are designed to further: the narcissistic recognition of the Same.

Considered from this standpoint, Freud's discussion of play in *Beyond the Pleasure Principle* illustrates another aspect that is missing from his earlier treatment of the subject, and it is a lack that is all the more serious since it touches on a central aspect of jokes. In his initial determination of play as the origin of jokes, Freud is unable to account for one of the most decisive aspects of the Witz as a linguistic phenomen: the place of the other in relation to language. In his account of the Fort-Da game, that place is indicated even if it is never mentioned as such by Freud. It is marked in the punctuation that Freud gives to the phrase, "Fort! Da!"—the exclamation point that characterizes the utterance as one directed to another person, endowing it with an imperative (Go!), rather than merely a constative tone. Indeed, the very essence of such play as a power-game resides in the manner in which a constative use of language transforms itself into a performative, perlocutionary, "symbolic" one, intent on producing effects, and thereby implying determinate addresses. By thus speaking, exclaiming, commanding, the child seeks to break that "solitude" to which Freud refers. The commanding subject of Freud's Fort-Da! game positions itself in relation to another: not merely the absent mother, but an other specifically summoned by the command itself. Indeed, if this other seems destined to replace the absent mother and to revenge the child, it would provide us with yet another reason for regarding the Symbolic as a lure of the Imaginary, as the discursive continuation of the ambivalent strategy of narcissism.

Freud, to be sure, will have nothing of this in his endeavor to trace the joke back to an origin that is as pure as it is innocent: the pleasure of play—child's play. For such play is designed to provide the ground and kernel not merely of the joke alone, but also of the theory that seeks to comprehend and to master the joke. This theory, we recall, seeks to succeed where others—Freud's *predecessors*—have failed: to organize the "disjecta membra" of the joke into an organic whole. But the psychogenetic derivation of the joke from play is still lacking what is perhaps the most characteristic aspect of the joke. And that, we repeat, is no laughing matter.

The Shaggy Dog

If Freud's psychogenesis of the joke, his attempt to derive it from play, does not have the last word, it is because the determination of the joke as "developed play" fails to account for the effect that every joke must produce in order to be one: that of laughter. Freud, it is true, does endeavor to provide an "economic" description of laughter, one that would relate it to play, or rather to the inhibition of play through the critique of reason. Laughter, he asserts, results when the energies that are otherwise consumed in the maintenance of critical inhibitions are momentarily liberated from this task by a joke and thereby channeled into laughter. But already this explanation presupposes a shift in the economic model implied by Freud's notion of "saving": for laughter results not from energy saved, but rather from *a redistribution of energies within a conflictual force-field*. In Freud's terminology, the word "saving," *Ersparung*, is replaced by the more dynamic, conflictual "relief," *Erleichterung*. The question now becomes, not who *saves* what, but who is *relieved* of what and how? The joke begins to emerge, not as the development of a pure, original, and innocent play, but as the effect of a state of tension.

In this sense, Freud's attempt to theorize the joke as the saving of energy is interrupted by that curious aftereffect, which, while not pertaining to the joke as such, is nevertheless indispensable to its function and, hence, to its essence: laughter. Concerning this laughter, Freud insists on two points: first, that it is tendentially an explosive, uncontrollable, convulsive movement that is difficult to domesticate or even to understand; and second, that it is exclusively the listener, the addressee of the joke, and not its narrator, who can laugh. The narrator thus depends not only on laughter, but upon the laughter *of another* to succeed with the joke.

This dependence on the laugh of the listener—the "third person" as Freud calls him—adds a new wrinkle to the already exceedingly complex "characterization" of the joke. For up to now, Freud has already operated a curious inversion of the traditional relation of language and meaning, outside and inside, in that he has relegated meaning to the "envelope" (Hülle) of the joke, and placed its linguistic "expression" as play in its center (Kern). What he now proceeds to do is to further dislocate the joke by splitting that center, or rather by displacing it: the indulgence in play no longer suffices to define a joke (this would leave laughter fully unaccounted for); rather, it is the rechanneling of inhibition in and as laughter that must be explained. Inhibition is no longer merely a negative obstacle standing in the way of play: it becomes a positive precondition of laughter.

Such decentering of the joke recalls Freud's approach to the dream, which only comes to be in its aftermath, in its (re-)narration or repetition, which is also its (further) distortion (Entstellung). The joke too is ent-stellt: dislocated and distorted in and as the laughter it must evoke but from which it is separated. In contrast to the dream, however, the dis-location that constitutes the joke post facto, as it were, cannot in any way be conceived or confined within a closed, "intrapsychic" space; on the contrary, Freud writes, comparing it to the dream,

a joke . . . is the most social of all the mental functions that aim at a yield of pleasure. It often calls for three persons and its completion requires the participation of someone else in the mental process it starts. (*Joke*, p. 179)

The question, then, that the relation of the joke to laughter imposes on Freud concerns the peculiar role of this other, the third person, in regard to the joke: "Why is it, then, that I do not laugh at a joke of my own? And what part is played in this by the other person?" (*Joke*, p. 144)

The fact that the "first person"—the joke-teller—cannot laugh at his "own" joke, indicates that the lifting of inhibitions must function differently in the listener and in the teller. In the case of the former, the energies that are freed (from maintaining inhibitions) by the joke are not bound to other mental representations by further intellectual activity and hence can be channeled into laughter.[17] In the case of the joke-teller, however, inhibitory cathexes are not simply dissolved, they are shifted to the narration of the joke itself, which absorbs the energy, "binds" it, and hence prevents it from being converted into laughter, except, as Freud notes, "par ricochet" (*Joke*, p. 156). Thus, it is only through the effect produced upon the listener, who is moved to laughter, that the teller can "relieve" himself: "It [the joke-process] seems not to come to rest until, through the mediation of the interposed third person (*der eingeschobenen dritten Person*) it achieves general relief through discharge" (*Joke*, p. 158).

With the "interposition" of the Other, the "third person" who listens and laughs, Freud's effort to theorize the joke gains in complexity but loses in the coherence that he had initially set himself as goal. Instead of a harmoniously organized "whole" we find a scene with three protagonists: a jittery if genial "first person," marked by a tendency toward exhibitionism (*Joke*, p. 143); a voyeuristically inclined third person, "corrupted" (*bestochen*) by the promised "gift" of pleasure (*Joke*, p. 148), and a "second person," who need not be a "person" at all, but rather an inacceptable idea. And yet, if this scene appears to lack the unity that Freud had declared to be his goal in constructing a coherent theory of jokes, the relations of its principal figures coalesce when Freud, again apparently only in passing, on the margins of the main text or argument, as it were, recounts another kind of story.

He comes upon this story in the context of his discussion of the "tendencies" of the joke, which he divides into the main categories of "hostile" or "obscene." In previous studies of jokes, Freud notes, the obscene variety of tendentious joke has been given far less attention than has the aggressive type, perhaps because of a taboo. Within the variety of obscene jokes, Freud turns his attention to a "borderline case" (*einen Grenzfall*), which, despite or perhaps even because of its peripheral position, "promises to shed light on more than one obscure point" (*Joke*, p. 97). This marginal case of joking is that of "smut" or the dirty joke (*die Zote*).

Freud begins his discussion of the dirty joke by reviewing the traditional conception of it, according to which it entails "the intentional bringing into prominence of sexual facts and relations by speech." But this definition is inadequate, for the simple reason that the dirty joke cannot be satisfactorily described exclusively in terms of its content or object: it must be grasped as discourse that is not merely about but also directed at a particular addressee. The key to the dirty joke resides in this addressee:

The dirty joke is thus originally directed towards women and may be equated with attempts at seduction. If a man in the company of men enjoys telling or listening to dirty jokes, it is because the original situation, which owing to social inhibitions cannot be realized, is simultaneously imagined. A person who laughs at the dirty joke he hears, laughs as though he were the spectator of an act of sexual aggression. (*Joke*, p. 97)

If the thematic object of the dirty joke ranges it among the category of "obscene" jokes, it also places the joke simultaneously among that of the "aggressive" variety, thus blurring the distinction between the two types. It is therefore not by a static taxonomy that one can hope to grasp the essence of the dirty joke, but rather by reviewing its development, the story of which Freud proceeds to tell. Its point of departure, as already indicated, is a frustrated attempt at seduction, but one in which we already find the trio of personnages that will characterize the joke-structure itself:

The ideal case of a resistance of this kind on the woman's part occurs when another man, a third person [*eines Dritten*], is present at the same time, since in that case immediate submission of the woman is as good as out of the question. This third person soon acquires the greatest importance in the development of the dirty joke. (*Joke*, p. 99)

The significance of this "third person" for the dirty joke, Freud continues, resides in the manner in which "he" comes to replace "the female" (*das Weib*) as the primary addressee of the joke:

Gradually, in place of the woman, the onlooker, now the listener, becomes the person to whom the dirty joke is addressed, and owing to this transformation it is already near to assuming the character of the joke proper [*des Witzes*]. (*Ibid.*)

It is only through the simultaneous presence, and interference, of a third person that the dirty joke is really constituted as a joke. The dyadic relationship implied in the relation of subject to object, seducer to seduced, must be disrupted by the presence of another, and this, as we shall argue, endows the joke with its peculiar logic, one which is also that of all articulations of the unconscious and which defies the constitutive rule of traditional logic, *tertium non datur*. For wherever jokes are concerned, and wherever the unconscious is at work, there must be a third, excluded from but also including the other two, *con-cluding* as well. If there is a logic of the unconscious, both the joke in general and the dirty joke in particular point to its basic rule: *tertium datur*.[18]

And it is precisely this rule—a bad joke by any traditional standard of logic, and yet no worse as a joke for its badness—that makes the joke a laughing matter. For it is only with the advent of the third person that a space is opened in which laughter can break out. Freud tells us the story of how this comes about. At first, the third person appears as an interloper, thrusting himself between the desiring first person and the desired second. The mere presence of this other man inhibits the fulfillment of desire. The third person, the other man, embodies the moral code and its interdictions. But then, "gradually," a change transforms the relation of first and third persons: their rivalry or conflict is replaced by a kind of complicity in which the aggressive tendency is displaced onto "the female," who remains inaccessible. And the attempted seduction is similarly displaced from the unattainable woman to the other man:

Through the first person's smutty speech the woman is exposed before the third, who, as listener, has now been bribed by the effortless satisfaction of his own libido. (*Joke*, p. 100)

The "satisfaction" that the dirty joke procures for its participants, and first of all for the third person, is evidently related to the imaginary mastery exercised over the desired but inaccessible woman. If, as Freud remarks, sexuality was originally closely bound up with sight (*Schaulust*, voyeuristic pleasure, as well as its inversion, *Exhibitionsdrang*), the dirty joke reenacts this scopophilic aspect, by ex-posing through verbal imagery the absent object of desire, and thereby producing, as laughter, the convulsive discharge of energy previously frustrated by the woman's inaccessibility. In this respect, Freud includes the dirty joke among the more general category of psychic acts bent on "undoing renunciation and retrieving what was lost." (*Joke*, p. 101)

But this explanation cannot account either for the necessity of a third person's being present or for the phenomenon of laughter. Nor can the "loss" of the desired object as such suffice to motivate the existence and efficacy of those inhibitions that normally stand in the way of the kinds of representation practiced by the dirty joke. Indeed, toward the end of Freud's discussion of the dirty joke, it becomes evident that its operation entails more than merely the actualization or making-present of what has been "lost." Freud is describing one of the favorite techniques of the dirty joke, that of "allusion — that is, *replacement by something small*, something remotely connected, which the hearer reconstructs in his imagination into a complete and straightforward obscenity" (*Joke*, p. 100, my italics). "Something small," *Das Kleine*, is described in *The Interpretation of Dreams* as a phrase designating (female) genitals; in later texts it will be interpreted as symbolizing both the penis and the child.[19] Here, the technique of "replacement by something small" used by the dirty joke designates not merely the general tendency of the joke to use indirect means of articulation to escape censure and critique, but more important, a conception of sexuality quite different from that which Freud's rather realistic account of the dirty joke would seem to suggest. The "sexual" aspect of these jokes would, in this reading, consist not so much in the effort to compensate for a loss by imaginary representation as in the use of certain techniques of substitution. The pleasure afforded by such jokes would then be more closely tied to games of substitution than to imaginary actualization or restoration.

Such a notion of sexuality as substitution rather than as presentation or reparation seems in any case necessary if one is to understand the importance that dirty jokes assign to the excremental:

The sexual material which forms the content of smut includes more than what is peculiar to each sex; it also includes what is common to both sexes and to which the feeling of shame extends—that is to say, what is excremental in the most comprehensive sense. This is, however, the sense covered by sexuality in childhood, an age at which there is, as it were, a cloaca within which what is sexual and what is excremental are barely or not at all distinguished. (*Joke*, pp. 97-98)

Just such a distinction will, in fact, be introduced by the development of the sexual significance of the excremental. Together with this emerges "the history of the first prohibition that the child encounters" and that will prove to be "decisive for its entire development" (S.E. 7, 187). On the one hand, this prohibition consolidates the distinction of self and other, inner and outer, own and alien, proper and improper, by valorizing the first term of the opposition positively, the second negatively: "The 'Anal' becomes henceforth the symbol of everything that is to be rejected, to be cut off from life" (*ibid.*). In so doing, the prohibition strengthens the ego's narcissism. On the other hand, and simultaneously, the same prohibition drives the ego ever further into what can best be designated as a *crisis of narcissism*, which culminates in the "castration complex." For the prohibition separates desire from its objects, the body from its products, the ego from others. In adults, it is precisely the ambivalent nature of this "first" prohibition that characterizes what must be regarded as the quintessence of character as such, the so-called "anal-character," with its tendency to exaggerated orderliness, frugality, obstinancy etc.

Something very much like these "characteristics" seem also to "characterize" Freud's own theoretical endeavor in seeking to ferret out the hidden "character" of the joke. First, he seeks to accumulate and to order a confusing proliferation of "examples," above all by subsuming them under the general concept of "saving" or economizing (*Ersparung*). Then, he seeks to develop this notion of economy in two principle directions: as the development of an original, "pure" pleasure in play (playing with feces is, of course, one of the first expressions of anal eroticism, and the first object of that "first prohibition"); and as the "lifting" (*Aufhebung*) of an inhibition standing in the way of such play—an inhibition that is "discharged (*abgeführt*) as laughter and thereby produces "relief" (Erleichterung). Moreover, the joke-pleasure is presented as a gift to the third person, and as such becomes the successor of the very first gift that the child offers: his feces.

But perhaps all this is merely wit gone wild, overingenious analogizing lacking the necessary discrimination. Perhaps. But anyone sensitive to the language Freud uses to describe the "making" of the joke itself will find it difficult to reject this "characterization" out of hand:

We speak, it is true, of "making" a joke, but we feel that when we do so we behave differently from when we give a judgment or make an objection. A joke has quite outstandingly the character of being an involuntary "discovery" [*Einfalls*]. One has no idea a moment beforehand just which joke one will make, and which then needs only to be clothed in words. *Rather we feel something indefinable, which I can best compare with an "absence," a sudden discharge [Auslassen] of* intellectual tension, and then, with one fell swoop [*mit einen Schlage*], the joke is there, as a rule together with its verbal costume [*Einkleidung*]. (*Joke*, p. 167, my italics)

Small wonder that Freud is so bent upon distinguishing the joke's envelope from its core, Hülle from Kern; and also small wonder that in the process of establishing such distinctions, the latter tend to turn themselves inside-out: the outer garment of verbal play reveals itself to be the inner nucleus of the joke, while the semantic material that usually makes up the interior domain is here only a facade. The prohibited game returns in and as this smearing of oppositions that are seemingly clear-cut. Is this then the "hidden character" of the joke? Of its theory? Its proper meaning?

And yet, perhaps Freud's theory, like the joke it describes, has no meaning that would be purely and entirely "proper." Perhaps it too only "makes sense" in and through another, a third person, who is neither simply a part of it nor simply distinct from it: the reader, whose role would not be so different from that of the listener in the joke. That "first prohibition," we recall, requires a third person for its implementation. The history of that prohibition, and the third instance it entails, is also that of the narcissistic striving of the ego to be, or become a "first person." The history of this ego thereby emerges not as that dialectic of Self and Other as which it is generally construed, but as an Auseinandersetzung that entails three participants, three "persons." Let us briefly recapitulate the history of this *Auseinander-setzung*. It "begins" with an impossible and yet self-evident presupposition:

For the male child it is self-evident to presuppose (*vorauszusetzen*) that all persons that it knows are possessed of genitals like his own, and therefore impossible to reconcile the lack of such with his idea of these other persons. (S.E. 7, 195)

The narcissistic belief in the continuity of Self and Other, which underlies the self-evident presupposition of the child, is severely challenged by the first prohibition that occurs in the anal phase, which establishes the idea of separation, and installs an unbridgeable gap between desire and the desired. But this development culminates decisively only in the castration-complex, where the (male) child must renounce, once and for all, the object of its narcissistic desire, and hence abandon the self-evident presupposition that all others are really just like himself, "possessed of genitals like his own." The recognition of others can no longer be modeled on the recognition of the same; the ego is forced to confront the nonego differently. The latter can no longer be regarded as merely a variation of the first person, distinct from and yet subordinated to it. The other is also no longer simply "out there," removed from the ego. And it is precisely at this point that the "third person" *comes in*: that is, enters the scene as the intrapsychic instance or agency (*Instanz*)[20] that is also the repository of the metapsychic values that constitute a culture: the superego. This superego is heir to the ambivalence that characterizes the narcissism of the ego from the very first: from its refusal to accept an other that would be radically different from its self (that is, from its self-image). In this sense the superego embodies both "the heir of the original narcissism" (S.E. 18, 110) and its constitutive limit. "Through its installation (*Aufrichtung*), the ego has both taken control (*sich bemächtigt*) of the oedipus complex, and also submitted to the Id" (S.E. 19, 36). Through its "installation" of the superego, the ego in a certain sense acknowledges the alterity that it has hitherto sought to exclude; but such "acknowledgment" is itself marked by ambivalence. On the one hand, it entails the effort by the ego to assimilate and incorporate the nonego; on the other, it creates a structure of differential articulation that can never be reduced to pure identity, for the superego places the ego in the most classical of double-binds. "Be like me!" it tells the ego, "Be yourself!" And yet, to be oneself is precisely to be *different* from the ideal imposed upon the ego by its "ideal." The superego represents the unattainable identity of the ego, toward which it must strive but which it can never attain. And this relation of superego and ego is precsely one of "third" to "first" person. For the superego speaks the language of the ego, but in the syntax of the id. It is, as Freud writes, "composed of word-representations (concepts, abstractions)" in accordance with its "origin from things heard" (*Herkunft aus Gehörtem*); but the affinity of its discourse with that of the ego is deceptive, since it derives its "cathecting energy . . . from sources in the Id" (S.E. 19, 52-53). The most striking manifestation of this impossible communication is surely that described by Daniel Paul Schreber: the voices that he heard addressed him, as Freud notes, "characteristically in the third person" (S.E. 14, 95).

The "third person," linguistically and psychically, as Benveniste has observed,[21] is distinguished from the second precisely by being a "nonperson," irreducible to the self-identity of an ego (or to its negative form, an alter-ego). The third person therefore does not merely join the first and second to form a trio of individuals, of egos: its "presence" marks the constitutive dependence of the ego as such on something that can never be fully assimilated to any form of self-identity. The "prohibition" that this third person installs—*aufrichtet*—does not, therefore, come upon the subject from without: it dislocates (entstellt) it from within, as it were, turning it inside-out, turning the "ego" outwards toward the superego, but also the (dirty) joke toward its "listener" or "spectator."

Thus, when Freud describes how the third person first hinders the accomplishment of the seduction, and then changes from an interloper into an ally, it is also the structural "resolution" of the Oedipus complex through the installation of the superego that he is anticipating. Whether this implies that the dirty joke is oedipal in structure, or conversely, that the Oedipus complex is a "dirty joke," is a question that will hardly permit a univocal response. But what can be asserted is that their relationship marks the manner in which the ego is subjected to an other in the process of articulating itself. Interdictory tribunal and ideal in one, this other—the third person—is the instance that must decide the fate of every "first person," qua ego. Through it, the ego encounters that measure of alterity which it can never either fully appropriate or flatly reject, since its future articulation depends on its relation to the superego. The paradoxical result of this relation, is that—in the psychic development of the subject no less than in the operation of the joke—the "third" person emerges as the condition of possibility (and impossibility) of the first. The resolution of this "paradox," or rather its articulation, is that possibility and impossibility of being a "first person," an "ego," compose that "being" as one of *imposability* (if not of imposture). The first person becomes himself, a Self, only in and through the struggle to *impose* that Self on and at the expense of the third person. The process of this imposition is condensed—and, in the diachrony of Freud's development, anticipated—in the tripartite structure of the joke, and in particular in the scenario of the dirty joke, to which we now return.

The third person has the power to decide the fate of the joke and hence of the "first person" who tells it. For if that joke does not succeed, as evidenced by the laughter of the listener, the first person is reduced to a nonperson, insofar as the joke is concerned. For the joke, we recall, is no joke without the laughter of its listener.

This dependence of the first person, the ego, on the third person, as articulated in the joke-process, allows us to discern what many readers of Freud have sought in vain: the precise dynamics by which the intrapsychic realm of individual subjectivity is mediated by or interacts with the intersubjective order of society. What we have referred to as the narcissistic ambivalence of the ego constrains the latter to displace its identity—which is always "ideal"—onto an instance that can only operate effectively as the ambivalent/ambiguous union of specular other (superego as ego-ideal) and of unrepresentable other (superego as derivative of the id). These two indispensable but profoundly heterogeneous aspects of alterity, inseparably bound together in the superego and its avatars, produce a curious but significant phenomenon: the "incarnation" of the superego in the third person of the joke—or, more generally, in the addressee necessarily implied by *every* articulation of the unconscious—requires that other to be *both* a determinate individual, acting with a measure of conscious volition, *and* one who is not fully conscious or in control of his acts. Thus, the decision to tell or listen to a joke depends on a conscious act, whereas the effect that decides the fate of the joke—laughter—lies precisely outside the control of consciousness, consisting as it does in a temporary breakdown of such control.

And laughing is a peculiar act, if indeed it can be considered to be an "act" at all: that is, an activity consciously prepared and executed. For what characterizes laughter, at least as Freud describes it in relation to the joke, is that it is only partially volitional. This designates the person who laughs as a "third" in the strongest sense: as a *persona*, a mask, through which *it* (id) laughs. The listener can be disposed to laugh, but even that disposition cannot be consciously decreed; laughter of the explosive kind described by Freud cannot be forced, calculated, or fully understood. It must be spontaneous, automatic, no more subject to conscious volition than the "making" of the joke itself.

For such laughter is characterized, by Freud, above all as a form of non-knowledge, "so that with jokes we almost never know what we are laughing about." (*Joke*, p. 154) Freud insists on this aspect of the laughter provoked by jokes, although it becomes clear, through his discussion of the function of "inhibition" in the mechanism of laughter, that the nonknowledge he describes as its constitutive condition is in fact another kind of knowledge, rather than pure ignorance. This other knowledge entails above all a diversion of conscious attention: "Laughter is in fact the product of an automatic process which is only made possible by our conscious attention being kept away from" the object that will provoke laughter. (*Joke*, p. 154). Laughter thus requires the diversion of consciousness or, it might be said, a certain divarication of the mind. The conscious part can be "kept away" from the object that will produce laughter only by simultaneously being drawn and bound to other representations or expectations, like that of an "intelligible context" or overall meaning to be transmitted by the joke.

It is this expectation of a meaning that thus becomes one of the negative preconditions of the joke, even though such expectation is qualified by the even more comprehensive fact that the joke entails a kind of contract on the part of its participants. A joke is almost always announced as such in advance, explicitly or implicitly, and this entails the expectation of a certain surprise, diversion, laughter. But however inevitable such an expectation may be, the particular "object" of the joke must remain removed from consciousness if the joke is to succeed. All that can be determined, in general, about that object—and it is highly significant for Freud's conception of jokes—is that hearer and teller must share the same inhibitions that the joke is designed to neutralize for laughter to take place. This is tantamount to asserting that the "place" of laughter in the joke-process is socially determined, involving generally held "inhibitions" or taboos (as opposed to purely individual ones). In producing laughter, the joke thus represents a collective if temporary transgression of shared prohibitions. Jokes therefore are always specific to certain groups, which may be more or less extensive, but which are never simply universal. "Every joke," Freud observes, "calls for a public of its own" (*Joke*, p. 151).

The contract that binds the parties engaged in the joke thus diverges from that of liberal, bourgeois jurisprudence: the contracting parties agree to a process of exchange without being certain that they will be able to accomplish the obligations they incur. The listener cannot guarantee that he will laugh, and indeed his laughter, in not being "his" at all, indicates the extent of his nonautonomy, his "heteronomy." What the joke entails is the common agreement to attempt to overstep certain boundaries, of which the consenting parties—in particular the decisive third person—cannot even be fully aware before or during the joke. But since the outcome of this contract can never be known or decided upon in advance; since it depends not on conscious volition but on a relation of forces in which that "other part" will be decisive, the joke takes place in an ambience of curiosity, one that aims not simply at discursive knowledge, but at other forms of discovery.

"Discovery," however, should not be taken as an exclusively, or even primarily, cognitive activity. In the text that he was writing at the same time as the book on jokes, his *Three Essays on the Theory of Infantile Sexuality*, Freud argued that the "desire to know" (*der Wisstrieb*) develops from the "urge to see" (*der Schautrieb*) (S.E. 7, 194). The joke demonstrates the force of the desire to see (and to be seen). Underlying the interaction of curiosity, surprise, meaning, inhibition, and play in the joke is precisely the *Schaulust*: the aggressive "exposure" (*Entblössung*) of the woman in dirty jokes is perhaps only the most evident manifestation of the intimate affinity of wit and vision.[22] In a sense, all "three" persons are ex-posed by the joke (just as the latter itself is exposed in, and to, laughter). That the "second person" is always tendentially exposed by the joke is indicated precisely by the joke's general tendentiousness. The first person, Freud observes, will often be possessed of "an ambitious urge to show (his) cleverness, to display himself—an instinct that may be equated with exhibitionism in the sexual field" (*Joke*, p. 143). Structurally, the joke-teller exposes himself to the "decision" of the third person. But what then of this third person? In what way does he participate in the Schaulust, and to what extent is he exposed to, or by, the joke? And what if this "he" were a "she"?

Characteristically, the response to these questions is inscribed not in the body of the main text, but implicitly, on its margin: once again in a footnote, and once again, added long after that body was composed. This footnote, through its positioning, resembles (but is this perhaps only idle wit, overingenious analogizing?) laughter, in its *Nachträglichkeit* with regard to the main text: written long after the book itself, touching on a phenomenon for which "there is no appropriate name," and of which one cannot even say for certain whether it belongs to the category of jokes at all. This inscription is doubly marginal: appended in 1912 to a long footnote on "nonsense jokes," it is nonetheless "central" to the theory of jokes. As central, that is, as anything could be to a phenomenon in which the core functions as envelope, and the envelope as essence.

But let us first look at the note "proper," added to the conclusion of Chapter Four ("Pleasure and the Genesis of Jokes") and treating the problem of "nonsense jokes." The latter, Freud writes, have been somewhat neglected in his discussion and therefore merit "supplementary consideration." The note begins by stressing that it would be a mistake to conclude that "nonsense jokes" are the primary or exclusive form of the Witz. Such jokes embody only one of the two essential components of the joke-process, the play with thoughts, which evokes pleasure through the lifting of inhibitions; the other, more original component of joke-pleasure, that deriving from the play with words, is independent of such nonsense-effects. Freud thereby recurs to the hierarchical opposition of play and inhibition, rhyme and reason, words and thoughts, with which he seeks to organize the diverse manifestations of the joke into a coherent whole. For only in this way can he hope to collect the membra disjecta—the debris of his predecessors—into a theory capable of characterizing the essence of the joke, and not consisting merely in a series of anecdotes.

But, Freud immediately acknowledges, it is precisely the duality of the joke, "the twofold root of pleasure in the joke," that is itself the root of the difficulty encountered throughout his own study; what Freud elsewhere refers to as the "Janus-face" of the joke, its double or duplicit aspect," gets in the way of a concise formulation in general statements about jokes" (Joke, p. 138). In other words, the ambivalent nature of the "pleasure" produced by jokes "gets in the way," i.e. inhibits, the attempt to comprehend its meaning in a unified theory. It is here that Freud arrives at his most lapidary—and as we have seen, problematical—formulation of the joke as "exhibiting a core [Kern] of original pleasure in play and an envelope [Hülle] of pleasure in the lifting of inhibitions."

No sooner is this distinction formulated, however, than it begins to unravel at the seam. Freud's binary classification, which seeks to describe "nonsense jokes" as the envelope of inhibitory pleasure, immediately demands further qualification: "The nonsense that still remains in a conceptual joke acquires secondarily the function of riveting our attention by bewildering us," and thus "serves as a means of intensifying the effect of the joke." But if every joke must produce laughter, and if laughter derives from the deviation and neutralization of energy otherwise absorbed in inhibitions, then this "secondary" function of nonsense in the joke would have to be no less necessary for its functioning than the inhibitions themselves. The clear-cut distinction suggested by the opposition of Hülle and Kern, the distinction between the transgressive and expressive aspects of the joke, would thereby lose its pertinence, since it would be impossible to say just where the inhibitions stop and the game (Spiellust) begins.

It is this equivocation—the effort to arrive at a univocal characterization of the joke's duplicity—that compels Freud to return to the problem of "sense in nonsense," first in the main body of the note just reviewed, and then, years later (in 1912), when he adds an appendix to this already extensive footnote. This belated supplement concerns "jokelike" productions" that lack a proper designation and that Freud at first characterizes as "idiocy in the guise of jokes" (*witzig scheinenden Blödsinn*). Freud's German, unlike the English translation, reminds us that this "idiocy" is still a form of *sense*: it is "*Blöd-sinn*," a meaning that is inane because it is has "bared" or "exposed" itself (the German "blöd" is etymologically related to "*bloss*" = *bare*) as in the *Entblössung* of the dirty joke. Like the latter, such inanities constitute a borderline case of the joke; if Freud nevertheless mentions them here, it is presumably because, like the dirty joke, their very marginality can help to illuminate the central problem of sense and nonsense in the joke.

One of the examples Freud cites of this kind of joke is the following: "'Life is a chain-bridge' says one man. — 'What do you mean?' asks the other. 'How should I know?' is the reply." (*Joke*, p. 139) The problem, of course, is that the listener—here, the reader—never knows in such cases whether to laugh or to cry. Or to get angry. This, according to Freud, is precisely the point of such "extreme examples":

These extreme examples have an effect because they rouse the expectation of a joke, so that one tries to find a meaning [*Sinn*] concealed behind the nonsense [*Unsinn*]. But one finds none, they really are nonsense. Under the influence of that play of mirrors [*Unter jener Vorspiegelung*] it has become possible, one moment long, to liberate the pleasure in nonsense.[23] (*Joke*, p. 139)

The kind of joke Freud is discussing (if it is a joke at all) deludes the listener, but in a very "characteristic" manner: it presents him with a mirror of his desire "to find a meaning concealed behind the nonsense." (S.E. 5, 506) It is this desire that makes the joke possible, and the example that Freud cites clearly mirrors its peculiar character. "The expectation of a joke" consists in the desire to make sense of the enigmatic assertion with which the joke begins. If the joke then refuses to provide the meaning it dangles before the listener, then its operation cannot be described as pure and simple nonsense. For such jokes "play" games with the desire of the listener to find "an intelligible context," the desire that, as we have seen, is at the origin of "secondary elaboration." This desire involves nothing less than the narcissistic striving of the ego to unify, bind, and synthesize, and thereby to construct that meaningful, self-contained *object* against which it can situate itself as an equally meaningful, self-contained subject, a self-consciousness. By rousing this "expectation" and then leaving it unsatisfied, turned back upon itself, such jokes function in a manner very reminiscent of the discourse of the analyst, who refuses to engage in a meaningful dialogue with the analysand precisely in order to confront the latter with the desires that motivate questions in search of an answer.

Freud, to be sure, does not mention the affinity such "joke-like productions" bear to analytical discourse. He is, after all, only discussing a marginal phenomenon of a subject-matter that itself is marginal in relation to psychoanalysis "proper." But if we bear the similarity in mind, his concluding remark assumes particular significance:

> These jokes are not entirely untendentious: they are "shaggy-dog stories," and give the teller a certain pleasure by misleading and annoying the listener. The latter then mutes this annoyance by resolving to become a story-teller himself. (*Joke*, p. 139)

If the discourse of the joke-teller is not free from aggressive tendencies in regard to its addressees, and if the latter "mute" their frustration by resolving to become tellers in turn, — that is, a "first person," an "ego" — then this opens up a variety of perspectives concerning the genesis both of analytical discourse and of the ego as such. Both would be the effect of a certain "transference" passing from "third" to "first" person through a process of narration that would thus emerge as the general context of both the psyche as psychoanalysis describes it, and of psychoanalytical discourse itself. That Freud would have no particular interest in stressing this "witty" connection is clear enough. For who could then decide for certain whether psychoanalysis had succeeded in comprehending and controlling the joke — as Freud had set out to do — or whether the joke had once again turned the tables on psychoanalysis, revealing it to be nothing more or less than a particular kind of witty story?[24]

And indeed, the story here in question is of such a dubious kind that it would hardly serve to enhance the reputation of the "science" Freud was obliged to defend. And yet, that it is just here that Freud stumbles upon a name for these jokes, for which as he has noted "there is no appropriate name," should give us further pause to dwell on the relation of joke and psychoanalysis. For the term that I have translated as "shaggy dog story," and which the Standard Edition renders as "take-in," is already familiar to us: it is "Aufsitzer," the same word used to describe the position of the dream-navel in regard to the "unknown." If dreams, as Freud claimed, provided psycho-analysis with the "royal road" to the unconscious, the *posture* that psychoanalysis necessarily assumes in negotiating that road is, in-exorably, that of the Aufsitzer.

To suggest that the psychoanalytic movement *moves* with the gait of an Aufsitzer is not, of course, to disqualify it as a pure and simple imposture, but rather to indicate the manner in which a theory that attempts to take the unconscious into account is inevitably con-strained to impose itself. To relate this manner of imposition to a "bad joke" such as the Aufsitzer would constitute a criticism only if we were to forget what Freud takes pains to stress: that bad jokes are no less effective than good ones. To condemn psychoanalysis as an Aufsitzer is only possible if it could be judged from a standpoint or tribunal—an *Instanz*—situated above or outside the story it seeks to judge. Such a court of appeal—the standpoint of the ego—is, how-ever, precisely what psychoanalysis irrevocably dislocates. And it does so by indicating, and indeed by itself exemplifying, how any such standpoint is inevitably inscribed in the very scenario or story it seeks to retell.

This is doubtless why Freud is constrained, many years after the publication of his theory of jokes, to return to the problem of "sense in nonsense" and to address himself to that most shadowy of addresses, the Aufsitzer. For if the ego's expectation of a mean-ingful whole is the implicit but inescapable condition of the joke, then nowhere is this condition more powerfully put into play than in the Aufsitzer, the "take-in" that is also a "come-on." What makes this most dubious of all joke-types so hard to take, is that we, as listeners at least, do not "take" it at all—rather, it takes *us* for a ride, on a road that is anything but regal. For at the end of the road all we find is nonsense: "They really are nonsense," Freud states, thus seeking to reassure us, and himself as well.

But if the Aufsitzer is "nonsense," it is also the quintessence of the joke, the joke played on "the expectation of a joke," as well as on our expectation of a theory capable of comprehending the joke. For that theory, as we have seen, is predicated on the possibility of discovering the concealed character of the joke as such, and hence of separating its outer Hülle from its inner Kern. The Aufsitzer, however, demonstrates the impossibility of telling the two apart, of discriminating what wit has brought together. And its demonstration is even more telling if we straddle the borders of the two languages with which we have been concerned, and consider for a moment the English translation that most closely approximates the German for "shaggy-dog story." Attempts to trace the etymology of this expression have been inconclusive, ohne Abschluss. Most such speculation has focused upon the more substantive part of the term, its canine "kernel," but with little success.[25] But if the *Pudels Kern* has thus proved to be a blind alley, perhaps it is time we cast another look at its Hülle; *shag*, even today (in British English, at least) means precisely what *Zote*, the German word used by Freud to designate the dirty joke, used to mean. For *Zote* stems from *Zotte*, signifying "unclean hair, pubic hair, unclean woman."[26] In short, both the Zote and the shaggy-dog story designate the kind of disreputable, tangled knot that Freud sought either to ignore, in his story of "castration," or to describe as the site of something far more visible and palpable: the mushroom rising from its mycelium. Zote and the shaggy-dog story thus emerge as versions of the thallus, out of which the phallus rises and falls. But this rise-and-fall of the phallus is already inscribed and prescribed in the Zotte, which also signified "hanging (animal) hair, fleece, rags, bits and pieces, bush," whereas the verb, *zotteln*, was used to designate a movement of "swinging back and forth."[27] Even more than the Zote, then, the shaggy-dog story leaves us "hanging" —not, however, in the middle of nowhere, in pure "nonsense," but in the midst of all those narcissistic fantasies through which the ego negotiates its way, from the "anal" to the "phallic" stages, and beyond. That *beyond*, which is also a *before*, is situated in a space that can only be described as thallic. For it is not the presence or absence, the possession or loss of an object that characterizes that space, but rather the texture and rhythm of the elements that inhabit it, "swinging back and forth."

Freud, who set out to unify and to totalize the membra disjecta of all previous joke-theories, arrives here not so much at the organic whole he desired as at its shaggy fleece. Instead of baring the essential characteristic of the joke, its innermost Kern, he is left, not unlike Goethe's Faust, with only a veil—or rather, with a patchwork quilt. Have we, has Freud, been "fleeced"? By the "representative of 'the others,'" that elusive third person, and first reader? Has Freud's theory turned out, once again, to be corrupted by unsavory wit, the very malady it was designed to cure?

Such questions, it is clear, cannot be answered here; the response they solicit must come elsewhere. All I can do, here and now, is to mute my frustration at so much uncertainty by resolving to tell you the following story which I heard many years ago[28] and at which, if I remember correctly, I once laughed:

A Jew and a Pole are sitting opposite one another in a train. After some hesitation, the Pole addresses the Jew: "Itzig, I've always been a great admirer of your people, and especially of your talents in business. Tell me, honestly, is there some trick behind it all, something I could learn?" The Jew, after a moment's surprise, replies: "Brother, you may have something there. But you know, you don't get anything for nothing—it'll cost you." "How much?" asks the Pole. "Five zlotys," answers the Jew. The Pole nods eagerly, reaches for his wallet and pays the Jew. The latter puts the money away and begins to speak: "You will need a large whitefish, caught by yourself if possible; you must clean it, pickle it, put it in a jar, and then bury it at full moon in the ground where your ancestors lie. Three full moons must pass before you return to the spot and dig it out. . . ." "And then?" replies the Pole, puzzled: "Is that all?" "Not quite," smiles the Jew in response. "There are still a few things to be done." And, after a moment's pause: "But it will cost you." The Pole pays, the Jew speaks, and so it goes from Cracow to Lemberg. The Pole grows increasingly impatient, and finally, having paid all his money to the Jew, he explodes: "You dirty Yid! Do you think I don't know your game?! You take me for a fool, and my money to boot—*that's* your precious secret!" And the Jew, smiling benignly: "But Brother, what do you want? Don't you see—it's working already!"[29]

III. Love Stories

One hot summer afternoon, as I was walking through the empty streets of an unfamiliar Italian city, I came upon a part of town about whose character I could not long remain in doubt. At the windows only heavily made-up women could be seen, and I hastened to leave the narrow street at the very next turning. But after I had wandered about aimlessly for a while, I suddenly found myself once again in the same street, where I began to cause a stir, and the only result of my hurried departure was that a new detour led me for the third time to that place. At that point a feeling came over me that I can only describe as uncanny. . . .

S. Freud, *The Uncanny*

The Analyst's Desire: Speculation in Play

Nothing more characterizes the response to Freudian thought than the manner in which its most speculative supposition, the death drive, has been received. As late as 1957 Ernest Jones, commenting on the reception of *Beyond the Pleasure Principle*, could observe:

The book is further noteworthy in being the only one of Freud's that has received little acceptance on the part of his followers. Thus of the fifty or so papers they have since devoted to the topic one observes that in the first decade only half supported Freud's theory, in the second decade only a third, and in the last decade none at all.[1]

Yet, at the very time that Jones was writing these lines, another psychoanalyst—whom Jones evidently chose to disregard—was at work developing an interpretation of Freudian theory for which the death drive was to serve as the exemplary articulation. For Jacques Lacan what the death drive sought to conceptualize was nothing less than "the relation of the subject to the signifier," in which, he held, the fundamental insight of psychoanalysis consisted.[2]

To the extent to which Lacan's "return to Freud" has increasingly influenced recent discussion of psychoanalysis, above all in France, but not only there, his revalorization of the theoretical importance of the death drive has tended to impose itself as a kind of shibboleth: the *Todestrieb* has gained wide acceptance as a kind of regulative idea of psychoanalysis. For instance, in his "Presentation" of Sacher Masoch, Gilles Deleuze describes the Freudian move *beyond* the pleasure principle as an inevitable consequence of this principle itself.[3]

121

Eliminating empirical observations as a possible factor in Freud's move (since observations as such could never call the pleasure principle into question), Deleuze locates the force impelling Freud to revise his previous position in the conceptual structure of the pleasure principle: the latter, Deleuze argues, is not really a principle at all, for it never explains phenomena in terms of causal factors; it only describes, in a general manner, without ever confronting the problem of how or why "pleasure"—or the avoidance of tensions—could or should regulate all psychic activity. This decisive theoretical omission, the "unprincipled" character of the pleasure principle, is therefore what leads Freud to seek further for the answer to the riddle of mental life.

Deleuze describes this search as taking place in two phases. First, Freud returns to one of his earliest ideas, that according to which psychic energy is necessarily involved, to varying degrees, in a process of binding (Bindung), which in turn serves as a precondition for the discharge, or evacuation (Abfuhr) of energy: i.e., for pleasure. The process of binding thus emerges (or reemerges) as a structural condition of the pleasure principle. But, Deleuze continues, it is not difficult to see that the idea of binding is a precursor of the later notion of *eros*, which will name the tendency towards unification, the formation of ever-greater unities. Eros, in this perspective, would name the generalized function of binding. This, however, leads Freud to the second phase: for, in order to conceptualize the notion of binding, Freud cannot avoid resorting to that of *repetition*: as a temporal process, binding is inconceivable except as a form of repetition. Repetition, however, forces Freud beyond the pleasure principle, taken in any simple sense, for it inevitably points back toward—and depends on—something anterior to itself, and which is hence prior to all binding of energy. Thus, if repetition is a necessary aspect of the binding of psychic energy, and hence of the pleasure principle, it nonetheless disarticulates this "principle" by pointing to a realm that is prior to it, not merely chronologically, but logically and structurally. If repetition is indispensable to the process of binding, it simultaneously is out-of-bounds, indicating that the forces at work may themselves be groundless.

That Freud's effort to reach a founding principle for psychic activity should thus lead not to a foundation but to an *abyss* (or more prosaically, to an infinite regress), is taken by Deleuze to be the sign of a "truly philosophical reflection," the essence of which is to be "transcendental."[4] Transcendental thought, according to Deleuze, is characterized by its inability to leave well enough alone: that is, by its incapacity to stop where it would like to, for instance at the discovery of eros. Instead, transcendental thought is impelled by its own impetus beyond such comforting, reassuring discoveries, "into the groundless" abyss.

For Deleuze, then, the death drive is just such an aporetic conception, the sign of true transcendental-philosophical speculation. Driven by the desire to get to the bottom, to the ground of the pleasure principle, Freud makes his way back to the idea of binding, which in turn involves him in repetition, and finally impels him over the brink, to the death drive.

This interpretation of Freud's trajectory has the virtue of setting his speculative activity in a necessary relation to the apparently less speculative, more empirical or clinical work that preceded it. And yet, inasmuch as Deleuze's account tends to place the aporetical concept of repetition in the position of transcendental subject, determining the movement of Freud's thought, it risks assimilating that thought to the very philosophy it incessantly sought to question. For the specificity of psychoanalytical thinking tends to dissolve to the extent to which the unconscious is equated with, or conceived of as a "transcendental" subject, however aporetic and "groundless" the latter may be construed. "To transgress" is not necessarily the same as "to transcend." To get at the difference, we need only retrace the manner in which Freud's speculation in *Beyond the Pleasure Principle* gets off the ground:

What now follows is speculation, often far-fetched speculation, which the reader will appreciate or ignore according to his particular perspective [Einstellung]. Furthermore, an attempt to exploit an idea consistently, out of curiosity as to where this will lead. (*Beyond*, p. 18)

According to Deleuze, Freud's *curiosity* here would be the manifestation of that transcendental mode of thinking that is destined to pursue its object so relentlessly that it lands in the bottomless, aporetic abyss. Freud, however, gives us a quite different account of curiosity. In his *Three Essays on Sexual Theory*, where he first thematizes the question of *Wissgier* (the urge to know), Freud emphasizes that it is "not theoretical, but practical interests that set the child's investigative activity in movement" (S.E. 7, 194).

And, from a Freudian perspective at least, nothing is less certain than the generally held conviction that such "practical interests" are any *less* decisive in the quests and investigations of adults. Hence, Freud's account of the "practical interests" presiding over the early development of the "urge to know" merits our attention. The interests at work in the child's first "sexual theories" reveal the concern with origins to be part of the ego's narcissistic effort to consolidate its organization through the "temporalizing-temporizing," i.e., narrative articulation of alterity (as origin, loss, separation). The phantasm of the maternal phallus represents difference as absence, the Other as a variant of the Same, repetition as recognition. In so doing, the narcissistic notion of an original bond or binding, indispensable to the ego's representation of itself, is constituted in the form of an invisible, concealed object that the child seeks to rediscover or reveal. If such inquisitiveness and curiosity—the child's *Forschertätigkeit*—leads inevitably to the crisis of castration, and through it to a restructuring of the ego in which its narcissistic identity is definitively displaced, this process (as we have argued in reference to Freud's second topology) is radically different from the kind of "bottomless pit" that Deleuze—but also Lacan—seem to have in mind. Images such as that of an "abyss" or a "béance" are still situated within the phantasmatic orbit of a narcissism that endeavors to reappropriate alterity by structuring it in terms of oppositional categories (plenitude/emptiness, presence/absence, visible/invisible). In particular, Deleuze's notion of "transcendental speculation" remains indebted to a form of narcissistic narrative that Freud's second topology re-places and dislocates. If the sequel to "castration" entails a story that is radically different from the "sexual theories" of the child, this difference cannot be described either in terms of a "transcendental" logic or of a pure "signifier." For this story tells neither of an (absent) origin nor of an abyss: it leads elsewhere, into regions that are both more and less determinate than any negative ontology (or epistemology) can hope to describe.

From these regions, a certain narcissism is never simply absent, although its role is anything but sovereign. Just such an absence, however, has been implied by the Lacanian and post-Lacanian tendency to erect the speculation of the death drive into a transcendental principle of psychoanalytic theory, thereby choosing to overlook the fact that for Freud, at least, speculation and narcissism are never completely separable. The possibility that the trajectory that Freud followed in moving first to the repetition-compulsion, and then to the death-drive, could itself be part of the original narcissistic narrative of origins, has received even less consideration on the part of French Freudians than on that of their Anglo-American counterparts.[5]

Both groups, it is true, have shared the conviction that Freud articulated the death drive as an alternative, or even antidote, to the power exercised over his thought by the theory of narcissism. Lacan, as we have noted, construes the death drive as epitomizing the subject's relation to the signifier, and as such, as the paradigm of the "symbolic" order of desire, which he tends, implicitly or explicitly, to oppose to the "imaginary" realm of the narcissistic ego, the self-alienated and necessarily self-alienating *moi*.[6]

But the tendency to conceive of the death drive as entailing a radical alternative to narcissism extends far beyond the limits of Lacanian orthodoxy. Jean Laplanche, who has justly warned against the temptation of confusing the critique of ego-psychology with the resolution (or elimination) or the problem of the ego, has described the introduction of the death drive as the attempt by Freud to restore a certain balance to his thought, which was in danger of being captivated by the notion of narcissism.[7] And for Deleuze, as we have seen, the transcendental character of Freud's speculation on the death drive is, at least implicitly, opposed to the identificatory movement of narcissism.

On the other hand, the more traditional attitude toward the death drive shares the same predilection, only with a negative appreciation. Jones, for instance, argues that the discovery of narcissism stood in opposition to the hypothesis of the death drive and led Freud to "ideas . . . of a very different kind," by which Jones means the second topology of id-ego-superego. These two opposing tendencies in Freud's thought, Jones maintains, overlap only in the personal psychology of Freud himself. Dismissing any valid theoretical interest in the death drive, Jones views it primarily as a symptom of Freud's personal effort to conserve the (narcissistic) belief in his own immortality through a theoretical construction amounting to a sublimated "introjection" of a "father-image." For Jones, then, narcissism indeed presides and prevails over the conception of the death drive; but whereas he reaches this conclusion only with reference to Freud's personality, Jones's interpretation, especially if taken in conjunction with that of Deleuze, suggests another possibility: that the hypothesis of the death drive emerges not simply as a symptom of Freud's (individual) desire, but also and above all as a result of the exigencies of his thought, of psychoanalytical thinking itself. The power of narcissism, then, would entail not simply the symptom of an individual subject, "Freud," but rather the theoretical project of psychoanalysis itself, putting its limits into play.

In a certain sense, therefore, what is at stake here is the possibility of elaborating and rethinking what Deleuze has called the "transcendental" nature of speculation in terms of a certain notion of narcissism, one that is never fully explicated in the writings of Freud, but which is all the more powerfully at work in his texts because it remains, in part at least, implicit. This is the supposition that the following reading seeks to explore.

Let us begin, then, with the notion of binding, which, as Deleuze has rightly emphasized, implies a process of repetition. That process, however, displays an aspect that Deleuze does not mention, perhaps because it seems so self-evident. Nevertheless, if we consider it for a moment, we will recognize that this aspect of the binding process is an indispensable constituent of the pleasure principle itself. For the concrete form that repetition takes within the binding process is that of the representation (Vorstellung): if psychic energy distinguishes itself from other forms of energy by its quality of being bound (or bindable), what it is bound *to* is a representation. Even in the "primary process" this fact still obtains, despite Freud's emphasis on the "unbound" quality of psychic energy in that primary state. For what Freud is describing, in contrasting primary with secondary processes, is a difference in degree, not in kind, at least insofar as the question of binding is concerned. Even the instability of cathexes in the primary process is relative to the greater stability of the secondary process: it is not an absolute. This is why the "primary" process is not simply primary, but depends—psychologically and logically—on the secondary process, in the sense we have already discussed.[8]

Freud addresses this problem from the very beginning. In *The Interpretation of Dreams*, he describes the interrelation of binding, repetition, and representation in the primary process:

> The first psychic activity, therefore, aims at a perceptual identity, that is, at the repetition of the perception tied [*verknüpft*] to the satisfaction of need. (S.E. 5, 566)

The primary process, in this description, despite (or because) of its unbound quality, strives to constitute a perceptual identity, a representation that repeats an earlier perception, rendering it susceptible of being recognized. This account, however, raises two questions. First, if the earlier perception is described as being "tied (verknüpft) to the satisfaction," what factors are at work in creating this bond? Second, the apparently spontaneous character of this *Verknüpfung* indicates that, for Freud's manner of conceiving the pleasure principle, two elements are required: discharge, but also representations. Indeed, these two elements seem to converge: the constitution of representations as a process of binding through repetition appears not merely as a *condition* of discharge; it tends to merge with discharge itself.

The question that thus emerges, is: what is the precise relation between this tendency to bind, to produce perceptual identities (or—for this seems to be the equivalent—to produce representations), and the tendency to seek discharge or reduction of tension? In what sense can the binding of psychic energy as representation comport or further a discharge? This question, once articulated, will loom ever larger in the thought of Freud, inasmuch as the nexus between "satisfaction" and perception or representation will continue to provide the matrix for all further elaborations of the processes of binding and of repetition.

If, then, the binding of psychic energy constitutes not only a condition of discharge, but tends to be identified by Freud with discharge itself, it can only be because what Freud describes as Abfuhr—the evacuation of energy—cannot be considered in purely economic terms, as entailing merely the quantitative reduction of tension; it must be situated topologically, that is, related to particular psychic systems or localities. This is what leads Freud to construct his first topological scheme of primary and secondary processes. But it is evident that this initial topology is incapable of accounting for the relation existing between the notion of discharge and that of binding, between the reduction of tension and the cathexis of representations. It is only in Freud's second topology, consisting of concepts that do not merely describe conflict, but which are themselves conflictual, that the basis for a response to this problem is developed. The particular system for which the formations (cathexis) of representations can, in and of itself, be a pleasurable activity, entailing the discharge of energy or reduction of tension—that system can only be the constitutively ambivalent, organized part of the psyche that Freud designates as the ego. If the ego organizes itself through a process of narcissistic identification, then the formation of perceptual *identities* must be the first and indispensable step in that process. Stimuli, impressions, tensions are rendered recognizable, identifiable through a process of repetition in which that which is repeated comes increasingly to be apprehended as the same. "Remembrance" quite literally remembers the disparate impressions as the perceptual object or identity (which therefore is never simply immediately present to consciousness, but always already a product of memory). By thus (re-)assembling the object, the ego gets its self together. And, at least in this initial phase, the struggle for order entails the reduction of alterity and the subordination of difference to identity. In the context of this struggle, the very formation of perceptual identities per se, the process of object-formation and, correlatively, the recognition it entails, would as such become a source of narcissistic pleasure for the ego, that is, for that portion of the psyche laboring on the constitution of its sense of self.

None of this is ever made fully explicit by Freud; and yet it is everywhere implicit. For instance, in the remark made in a footnote at the beginning of *Beyond the Pleasure Principle*, where he observes that "what is essential, to be sure, is that pleasure and unpleasure (*Lust und Unlust*), as conscious sensations, are bound (*gebunden*) to the ego" (*Beyond*, p. 5). The question, of course, is whether pleasure and unpleasure can be conceived as operating independently of the ego; whether, in other words, the "reduction of tension" can be construed apart from the process by which the subject puts itself in the position to recognize the same: first as a perceived object, occupying a fixed place, then as the site that in turn it can occupy (besetzen: "cathect," "invest").

All this would amount to a revision of the generally held conception of Freud's thought as dualist, constituted of oppositional categories such as primary/secondary process, pleasure/reality principle; such oppositions would have to be relocated within the conflictual continuity of narcissistic ambivalence. Thus, instead of the static duality of the opposition, Freud's thought would develop according to the paradigm of a dynamic disunity of which narcissism is the organized, if ambiguous, part. "Pleasure" would thereby no longer be the attribute of a self-identical system, but rather a function of the ego's effort precisely to organize such a system. Pleasure, in short, would have to be rethought as a function of narcissism—and hence, of the ego.

Thus, in our previous discussion of Freud's theory of play, we have argued that the allegedly "pure" pleasure the child takes in play, consisting in repetition and recognition, cannot, as Freud suggests, be opposed to the later development of the rational, critical intellect, since the latter is in fact the continuation of the narcissistic process of recognition and repetition of the same that already informs the play it replaces; the form of recognition changes, but not its essential function. What is decisive is the faculty to identify, to recognize, to repeat as the same, first in the *form* of the word, then in the *objects* it signifies. Far from ignoring the differences between the two, the process of identification alone permits the rigorous determination of those differences, in terms of an increase in the power to recognize sameness in difference (or, viewed from the other side, an increase in the power to exclude and to subsume, to *repress*). Verbalization, and then conceptualization, would thus not simply put an end to the preverbal and verbal pleasure of play (pleasure in the recognition of phonic or graphic similarities, for instance), but would prolong the narcissistic pleasures of the ego by extending its "grasp," by strengthening its grip on the other, in order to determine the latter verbally as identical-to-itself.

Summing up: if Freud in *The Interpretation of Dreams* can describe rational thought as a "substitute for hallucinatory desire" (S.E. 5, 567), it is not simply in a limited, functionalist sense (both hallucinated wish-fulfillment and thought have the same goal, the reduction of tension), but because both strive for that goal by the same overall procedure: the identifacatory appropriation of the other in the service of the narcissistic constitution of the ego.

We need only contrast this account with that of Deleuze to become aware of the issues it raises. For Deleuze, what is at work in the Freudian speculation, in the trajectory it follows from binding to repetition to the death drive, is something not susceptible of further analysis: "transcendental-philosophical" speculation, the search for a foundation that irresistibly precipitates itself into the precipice of the unfounded and the unfathomable. What emerges from our reading, by contrast, is an aspect of speculation that Freud was ready to criticize in others, but which he sought to justify in his own work: the narcissistic striving to rediscover the same. Thus, the earlier, anterior moment that all repetition necessarily implies, does not lead us to the unfathomable, as it does Deleuze, but to the more determinate, if ambiguous narcissism of the ego as the ambivalent condition of the "pleasure principle."

If, then, repetition leads to narcissism, what of the death drive? Does it articulate, or adumbrate, something radically different? The French Freud discussion, in support of its positive response to this question, often refers to the "silence" attributed by Freud to the death drives, to his statement that "the death drives are essentially mute (*stumm*) and the sounds of life generally proceed from Eros" (S.E. 19, 46). What possible justification can there be, from a Freudian perspective at least, in suggesting that "this transcendent, mute instance" (Deleuze) might be just another form of the narcissistic language of the ego?

Only this, perhaps: if we listen closely, or rather, if we read attentively, we may remark that the very *Stummheit* of the death drive precludes it from ever speaking for itself; it is inevitably dependent on another discourse to be seen or heard. And that discourse, however much it may seek to efface itself before the "silence" it seeks to articulate, is anything but innocent or neutral. The death drive may be dumb, but its articulation in a theoretical and speculative discourse is not. To insist upon the silence of what one is at the same time speaking *for*, is, whatever else it may be, a theoretical Fort-Da game par excellence: now you see it, now you don't. Nor is such a game without its own particular history, as we shall soon discover.

The silent pathos of the death drive has, at any rate, depended upon a certain nonreading of the text in which it is inscribed. Only such a nonreading could render plausible the transcription of *Todestrieb* as a *term*, a *maître-mot* terminating a movement, and be it as one that is . . . interminable.

For only such a nonreading could ignore the manner in which the very impulse that drives Freud beyond the pleasure principle to repetition, and beyond repetition to the death drive, also impels him to move beyond the death drive "itself," toward a very different "place," which has little in common with Deleuze's transcendental Abgrund. That other place is far less profound, indeed; it is hardly even "flat."

But we are already hurrying ahead when instead patience is needed for the route that lies before us. Let us begin our rereading of *Beyond the Pleasure Principle* with Freud's discussion of repetition, to be sure, but also, and above all, of its *Zwang*, the compulsive power it exercises. If Deleuze tends to skip quickly over the question of experience and empirical observation, to arrive at what he holds to be the essentially transcendental structure of Repetition Itself, Freud, by contrast, is more prosaic. He situates his discussion of repetition in a more familiar field, that of the analytic session. This site is worth remarking, since it is here and only here that Freud discovers what he considers to be conclusive proof of the existence of repetitive phenomena that defy the sway of the pleasure principle. The precise place in which such evidence emerges, then, the scene of the repetition-compulsion, is none other than that of psychoanalytical transference:

> The patient cannot remember the whole of what is repressed in him, and what he cannot remember may be precisely the essential part of it. *Thus he acquires no sense of conviction of the correctness of the construction that has been communicated to him.* He is *compelled [genötigt] to repeat* the repressed material as a present experience instead of, as the physician would prefer to see, remembering it as a part of the past. (*Beyond*, p. 12, my italics)

The compulsion here is that with which past experiences are repeated by the analysand, instead of being remembered (i.e., recognized, as a memory-representation). But the force of the transference makes itself felt not merely by its power to elude the memory of the analysand; no less important is the manner in which the repetition of transference imposes itself upon "the physician," who "would prefer to see" the patient remember instead of unconsciously repeating the past. The goal of the analyst is to bring about the recognition of repetition:

> He must get him . . . to recognize that what appears to be reality is in fact only a reflection of the forgotten past. (*Beyond*, p. 13)

The repetition thus desired by the analyst is one in which repetition is recognized as such, the past is repeated as the past, i.e., remembered, identified. It is this determination of repetition—as an object of recognition, identical-to-itself—that endows the analyst with that "measure of superiority" that Freud, in his discussion of polemics (cited earlier), saw as an essential aspect of the analytical situation. Now, however, we discover, with Freud, that the very lever of analysis, transference, tends to call that "superiority" into question. What makes analysis possible also endangers it. For transference designates the propensity not merely to repeat without knowing it, but also to resist the effort of the analyst to facilitate such recognition, for instance by constructing an interpretation. To the extent that the analysand is submitted to the power of transference, he or she may choose to reject or ignore "the construction communicated," thus defying the will or wish of the analyst. It is precisely in such situations that Freud seems to perceive a repetitive power that defies the pleasure principle:

The new and remarkable fact that we must now describe is that the repetition-compulsion also brings back those past experiences which include no possibility of pleasure and *which even then could never have brought satisfaction, not even of drive-impulses that have since been repressed.* (*Beyond*, p. 14, my italics)

If Freud rather precipitously interprets such phenomena of analytical transference as deriving from experiences that could never have been sources of pleasure, and hence whose repetition calls that principle into question, what his account textually describes is something quite different. For the pleasure that the patient's transference resists and defies is not that of a hypothetical past about which any assertion can only be a conjecture, but rather that of the analyst himself, who sees his interpretive constructions rejected or ignored by a patient who refuses to recognize repetition for what it is: that is, as more of the same, and instead insists on repeating without knowing it. What the repetitions of transference call into question, then, is not the pleasure principle as such, but the pleasure of the analyst.

But if the analyst's desire is thus put into play in his transferential interplay with the patient, and if the pleasure of seeing his interpretations recognized as correct is thereby denied the analyst, there is another pleasure still available to him, especially if his name is Freud: the pleasure of recognizing what it is that stands behind the patient's refusal to recognize. Precisely the absence of recognition in the analysand now becomes the object of a new recognition by the theoretician. "The new and remarkable fact" with which Freud confronts us resides in his conviction that such repetitions draw their force not from the ego—which is otherwise the only source of "resistance"—but from the "unconscious repressed material" (*des unbewussten Verdrängten) (ibid.)* Freud thereby seems to take for granted that the ego of the analysand could never have the power to resist the desire of the analyst with such tenacity, were it not reinforced by other, more powerful forces.

And yet, when he attempts to locate those forces—at least in the intrapsychic domain—he cannot avoid contradicting himself, describing the repetition-compulsion as the "expression of the force of the repressed" (*ibid.*). The contradiction is blatant: for if the experiences or representations thus repeated could not have been a source of pleasure, neither originally nor even of "drive-impulses since repressed" (*selbst nicht von seither verdrängten Triebregungen*), then it is difficult to see how such repetition could have anything to do with repression either. For nothing is ever "repressed" that is not, in some way, an object of desire, and hence a possible source of pleasure.

One might be tempted to conjecture that just such contradictions were what impelled Freud to attempt to move beyond the pleasure principle. Yet the text of this essay provides no explicit support of such a surmise: Freud never appears to have recognized, much less reflected upon the problems raised by his description of the repetition-compulsion as a manifestation of repression, on the one hand, and as being independent of the pleasure principle on the other. Nor does he qualify or even temper that assertion. Rather, he simply drops it. In so doing, his procedure recalls the mechanism of *isolation*, which, we remember, provides the ego with an alternative to repression.

A possible reason for this strange abandonment begins to emerge when we consider the direction in which the emphasis on repression inevitably leads: toward a discussion of "infantile sexual life" and thus into a realm that up to this point at least, has been unthinkable apart from the domination of the pleasure principle and the domination of narcissism: "The failures" of infantile sexual striving, "loss of love . . . leave in their wake a lasting impairment of self-esteem as a narcissistic scar." Freud observes, as though he might then attempt to derive the repetition-compulsion from such narcissistic reverses: "There are a limited number of types that recur regularly (in later life)" (*Beyond*, p. 15).

But to derive the repetition-compulsion from the "scars" of narcissism is hardly, in and of itself, to move decisively beyond the pleasure principle. Everything depends on the manner in which those scars are conceived. At first, it seems that Freud conceives them here in an extremely realistic manner: "The physical development of the child" is described as responsible for the reverses imposed on its narcissism. All the easier, one might conclude, for the adult to surmount them. Such, however, is seldom the case, Freud continues. Indeed, were it otherwise, the repetition-compulsion would be much less widespread than it is: for Freud now proceeds to cite a variety of instances, drawn from "the life of nonneurotic persons." Everywhere, it seems, Freud suddenly finds the evidence he is looking for:

Thus we have come across people all of whose human relationships have the same outcome: the benefactor who is abandoned in anger after a time by each of his protégés, however much they may otherwise differ from one another, and who thus seems destined to taste all the bitterness of ingratitude; the man whose friendships all end in betrayal by his friend; the man who time after time in the course of his life raises someone else into a position of great authority, either for himself or for the public, and then, after a certain interval, himself upsets that authority and replaces him with a new one; the lover, each of whose amorous relationships passes through the same phases and reaches the same conclusion. (*Beyond*, p. 16)

Everywhere Freud finds . . . the *same*: the same story of ingratitude, betrayal, inconstancy, love—like the child, who not finding what it is looking for, is destined to repeat that search ever after as an adult. Without knowing it, of course. Which is precisely where the analyst comes in: he *knows* what he is looking for, and what the other is looking for as well. For the analyst is one who knows all the stories, knows them all as the story of the same. And if the analyst's knowledge is rejected or ignored by the patient, then this too is part of the same old story, "transference," "resistance." If this resistance resists all the efforts of the analyst to bring about a cure, then the man in power "himself upsets the authority" he has installed, the "pleasure principle," and replaces it "with a new one," the repetition-compulsion. But the new one, as in the story Freud tells, is in reality only more of the same.

Thus Freud continues to recount stories, drawn not from the experience of psychoanalysis, but from "the lives of normal people":

There is the case, for instance, of the woman who married three successive husbands, each of whom fell ill soon afterwards and had to be nursed by her to death [*von ihr zu Tode gepflegt werden mussten*]. (*Beyond*, p. 16)

This case, Freud remarks, is even more impressive then the previous ones, since it entails "a *passive* experience" in which the subject has no control over the recurrent destiny she encounters. Is it an accident that the subject of such passivity is female? All she can do, in any event, is to nurse her husbands *to death* (*not*, as the Standard Edition translates, "on their death-beds"). And thus, the first, veiled appearance of the "death drive," here in the stories Freud recounts to demonstrate the ubiquity of the repetition-compulsion, takes the form of "three successive husbands," each "nursed to death" by "the woman" they have married.

Thus, if Freud's initial stories deal with men, betrayal, and ingratitude, death enters the scene with—as?—the passive female. In this perspective, the final story Freud tells in this series appears to condense and conclude the previous tales:

The most moving poetic representation [Darstellung] of such a trait of destiny [*Schicksalszuges*] has been given by Tasso in his romantic epic, *Gerusalemme Liberata*. Its hero, Tancred, unwittingly kills his beloved Clorinda in a duel while she is disguised in the armour of an enemy knight. After her burial he makes his way into a strange magic forest which strikes the Crusaders' army with terror. He slashes with his sword at a tall tree; but blood streams from the wound and the voice of Clorinda, whose soul is imprisoned in this tree, accuses him of once again injuring his beloved. (*Beyond*, p. 16)

This second story of repetition and death is no longer equivocal: this time, the victims are not "nursed to death," but murdered, albeit "unwittingly." Tancred is *active* as only the unconscious can be: he acts without knowing it, and his act is to kill the woman he loves. This story, coming as it does after that of the "nurse-unto-death," provides a curious counterpoint to the latter. The Schicksalszug that Freud asserts it represents, is not simply the recurrence of destiny, but a recurrent fatality linked to the female: she either eliminates the male or is eliminated by him. But nothing is more difficult to do away with than this persistent female: you kill her once, and her soul returns, "imprisoned in a tree"; you "slash with (your) sword at (the) tall tree," and a voice returns to accuse you. The activity of the subject, in this final story, consists indeed of a repetition, but what he repeats, actively, is the narcissistic wound that never heals without leaving scars.

Freud tells the stories of these scars, but instead of reading these stories as the signal of something else, he sees them as more of the same, as the manifestation of a new and more powerful *authority*:

If we take into account *observations such as these*, drawn from behavior in transference and from the destinies of men and women, we shall find the courage to assume that there is a repetition-compulsion at work in psychic life that overrides [*sich . . . hinaussetzt*] the pleasure-principle. (*Beyond*, p. 16, my italics)

Although Freud will immediately qualify his "observations," with the remark "that only in rare instances can we observe the pure effects of the repetition-compulsion" (*Beyond*, p. 17), and that in the case of children's play, at least, the repetition-compulsion "seems to converge" with "the pleasurable satisfaction of drives," the stories he has told have had the decisive effect of opening the door to doubt and calling into question the "familiar motive forces" of the pleasure principle.

For Freud, then, the stories he has told are not versions of the narrative of narcissism, but evidence of something radically different. And yet, when he seeks to describe that difference, it emerges as more of the same:

Enough is left unexplained to justify the hypothesis of a compulsion to repeat — something that seems *more* primitive, *more* elementary, *more* drive-like than the pleasure principle it overrides. (*Beyond*, p. 17, my italics)

For Freud, the stories have done their work, the case for curiosity has been established: "If a repetition-compulsion does operate in the mind, we should be glad to know something about it." Having thus "observed" the unobservable: the absence of the pleasure principle in analysis and in life (Fort!), the search for that which has evicted it (Da!) can now begin.

The *Fort!*

It is only after he has told his stories, presented as observations, that the game of speculation can begin in earnest. Up to this point, Freud insists, everything, including the hypothesis of the repetition-compulsion, has been derived more or less directly from observation. Speculation, by contrast, is determined not by empirical data, but by "the consistent exploitation of an idea, out of curiosity as to where it will lead."

But what is it that makes the exploitation of an idea consistent, "*konsequent*"? What regulates the sequence, the succession of thoughts that constitute the "exploitation" (*Ausbeutung*) of an idea? Nothing, it appears, if not the rule of a certain repetition itself:

It is impossible to pursue an idea of this kind except by *repeatedly combining* factual material with pure conjecture (*mit bloss Erdachtem*) and thereby diverging widely from observation. (*Beyond*, p. 53)

To exploit the idea of the repetition-compulsion is inevitably to submit to the compulsion to repeat it in ever-changing combinations that move ever further from "observation," which is otherwise, for Freud, the test of speculation and the antidote to its narcissistic tendencies. In the absence of, or distance from, the criterion of observation, the speculation that repeats the compulsion to repeat can be guided only by the consistency or consequence of its own operation—guided, that is, by the logical rule of noncontradiction. Such a contradiction mars, as we have seen, the first identification of the repetition-compulsion as a force acting both independently of the pleasure principle, and as the expression of the force of the repressed. Since, however, repression is always conceived as functioning under the sway of the pleasure principle, Freud is therefore compelled, by the principle of consistency, to seek another source for the force of the repetition-compulsion. This other origin Freud infers from the "regressive" tendency of the drives not merely to reduce tension ("pleasure"), but to reproduce (to repeat) an earlier state of affairs. Freud, in short, *temporalizes* the pleasure principle, and having done so, need only "pursue to its logical conclusion the hypothesis that all drives tend towards the restoration of an earlier state of things" (*Beyond*, p. 31) in order to arrive at the decisive derivation of the repetition-compulsion:

Let us suppose, then, that all the organic drives are conservative, historically acquired and directed at regression, at the restoration of *an earlier state*. . . . Those instincts are bound to give the deceptive impression of being forces striving for change and progress, whereas they are merely seeking to reach *an old goal* by paths old and new. Moreover *this final goal* can be identified. It would be in contradiction with the conservative nature of the drives if the goal of life were a state that had never before been attained. Rather, it must be *an old state, a point of departure* which the living being *once left [einmal verlassen hat]* and to which it strives to return along all the detours of its development. If we may assume it to be true without exception that every living being dies *for internal reasons [aus inneren Gründen]* —returns to the inorganic—then we can only say: *The goal of all life is death*, and going further back: *The inanimate was there before [war früher da] the animate*. (*Beyond*, pp. 31-32, emphasis mine except for the last two italicized passages)

Freud's derivation of the repetition-compulsion here follows the very procedure of repetitive combination prescribed as the method of consistent speculation: the drives are first described as "the restoration of an *earlier* state"; that state is then redefined teleologically as "an *old* goal"; the indefinite article is then replaced by the more determinate *this*: "This final goal," which in turn is even more definitively situated, in its next repetition, as "an old state, point of departure" for life as such. Finally, this point of departure is assigned a proper name, "death," and a proper place: there (da), before the animate.

Repetition is thus put in its place, there, before the Living. From this place, this absolute origin, the Living can be determined with perfect consistency as the logical consequence of that other place from which it comes and toward which it goes. By retracing the "organic drives" all the way back there, to a place where they are not, Freud seems to have accomplished the perfect theoretical game of "Fort! Da!": life disappears "there," it is Fort! by not being Da! The Fort!

is (the) Da! Freud tells us, both in being there, before the emergence of life, and also by remaining there, in the midst of the Living, which —*therefore*—"dies for internal reasons," "*aud inneren Gründen.*"

Freud's derivation thus presents us with a model of internal consistency: the repetitive movement of the drives is retraced to the one, single, self-identical origin, the Fort! which was There and is There and will be There, before, during, and after all is said and done.

There is only one problem: the problem of the *one*, or rather: of the *once*. The problem, that is, of the story, which requires not merely a One—an Origin—but also, a "Once": not merely an "ein" but an "ein*mal*." And it is this *mal* that is missing from Freud's perfectly consistent derivation. That is, it is there, da, inscribed in the text, but in a place that is difficult to situate. For the Fort that is There is such a bastion of identity, its walls so strong and impervious, that there seems hardly any space for life to emerge from it. And yet, we are told that "the living once left" that place, which was there, before. The problem, in short, is that Freud's Fort! leaves no place for the Mal: retracing repetition back to its origin, he leaves no room for the trace without which the Living can never emerge. Freud's Fort! therefore begins to look less like a point of departure or a final goal than like those mysterious, nonphenomenal phenomena that astronomers call black holes, and which, they conjecture, draw everything visible into their invisible mass, from which neither the Living, nor Light itself, can ever reemerge.

The same fate threatens Freud's speculative construction: what it seems to exclude, or at least fails to account for, is the force of resistance that would have been required for anything to escape the pull of that original Fort! and thus to originate. Life, and with it the speculative theory of the death drive, would have imploded by virtue of its very immanence and intensity. It would have vanished into its nucleus. And nothing would ever have happened.

A strange story. And yet by no means one that has been invented post facto, as it were, by an overimaginative reader. Or at least, not by him alone. For the very same problem is explicitly treated in Freud's text. It is just this problem of escaping the impulsive consistency of the speculative black hole—and can we still be certain, as Jones is, that this is a *father*-image?—that forces Freud beyond mere consistency, toward descriptions that begin strangely to sound more like stories than arguments. Or, more precisely, like stories within which speculations—such as that of the death drive—are inscribed. These stories no longer conform to the narcissistic scheme of beginning, middle, and end, as we can verify by rereading Freud's derivation of repetition, this time, however, restoring the passage we have hitherto omitted:

Let us suppose, then, that all the organic instincts are conservative, historically acquired and directed at regression, at the restoration of an earlier state. It follows that the achievement of organic development must be attributed to external, disruptive and diverting influences. The elementary living being would, from its very inception, have never wanted to change itself and would only have repeated the same course of life under conditions that remained identical [*sich gleichbleibend*]. But in the final analysis [im letzten Grunde] it must have been the history of our earth and its relation to the sun that has left us its mark (Abdruck) in the development of organisms. Every modification which is thus imposed upon the course of the organism's life is accepted by the conservative organic drives and stored up for further repetition. Those drives are bound to give the deceptive impression of being forces striving for change and progress.

Thus, we see that Freud neither ignored nor evaded the speculative dilemma of the black hole, of a Fort! so strong, so consistent, and self-contained that it could never be breached by the Life of which it was supposed to be the origin. To account for the origin of life, Freud must abandon the effort to think consistently about repetition by retracing it to a state so original that there would be no place for the trace. In short, Freud must *depart* from his attempt to think repetition as a movement of identity — to think, in short, repetition as such — and instead attempt to think it as departure. To do this, he must partition the origin so that the walls of its Fort! are no longer impervious to an exteriority, without which Life can never depart. For it is only as the effect of a double or split origin, an origin that is dislocated and disrupted by "external" forces — influences which leave their mark upon us — that the drives can be conceived as repetition. What they repeat, however, is no longer simply the "same" — the Fort! that is Da! — but rather a *da* that is *fort*: elsewhere, and yet also here: the "modification" or "alteration" (*Veränderung*) which is repeated as the imprint, the Abdruck of an irreducible alterity. This Abdruck, then, is what gives the drives their distinctive character. In the final analysis, "im letzten Grunde," what the drives repeat is neither a ground nor an abyss, but a violent process of in-scription, alteration, and perhaps above all: narration.

It is the last-named that most philosophical readings of Freud seem unable to conceive, precisely because in the final analysis, the letzer Grund is always conceived as a concept, albeit it an aporetic one, an *Abgrund*.

At some time [*Irgend einmal*] the properties of life were suscitated in inanimate matter by the intervention of a force that is still entirely inconceivable [*unvorstellbar*]. Perhaps it was a prcoess prototypically similar [*vorbildlich ähnlich*] to that which later allowed consciousness to arise in a particular stratum of living matter. The tension that then arose in what had hitherto been inanimate substance endeavored to cancel itself out [*sich abzugleichen*]; the first drive had emerged, the drive to return to the inanimate. For living substance at that time dying was still easy, the course of life was probably only a short one, its direction determined by the chemical structure of the young life. For a long time living substance may thus have been created anew, again and again [*immer wieder*], easily dying, until decisive external influences so transformed themselves that they constrained the surviving substance to diverge even more widely [*immer grösseren Ablenkungen*] from the original course of life and to follow ever more complicated detours [*immer komplizierteren Umwegen*] before reaching the goal of death. These detours to death, faithfully retained by the conservative drives, would thus offer us today the image of the phenomena of life. (*Beyond*, pp. 32-33)

Freud's effort to objectify, in the form of an event, the decisive but inconceivable (unvorstellbar: unimaginable, unrepresentable) intervention of that external, disruptive force, leads him to a narrative form of exposition whose introductory formula, "Irgend einmal," recalls the traditional "once upon a time" (*Es war einmal*) of the fairy tale. Freud's story, of course, does not constitute an explanation: to describe a series of intensifications that also comports a dislocation (ever wider divergence, ever more complicated detours) is not to account for the process by which the repetition of the same becomes the repetition of difference. Here, as elsewhere, the story leads us to that "capital X" about which we know nothing, the economic increase in energy and tension, the self-transformation of external influences that constrains the repetition of the same to diverge from itself and to become different. But Freud's story, which thereby repeats a problem with which we have become familiar, also transforms that problem, in two ways: first, by representing it as the (unrepresentable) origin of Life itself, and hence, of the external, real basis of the life of the psyche; and second, by suggesting that this unrepresentable *origin* is itself a kind of prefiguration—vorbildlich ähnlich—of the origin of consciousness. Suggesting, in short, that the unrepresentable (origin of life) may well be a representation of representation itself.

If Freud's story of the origin of life is thereby presented as a possible model of the origin of consciousness, the latter may be considered to be a repetition of the former. This is doubtless the sequence that Freud seeks to suggest in utilizing the word "vorbildlich": if the origin of life may well resemble that of consciousness, it is because the latter repeats the former, follows after it, is its consequence. This, of course, is the only logical, consistent way to conceive the relation of consciousness and life: first there is life, then there is consciousness. But if this sequence would hold for traditional psychology, its validity for psychoanalysis is less evident—first, because the realm of the psyche can no longer be identified with that of consciousness or representation; and second, because the mechanism of repetition that structures the drives, and hence, the psyche, does not conform to the laws of identity and of noncontradiction, which are the laws of consciousness. The opposition of consciousness and life, representation and presence, is precisely dislocated by the narrative that retraces repetition to the inexplicable intervention of exterior forces that leave their mark—for us to decipher, or rather, to repeat by reinscribing it elsewhere, that is, by retelling stories.

In any case, what is certain is that if we wish to learn more about that inconceivable, unvorstellbare intervention and inscription, we have no choice but to return to Freud's account of the emergence of consciousness, in the section of the essay immediately preceding that in which the story of life is told. In Chapter Four of *Beyond the Pleasure Principle*, just after he has formally announced the beginning of his speculation ("What follows is speculation"), Freud launches into a discussion of the limits of consciousness, as psychoanalysis has sought to put them in question. These limits Freud seeks to localize precisely by stressing the peculiar *position* of consciousness, situated "on the frontier between outside and inside." To understand consciousness, Freud argues, one must conceive of it topologically, for its borderline site determines its function, consisting in the transmission of "perceptions . . . coming from the outside world, and of sensations of pleasure and unpleasure, which can only stem from the interior of the psychic apparatus."[9] (*Beyond*, p. 18) To fulfill this task, consciousness must conserve its receptivity and sensitivity and therefore cannot accumulate "lasting traces" (*Dauerspuren*) that would sooner or later saturate it and thus reduce its ability to receive new impressions and to transmit them. Consciousness is thus opposed to memory, the guardian of traces, and indeed is described as having arisen "in place of memory-traces" (*Beyond*, p. 19). If Freud here returns or repeats arguments that go back to his *Project* of 1895, this repetition is not merely more of the same. For by thematizing the problem of repetition itself as the fundamental characteristic of the drives, all of Freud's earlier conceptions assume new significance. To assert that consciousness arises "in place" (*an Stelle*) of memory-traces—that is, both re-placing it and taking its place—is to demonstrate that the representations of consciousness, its perceptions, including those of pleasure and unpleasure, are all effects of a repetition (a memory-trace) that itself cannot be reduced to the logic of representation. The form in which such repetition, such memory-traces, articulate themselves, can only be that of a speculative narration. And indeed, this is precisely what Freud proceeds to do. Instead of seeking to represent the emergence of consciousness through a genetic argument, Freud appeals to our imagination, our ability to form representations, in order to represent the origin of consciousness:

Let us imagine [*Stellen wir uns . . . vor*] the living organism in its most simplified form as an undifferentiated vesicle [*Bläschen*] of excitable substance; then its surface, which is turned towards the outside world, is differentiated through its very position and serves as an organ for receiving excitation . . . It would then be easily conceivable that through the unremitting impact of outer excitation upon the surface of the vesicle its substance is permanently altered down to a certain depth. . . . A crust would thus have formed which at last would be so thoroughly scorched [*durchgebrannt*] that it offers the most favorable conditions for the reception of excitation and is incapable of further modification. (*Beyond*, p. 20)

If the story of life was "unvorstellbar," what Freud here asks us to imagine is hardly less so: an undifferentiated Bläschen, a kind of bubble, or possibly also a blister. Or a bubble that becomes a blister, through the friction of "outer excitation," by forming a crust, which solidifies its borders, demarcating and organizing consciousness in its relation to what it is not, the powerful excitation of the outside world. The emergence of consciousness in the living organism would thus be marked by the formation of a crust consisting of inalterable alterations (recalling our previous description of the operation of anxiety as the alteration of alterity). But the process by which such alteration comes about, the scorching of the organism, still remains to be explained, and this compels Freud to continue—that is, to repeat and to alter—his story of the Bläschen:

But we have more to say of this living vesicle with its receptive cortical layer. This little piece of living substance is suspended in the midst of an external world charged with the most powerful energies, and it would be slaughtered by them were it not provided with a shield against excitation [*Reizschutz*]. It acquires the shield in this way: Its outermost surface loses the structure proper to living matter, becomes as it were inorganic and now functions as a special envelope [Hülle] or membrane to resist excitation. . . . The outer layer has, however, by dying [*Absterben*] saved all deeper ones from the same fate. (*Beyond*, p. 21)

In thus telling the story of consciousness, Freud repeats—or anticipates—the story he will later tell of the origin of life itself. Only here, the story is altered by the account of alteration itself. For the scorching of the crust and its transformation into a Reizschutz is now described as a process of Absterben, of dying. The outer layers die to save the inner ones: the envelope sacrifices itself for the core. But that process of dying is now recounted as something very different from the "return" to an inorganic state as which Freud will subsequently represent it. To die, here, designates the manner in which the organism reacts to the impact of external forces, a process of alteration by which further alteration is arrested. To die, then, in the sense of the Bläschen, is to alter alteration until "no further lasting alteration" is possible. (*Beyond*, p. 20)

To describe the emergence of consciousness in this way is, of course, to raise questions rather than to answer them. For the kind of consciousness that Freud here asks us to imagine is very different from what we usually call consciousness; it is precisely not consciousness *of* anything, and even less is it self-consciousness. Rather, it is a defensive shield incapable of retaining any sensation, perception, or memory, a shield consisting in inalterable alterations. This shield therefore both protects against excess excitation—which would otherwise have a traumatic effect on the organism (the psyche)—and also transmits excitation from the outside to the inside of the organism. Such a double function, that of protection and of transmission, is what the Reizschutz is called upon to accomplish. Just how it does this is, of course, the problem.

Freud at first seeks to equate the operation of the Reizschutz with that of the primary process, in which there would be "no bound energy, but only energy capable of free discharge." (*Beyond*, p. 21) And yet, in the course of his discussion it soon emerges that such a state would be entirely unable to serve as the kind of shield and filter required; indeed, the state of fully unbound energy constitutes precisely the kind of "danger" that the Reizschutz is called upon to avert. Confronted with the problem of the trauma, then, Freud is compelled to recognize that the protection against excessive excitation necessarily entails "mastering the amounts of stimulus that have broken in and of binding them, in the psychical sense, so that they can then be disposed of." (*Beyond*, p. 24)

If the Reizschutz dies to save our soul, its death cannot be construed, as Freud initially would have it, as the formation of an essentially inert substance. On the contrary, it must be imagined as the development of a capacity to bind energy, which in turn implies the formation of quiescent cathexes, since the capacity of a system to bind energy varies in proportion with "the system's own quiescent cathexis." No wonder, then, that shortly after this discussion, Freud makes his now familiar reference to the "capital X." The analysis of the Reizschutz has led to the paradoxical conclusion that a certain death of organic substance must be consubstantial with a certain binding of energy. That is, the resuscitation of consciousness from the death of the body must necessarily entail both the binding and the transmission (i.e., a certain unbinding) of energy, and moreover, must entail both at one and the same time.

Which amounts to implying, however, that this time cannot be simply one and the same. Freud hints at a possible resolution of this problem in a remark that he inserts, parenthetically, in his discussion of the Reizschutz, concerning the mechanisms by which it accomplishes its task of protection. The unconscious, he reminds us, is timeless. "Our abstract notion of time," Freud continues, "seems to be wholly derived from the method of operation of the system Pcpt.-Cs. and to correspond to a perception on its own part of that method of working. This mode of functioning may perhaps constitute another way of providing a shield against stimuli" (*Beyond*, p. 22).

According to this remark of Freud's, "our abstract notion of time" would be the manner in which consciousness represents itself, its mode of operation, to itself. But both this mode of operation as such and its particular self-representation as time would then constitute aspects of the Reizschutz itself. By organizing excitation temporally, consciousness would bind energy and thereby protect the psyche against traumatic excess. Freud describes the general mechanism by which such protection operates in the paragraph immediately preceding this one: the excessive, unbound quantities of excitation are subjected to a process of "sampling," which Freud also compares with "feelers," which are all the time making tentative advances towards the external world and then drawing back from it" (*Beyond*, p. 22). But this process of sampling, which Freud describes here in quantitative and spatial categories, is also associated in his work with the formation of *signals*, and with thinking as such. In *The Interpretation of Dreams*, he writes that

> thinking must aim at freeing itself more and more from exclusive regulation by the unpleasure principle and at restricting the development of affect in thought-activity to the minimum required for acting as a signal. (S.E. 5, 602)

If, then, the qualitative aspect of the protective sampling of excitation entails the formation of signals—which, therefore, are always, tendentially, danger-signals—then the process by which such signals are formed would coincide with the articulation of a temporal structure capable of temporizing the traumatic effects of an excess of energy, effects that could then be projected as being exterior, anterior, or posterior to the position of the psyche.

The form such temporalizing-temporizing sampling (signalization) would therefore tend to assume would be none other than that of a narration, through which alterity is composed and organized. The "death drive" would then be merely another name for a story that seeks to organize the other, precisely by naming it. But in telling his stories, Freud inevitably names too much — and too little: "The relation of our earth to the sun," to those "external, disruptive and diverting influences," to that "still entirely inconceivable power," remains to be conceived, *vorgestellt*. Which is why Freud's speculation must continue to follow out its idea. For there is till one more story to be told.

Speculation: The Way to Utter Difference

If Freud's speculative effort to think repetition through to its ultimate consequences leads him to question "our abstract idea of time," this merely continues an interrogation that is as old as psychoanalytic thought itself. Already in *The Interpretation of Dreams* Freud recognizes a major difficulty of his "attempt to penetrate more deeply into the psychology of dream-processes" to consist in the necessity of "rendering the simultaneity of a highly complex configuration [*Zusammenhang*] through the successivity of description" (S.E. 5, 588). All of his subsequent efforts to construct a topology of the psyche bear witness to the complexity of that "simultaneity" and of the space it entails. If the space that Freud's conception of the psyche implies is difficult to represent—"unanschaulich" and "unvorstellbar" —it is because it is the theater of conflictual processes that do not take place "in" it as much as they produce the places they take. Conflicts of the sort psychoanalysis seeks to articulate take place as dislocation, Entstellung, and this cannot but affect the nature of those psychic "localities" its topologies seek to situate. The dislocation of psychic space disrupts the traditional idea of "simultaneity" as the coexistence of self-identical elements, each in their proper place; indeed, the very notion of a *proper place* is replaced by a conflictual dynamics of displacement, the movement of which is incompatible with the traditional conception of time as linear, irreversible succession. The Freudian notion of *Nachträglichkeit*, "belatedness" or "subsequence," is indicative of this dislocation of temporal successivity, designating not merely how certain psychic events develop their

146

significance "belatedly"—this in itself would in no way disrupt the traditional conception of time—but rather how events such as dreams or jokes only come to be in and through the production of after-effects from which they are distinctively separated and yet on which they necessarily depend: the dream, in the narration that disfigures it; the joke, in the laughter that displaces it. Such after-effects repeat the event they follow, but they also alter it, and it is precisely this process of repetitive alteration that renders the event effective, psychically "real."

If, however, the nature of psychic "reality" can be designated as one of repetitive alteration, the problem of psychoanalytical exposition (Darstellung) can no longer be the discrepancy between a subject matter that is "simultaneous" and a discourse that is "successive." Rather, it entails the relation between two kinds of repetition: the one entailing a movement of alteration, the other, of identification. To identify alterity, therefore, can only be to repeat it in a discourse that disfigures what it represents. Such a disfigural representation is what emerges in the course of Freud's speculation upon the repetition-compulsion, and the form it assumes is the compulsion to tell, or retell *stories*. These stories do not merely repeat an event that is inaccessible to the direct repetition of conceptual analysis; they repeat each other, in a sequence that is both successive and simultaneous. These repetitive narratives, in short, emerge as the ultimate con-sequence of Freud's "speculation."

That is why, after all is said and done, *another* story remains to be told; and why this other story is inevitably the most decisive, on which all the rest depend:

If, therefore, we are not to abandon the hypothesis of the death-drives, we must suppose them to be associated from the very first with life-drives. But we must admit that we are working there [*wir arbeiten da*] on an equation with two unknowns. (*Beyond*, p. 51)

The speculative reduction of repetition to the Fort! of the death drive has led Freud to a place—da—where he sees himself confronted not merely by the "capital X" that inhabits all metapsychological formulas, but to its duplication, "an equation with two unknowns." Small wonder, then, that of this place

science has so little to tell us . . . that we can liken the problem to a darkness into which not so much as a ray of an hypothesis has penetrated. (*Beyond*, p. 51)

If this darkness is impervious to scientific elucidation, it is precisely in the sense of a black hole of science itself: the effort to represent the origin of repetition, as the death drive; to render that origin observable, that has, as it were, absorbed all the light that science can shed into its impenetrable Fort! which is Da! If the pleasure principle has proven incapable of accounting for the phenomena of repetition, the construction of the hypothesis of a death drive, taken by itself, is equally untenable. Even the science of biology, which Freud has reviewed in the preceding chapter, fails to offer an explanation of how life could possibly have survived against the irresistible power of the death drive.

Freud has no choice, therefore, but to forsake the Fort! that is Da! and instead, to look elsewhere:

In a very different place we *do* meet with such a hypothesis, which however is of such a phantastic kind—surely more of a myth than a scientific explanation— that I would not dare to cite it here did it not *fulfill* just that condition whose *fulfillment we desire*. For it derives a drive from the need to reinstate an earlier state of things. (*Beyond*, p. 51, my italics)

The need for another form of repetition, to counterbalance that of the death drive (as repetition of the same), leads Freud back, once again, to the beginning: to a certain beginning. This time, however, it is not that of life itself, nor even of consciousness, qua organism: rather, it is toward the beginnings of our cultural consciousness that he finds himself ineluctably drawn. The beginning is, of course, a *myth*. For only this can, according to Freud, "fulfill the condition . . . whose fulfillment we desire." The repetition of the word "fulfill/fulfillment (*erfüllen/Erfüllung*) is rare enough in a stylist such as Freud to be worthy of attention; it bears witness, surely, to the power of the desire, the striving (*Streben*) that drives Freud towards that "very different place" (*ganz andere Stelle*) to which he assigns the name "myth."

And yet once he has thus named this other place, Freud immediately proceeds to modify this name in an attempt to unsay what he has said, under the pretext of clarifying it:

I mean of course the theory which Plato puts into the mouth of Aristophanes in the *Symposium*, and which deals not only with the origin [die Herkunft] of the sexual drive but also with the most important of its variations in regard to its object. (*Beyond*, p. 51)

The "myth" then turns out to be not a myth, "of course," but rather a theory, and Aristophanes merely the spokesman of Plato, the author of the *Symposium*. The "fantastic" aspects of this pseudo-myth are thus theoretically authorized, as it were, by Freud's attribution of the story to an author who, more than most, can be presumed to have known from start to finish what he really wanted to say. We will return to this attribution and this authorization in a moment. But let us first follow Freud as he makes his way ever further into this very different place, and having first set things straight concerning its fantastic appearance, now proceeds to tell, or rather retell the story, almost but not quite in his own words:

Our body, you see, was at first not at all formed as it is now; it was utterly different [*ganz anders*]. First of all, there were three sexes, not just male and female, as now, but also a third, which combined the two . . . the man-woman. . . . Everything about these humans, however, was double, they had four hands and four feet, two faces, double private parts etc. Thereupon Zeus was moved [*Da liess sich Zeus bewegen*] to divide each human in two parts, "as one slices quince apart for pickling . . . Because now the whole being had been cut in two, yearning drove [*trieb*] the two halves together; they entwined themselves with their hands, interlaced with one another *in the desire to grow together.*" (*Beyond*, p. 51-52)

Once he has thus retold the story, Freud hastens to furnish us with its theoretical interpretation, one designed to provide support for his previous speculations:

Shall we, following the hint of the poet-philosopher, venture the supposition that in the process of becoming animate living substance was torn apart into small particles which ever since have striven, through the sexual drive, to reunite? That these drives, in which the chemical affinity of inanimate matter persists, in their development through the realm of the protista, gradually overcome the difficulties set in their way by an environment charged with mortally dangerous stimuli that compel them to form a protective cortical layer? That these splintered particles of living substance thereby attain a multicellular condition and finally transfer the drive to reunite in the most concentrated form to the germ-cells? But here, I believe, the place has come to break off. (*Beyond*, p. 52)

Freud's interpretation, we discover, gives us: more of the same. Replacing the "phantastic hypothesis" by a theory placed in the mouth of a fictional character by "the poet-philosopher," Freud seeks to surmount the fiction and to restore the truth behind it: an original unity, "living substance," is split apart at the moment of its birth; repetition thus appears, once again, as the restoration of a previous unity, as a "reunification."

If this interpretation seeks to authorize itself by appealing to the authority of the author, the "poet-philosopher," this gesture both repeats and initiates what it seeks to confirm: repetition as a movement of the same, originating and seeking to return to a founding identity.

The text, as the expression of the "poet-philosopher" repeats what the latter intended to say: namely, that all repetition repeats an original identity, that it seeks to restore: the lovers, their original unity; life, its original death; the text, the original intention of its author. Freud's interpretation thus presupposes the authority of an original identity, the Author, and more precisely, an authorial consciousness and intention as the ground and guarantee of the meaning it attributes to the text. The essence of that meaning, and perhaps of meaning as such, is to portray repetition as a movement of sameness, deriving from an original identity.

But in thus interpreting the story of Aristophanes as a repetition of the same, Freud, curiously enough, alters that story. We need only reread the opening lines of the *Symposium* to discover that the question of who said what is just what sets the scene of the text, and sets it up so as to exclude the possibility of its ever being authoritatively resolved. This is why all the speeches of the *Symposium* are reported in a blend of direct and indirect discourse, something that Plato, the poet-philosopher, will specifically condemn in the *Republic*.[10]

The *Symposium*, of course, is generally considered to be an *early* text of the poet-philosopher. But just how early is precisely the question. For the text begins with Apollodorus telling Glaucon that just two days earlier he recounted the very same story Glaucon asks him to tell. The story concerns a dinner given by Agathon, which Glaucon assumes to have taken place in the recent past, with Apollodorus an invited guest. The latter, however, is quite amused at the assumptions of his interlocutor, whom he astonishes by informing that he was not present at the gathering and could not have been, since the banquet took place many years ago, "when we were still children" (173a). Apollodorus, it turns out, does know the story, but only through others, above all, through a certain Aristodemos, who, it appears, really did attend the dinner. "But even Aristodemos did not remember any more everything that was said," Apollodorus adds, "nor do I recall everything that he said to me" (178a).

This, then, is the starting-point, the point of departure for the speech that will constitute the major portion of the *Symposium*, and nothing is therefore less certain than what Freud so readily takes for granted: who precisely said what. For everything that is recounted is a repetition of a repetition, Apollodorus recounting the words of Aristodemos. And what really was said may never be certain, for it all took place "long ago, when we were still children."

The *Symposium*, then, begins with a series of repetitions, and it is difficult to know where, if anywhere, they stop. Freud, by contrast, is looking for something quite different: an authoritative account *of* repetition, not one that merely repeats what others (may) have said. He therefore needs authors and authorities and invokes as one such, "Prof. Heinrich Gomperz of Vienna," to establish the authenticity of the myth. The Professor is cited in order to situate the myth of the *Symposium* as the development of an earlier one, found in the *Upanishads*, which tells of the "emergence of the world from the Atman" (the Self or the Ego), as Freud recounts in a long footnote.

It is as though Freud, backed by the scientific authority of Prof. Gomperz, once again seeks to retrace a repetition (the myth of the *Symposium*) back to its source and origin (the *Upanishads*), to establish it as a repetition of the same. And yet, right from the start, something very curious happens: Freud invokes the authority of the specialist, Prof. Gomperz, to whom he attributes "the following suggestions concerning the derivation (Herkunft) of the Platonic myth"; but when he then proceeds to those "suggestions" ("I would like to call attention to the fact that"), he renders them "only in part in his (Prof. Gomperz's) words." It thus becomes virtually impossible to discern with certainty just who, in this long footnote, is saying what; that is, where the discourse of Professor Gomperz stops and where that of Professor Freud begins—or vice versa. In itself, of course, this would be a trivial matter, but where questions of authority and authenticity are at stake, it becomes an important, if undecidable, question. For the entire footnote serves primarily to line up authoritative support for Freud's interpretation of the "Platonic" myth by demonstrating the latter to be merely a repetition of another, an earlier story, whose meaning is clear, once and for all. It is to this end that Freud invokes Professor Gomperz, however vague that invocation turns out to be:

I have to thank Professor Heinrich Gomperz, of Vienna, for the following discussion of the origin of the Platonic myth, which I give partly in his own words. It is to be remarked that what is essentially the same theory is already to be found in the Upanishads. For we find the following passage in the *Brihad-âranyaka-upanishad*, 1, 4, 3, where the origin of the world from the Atman (the Self or Ego) is described: "But he (the Atman, the Self or the Ego) felt no joy [*hatte auch keine Freude*]; therefore [*darum*] a man has no joy when he is alone. Thereupon [*Da*] he desired a second. You see, he was as large as a woman and a man intertwined. This his Self he sunders in two parts; out of this [*Daraus*] husband and wife emerged. Therefore [*Darum*], measured against the Self this body is as it were a half, thus explained Yagnâvalkya. Therefore [*Darum*] this empty space here is filled by woman." (*Beyond*, p. 52)

No doubt that Freud here recognizes the possibility of escaping from the joyless solitude of the Fort! Da!, and, with the authority of Prof. Gomperz, of transforming it into a "There-fore" (darum), a logically compelling way of departing from the "there" (daraus). No doubt that this version of the myth provides Freud with a mirror-image of the fulfillment he desires: a self or ego alone is no more cause for rejoicing than is a death drive all by itself. For there to be joy, Freude, there must be a second, a double, a pair of opposites, joined together, to be sure, in holy matrimony. The other must be different, and yet dominated by the law of the same—that is the condition that Freud's speculation desires to fulfill.

But if the story he thus retells, partially in the words of another, authorizes such a desire, it also repeats the very problem that Freud has been seeking to avoid: for this narcissistic account of the creation of difference from identity cannot account for the creation—i.e., separation—itself. Except, that is, by pointing to the lack of Freude that renders that separation necessary, but not necessarily intelligible. The gap, in short, between a "therefore" and a "thereupon," a darum and a da, remains to be bridged. And yet, without this bridge, the fortress of the Fort! Da! has not really been breached.

This is why Freud may find comfort in discovering an earlier origin of the myth he seeks to found, but also why he cannot dispense with its "Platonic" repetition. For although the story that furnishes him with the hypothesis he desires is spoken by Aristophanes, Freud persists in treating the latter as a mere spokesman for the "poet-philosopher," for whom, as is well known, the comic dramatist had little sympathy. Yet this attribution—of Aristophanes' discourse to Plato—is only one of a number of alterations that Freud's reading of the *Symposium* imposes upon its "original" text. Let us, therefore, reread the latter as literally as possible, without prejudging the question of who, in the final analysis, im letzten Grunde, is really speaking, or who has the *last word*. Let us, in short, allow Aristophanes, at least for the moment, speak for himself. He begins his story thus: "Our body, you see, was at first not formed as it is now; it was utterly different." Wilamowitz, whose translation Freud cites, renders the Greek "physis" not, as is often the case, by "nature" but, more concretely, by "body." The story shows that the choice was a good one. For, in contrast to the alleged source in the Upanishad, Aristophanes' story concerns not abstract or incorporeal beings, a "self" or an "ego," but *bodies*. His story of love begins with the body. Not with the body as we know it today, to be sure, but with one that was "utterly different." Once upon a time (*pálai*). *Einmal*. . . .

And yet, when those bodies begin to be described, we discover that they were not quite so different after all. What was different was a certain duplication: a double-male, double-female, and that third kind, combining half of each, and which survives only as a name, androgyne. Everything was doubled in these beings, with one notable exception: the head. They kept their heads, as it were, single. Once upon a time, long ago.

In the context of Freud's speculations, one might be tempted to see in this initial state not merely duplication, doubling, but also: repetition. Repetition of the same, at the very beginning. But instead of jumping to conclusions, let us listen to Aristophanes, and to what he has to say at the end of his tale. The moral of the story, as Aristophanes describes it, seems to be not so very different from the interpretation of Freud:

The cause of all this is that our original nature was thus, and we were whole, and this very yearning and striving for wholeness is what we call love. And before this, as I have said, we were one, but now, because of injustice, we have been taken apart by the God and dispersed like the Arcadians before the Spartans. (*Symposium*, 192-193a)

Like Freud, and most other commentators of this text,[11] Aristophanes seems to state unequivocally that human beings were originally whole and one, and that only as a result of "injustice" were they condemned, punished and estranged from their original unity; that Eros entails the striving to return to this lost unity, to restore that original wholeness. This, at least, is what Aristophanes seems to want to say. Indeed, he seems to leave little room for doubt,

that our race would be blessed if we could succeed in love, and everyone was able to win his particular beloved, in order thus to return to our original nature. If this would be best, under the prevailing conditions the best will be what comes closest to that ideal, and that is to find the beloved who most conforms to our wishes. And therefore if we wish to celebrate in song the God to whom we owe this, we must indeed sing the praises of Eros, who nowadays shows us so much good in leading us to those for whom we bear affinities, but who also gives us hope that in the future, if only we prove our respect for the Gods, our original nature will be healed and restored, and we will be made happy and blessed. (193c-d)

Who would wish to spoil such a Happy Ending, or want to say anything different? This, at least, seems to be the effect intended by Aristophanes, for immediately after proclaiming this to be the moral of his story, he turns to the previous speaker, Eryximachos, the physician, with a remark that casts a somewhat different light on that moral:

This, oh Eryximachos, he said, is my discourse on Eros, one that is quite different from yours. As I asked you before, please don't make fun of it. (193d)

In view of this plea to be taken seriously, Aristophanes' commentary on his tale now appears as something of a *captatio benevolentiae*. And, as readers of the *Symposium* already know, his fears are not unfounded. Nor is he himself innocent in the affair. For earlier in the evening, as it had come time for him to speak, Aristophanes suddenly seemed taken by a fit of hiccoughs which caused him to change places in the order of speakers with Eryximachos, who also gave him the professional advice of sneezing and holding his breath in order to get over the attack. That such remedies were not without their effect can be surmised from the fact that Aristophanes is able to reply to the physician immediately after the latter has concluded his speech. But Aristophanes' response to the well-meaning inquiry of the doctor as to the state of his hiccoughs, can only be considered an impertinent provocation:

Of course it stopped, but not before it was treated with sneezing; and this, he added, makes me wonder why it is that the harmony of the body [one of the basic positions outlined by Eryximachos in the speech he has just delivered] should desire the kind of noise and tickling involved in sneezing; for as soon as I began to sneeze, it stopped straightaway. (189a)

Having presumably sneezed and snorted throughout much of the good doctor's discourse, Aristophanes now has the effrontery to cite his own cure as evidence against Eryximachos's panegyrics to love as the harmony of the body. Small wonder, then, that Aristophanes concludes his own speech with an eye cast anxiously in the direction of the physician. For the latter has already given him fair warning:

My good Aristophanes, take care! You mock me, as you are about to speak, and compel me therefore to become the judge of your discourse and to make sure that you too do not say anything laughable [*geloion*], whereas otherwise you could have spoken in peace. (189a-b)

If the scene of the *Symposium* is from the very beginning agonistic, with the different speakers vying with one another in their praises of Eros, the interchange of Aristophanes and Eryximachos introduces an unmistakable tone of aggressiveness. Henceforth, the speeches will not merely be in competition with one another, and therefore directed at addressees who are also judges: they will also engage the prestige and standing of those who deliver them. Which is why Aristophanes' reply to the physician's warning, while ironically half-hearted, touches the core of the problem:

Thereupon Aristophanes laughingly [*gelásanta*] replied: Well said, Eryximachos, and as far as I am concerned, let what I have said be unsaid. So don't lie in wait for me, since in any case I shall be concerned, not that what I intend to say will turn out to be laughable [*geloia*], for that would be all to the good and in accordance with my muse, but rather ridiculous [*katagélasta*]. (189b)

But if Aristophanes seeks to unsay what he has said, he knows, no less than Freud, that such an attempt at "undoing" must always leave traces. And if he thus chooses the physician, Eryximachos, to be his privileged addressee and judge, is this not his attempt to displace the verdict, upon which his joke, like all jokes, depend, from that other listener, who, for the moment at least, remains silent, awaiting his turn. For if Aristophanes insults and provokes Eryximachos, the author of the *Clouds* knows full well that his most redoubtable antagonist lies elsewhere. Eryximachos, however, speaks also for the silent Socrates when he reminds the satirist that, notwithstanding his efforts to unsay what he has said, he can expect to be held responsible for his words:

Now that you have done, Eryximachos replied, do you think you can get away as easily as that, Aristophanes? Take care, rather, to speak as one who will have to answer for what he says. (189b-c)

It is not simply fortuitous if it is a physician, Eryximachos, who is first charged with calling the mocking Aristophanes to order. From Plato to the present, the doctor has stood as one of the chief guardians of order in the *physis*, and hence as a model for order in the *polis* as well. It was Eryximachos who first launched the idea of replacing the usual after-dinner entertainment, music, with serious discourse:

Now that it has been decided . . . that each shall drink only as much as he likes . . . I would like to propose that we ask the lady flutist who has just entered to leave and either play for herself or, if she prefer, for the women inside, and that this evening we entertain ourselves with speeches. (176e)

The lady flutist having thus been excluded, the men, left to themselves, begin to speak seriously their *logoi* about Love. It is only consistent, then, that it is Eryximachos who has the task of calling Aristophanes to order in the name of seriousness and of reponsibility. And it is no less consistent that Aristophanes should therefore conclude his speech with a moral designed to disarm the suspicions he himself has provoked.

But what, then, of that speech itself? Aristophanes, it will be recalled, concludes by stressing that it has been very different from that of Eryximachos; he introduces it, however, in precisely the same way:

To be sure, Aristophanes said, I intend to speak very differently from the way both you and Pausanias have spoken. For it seems to me that so far people have not at all perceived the true force of Eros. Had they done so, they would have certainly built him the most marvellous temples and altars and made the greatest sacrifices in his honor. (189c)

If Aristophanes declares that he intends to speak in a very different manner from that of his predecessors, it is because he is convinced that there has been a problem of perception: the true power of Eros has not yet been properly recognized and therefore remains to be revealed. The discourse of Aristophanes, then, will be different in not taking Eros for granted, for self-evident, but rather as the object of a certain blindness, a kind of malady that he sets about to remedy. Aristophanes, therefore, repeats the gesture of the physician but at the same extends it to cover the operation in which he and the other speakers are engaged. For one can only seriously sing the praises of Eros if one knows what one is talking about. And this, Aristophanes insists, is precisely the problem. His discourse will thus be both revelatory, and pedagogic:

I will therefore try to explain his power as well, and you can then be teachers of the others. (189d)

This pedagogic intention, therefore, to reveal the true nature and power of Eros, to remove, that is, a certain blindness, may be what explains the vivid quality of Aristophanes' description of those ancient beings, whom he asserts, were so utterly different (all'alloia) from those we see today. And yet as we have already remarked, the difference to which Aristophanes refers is rather one of quantity than of quality: a difference, one might say, in economy. For if we look closely at Aristophanes' description of those double-beings, we discover them to have been very similar: to us, to themselves and to their parents:

Because the male was originally an offspring of the sun, and the female a child of the earth, while that participating in both was sired by the moon, which itself participates in both sexes. And they were round and went round, thus resembling their parents. (190b)

The world of the double-beings was one of resemblances, family and otherwise; and like their parents, they moved in circles, "making cartwheels", as children do "even today." If we compare Aristophanes' double-being with the Atman of the Upanishad, we can see that the solitude of the latter would seem out of place in the world of the former: never being alone, they would never need to create others. And if there is a beginning, it is already doubled, duplicated, full of repetition and of resemblance, circular: for "they were round and they went round"—while keeping their heads, that single, "common head shared by the opposing faces."

They kept their heads—or did they?

Freud's version of the story grows strangely vague at this point: that is, at precisely the point where the actual story, the dramatic conflict as it were, sets in: "Thereupon Zeus was moved. . . ." The German is even more suggestive: "*Da* liess sich Zeus bewegen . . . ." But where, *da*? If Freud is notably imprecise, Aristophanes is less so. What he has to say shows that Zeus had good reason to be moved. For the double-beings had begun to grow tired of the same, of turning around in circles, and had cast their eyes upward instead:

Now their force and strength were enormous, and their thoughts no less so, and what Homer tells of Ephialtes and Otos applies to them as well, for they wanted to invade the heavens and attack the gods. (190b)

Freud's "thereupon," that indeterminate but indicative "da," spatial and temporal at once, covers a desire that is distant and yet familiar: the striving to transgress the boundaries separating gods from men, rulers from ruled, the other from the same. And although Freud in his account omits the deliberations that lead Zeus to "be moved," Aristophanes does not:

For it was not expedient to kill them [the double-beings], and, as in the case of the Titans, exterminate the entire race, since that would have also meant the loss of all the tributes and sacrifices men give to the gods: but they could not simply be permitted to continue their blasphemous doings either. (190c)

The deliberations of Zeus indicate what Freud is at pains to ignore: that the law presiding over the *Fort(ress)-Da!* is none other than that of the *oikos*: the economy of appropriation and assimilation that characterizes the organization of the ego; in short, the economy of narcissism. In that distant place, utterly different from all that is familiar, we therefore encounter something all too familiar: the narcissistic effort to keep the other in its (proper) place, to subordinate alterity to an economy of the same. In the case, however, of an other that is all the more difficult to control because it is already a mirror-image of the same, radical measures are called for. The other must be altered, in accordance with the laws of narcissistic economics, and this is precisely what Zeus proposes:

I think, then, that I have found a means that will allow humans to survive and still compel them to cease their excesses for lack of strength. For now, he said, I shall cut each of them into two halves, which will make them weaker and also more useful to us, since there will be more of them, and they will walk upright on two legs. Should I observe, however, that they continue their blasphemous doings and refuse to keep still, he said, I shall cut them apart once again, and then they can hop around on one leg, like tops. (190c)

Zeus' strategy is doubtless decisive: by dividing the doubles he ups the ante while lowering the risk, and the move can be repeated. It is also fully in accord with the economic law that calls for a lowering in (unbound) energy and an increase in binding. If the energy of the doubles is dangerously unbound, bounding back and forth, as it were, through a mirroring in which the same becomes other and the other, the same, what Zeus suggests is to create a different kind of image; the image of difference "itself." Zeus therefore proposes, but it is Apollo—god of the sun, father of the male—who disposes; for after Zeus has made the first incision,

he ordered Apollo to turn the face and the half-neck around towards the cut, so that man, confronted with his cleavage, would become more moral, and the rest he ordered Apollo to heal. (190e)

"In the final analysis [*im letzten Grunde*], it must have been the history of our earth and its relation to the sun that has left us its mark . . ." Aristophanes, here, tells us just that story of the mark, left by wounds not of the spirit, but of the body; and these wounds, as both Freud and Aristophanes well knew, do not heal without leaving scars. Or "blisters," as with the scorched crust—scab?—of the Bläschen. Or finally, without marking the place in which all these strands come together to form a single, inextricable knot.

[Apollo] therefore turned the face around, pulled the skin from all sides up over what today we call the belly, and just as when one pulls together the strings of a purse, he drew the ends together and tied them up in the middle of the belly in what today we call the navel. The resulting wrinkles he smoothed out for the most part, and moulded the chest with the aid of a tool like that used by shoemakers to smoothe out creases in the leather, except for a few wrinkles that he left around the belly and navel to serve as a reminder of the ancient accident. (190e-191a)

The navel is left wrinkled, knotted, interrupting the smooth surface of the body, which, as Freud knew, serves the ego as its model.[12] The closure of the body, paradigm of the ego's organization, is both accomplished and interrupted by Apollo, the "sun," the intervention

of an exteriority, and serves as reminder "of the ancient accident."
No matter how economical the ego may be, its "purse" can never be
hermetically sealed, for just in the place where everything comes together, we find the scar and stigma of an ancient wound, an ancient
striving. And it is precisely this striving that emerges from the operation of Zeus and Apollo:

Once the figure had thus been cut in two, each part yearned for its other half,
and so they came together, held each other in their arms and pressed together,
intertwined. (191a)

This marks the spot where Freud *seems* to have found what he was
looking for: the derivation of life as a process of repetition from the
tendency to restore a previous unity. It is here, then, that he believes
that he has found Eros. But in Aristophanes' story, Eros is not yet
mentioned, and with good reason. For the striving that Freud takes
to be Eros is, in the version of the comic-dramatist, nothing other than
Thanatos, in the purest and most irresistible of forms. The sundered
bodies, he relates,

intertwined, and out of the desire to grow together they died from hunger and
other neglect, for they would not do anything apart. If, now, the one half was
dead and the other remained, the survivor sought out another and embraced it
. . . and thus they perished. (191b)

Had Aristophanes' tale ended here, as Freud's version does, there
would have never been Eros at all, but only death. The story would
have merely repeated, or rather anticipated, the Freudian black hole,
fortress of the impervious *da!* and, in the end, nothing would have
been left, not even death itself. But Aristophanes continues his story,
just as Freud must continue his search. And it is just possible that it
is precisely this continuation that provides what Freud so deeply desires. For Aristophanes tells of a second, repeated intervention, designed to save the moribund bodies from themselves, from their
deadly desire to be reunified and whole—to be, in short, a self:

Thereupon Zeus took pity and placed another means at their disposal, by shifting their private parts to the front, instead of on the side where they were before,
since previously they had reproduced not in one another but in the earth, like
crickets. Now, however, he shifted them to the front and thus allowed them to
reproduce in one another. (191b-c)

This second intervention does not merely repeat the first; it adds a
new direction: instead of dividing, cutting, and separating, it shifts,
dislocates, and rearranges the reproductive organs, bringing repetition,
as it were, to the fore. It is only with this dislocation, with the advent

of a certain Entstellung, that the fort(ress) da! is finally and irrevocably breached. And only here, in the story of Aristophanes, is Eros finally named:

Ever since this distant time, therefore, love is inborn in man, attempts to make one of two and to heal human nature. (191c-d)

Therefore, henceforth, the da! is fort!: not simply as a unity that has been lost, or a wholeness that has been separated from itself, but as an Entstellung that reinscribes the stories of loss and of separation in another text, one in which displacement becomes the "origin" of eros. For it is only when the organs have been displaced that they become capable of generating eros, and not merely thanatos; only then do they become *erogenous*:

Each of us is therefore a fragment of a man [*anthropou sýmbolon*], since we are cut like flatfish, and have become two from one. Therefore everyone is always seeking his other part. (191d)

For Aristophanes, it would seem, this erogenous, symbolic striving can never be separated from the narcissistic desire to become one; for him, the Symbolic therefore is indissociable from narcissism, from a certain mirror-image of the other. And yet, his story also marks indelibly the site, and the sight, of that image as the *navel*, reminder of the ancient accident or incident by which the sun left its imprint for us to decipher.

But what of that cipher left in just the place where we straddle, or fall for, the unknown? What of the "capital X" in which so much energy is bound up, the variable that both permits the "equations" of metapsychology and also casts them in doubt?

In short, can we be sure, as Freud seems to be (but only by not reading the story he recites), that we know just where the story stops, or where it is going? Where the myth ends, and where theory begins? The lovers, at any rate, are least able to say what it is they really desire:

When, then, one meets its true, proper half, be he a pediast or anyone else, the two are overcome by amorous union and love and do not wish to part for even the shortest time; and those who spend their entire lives together would not even be able to say what they want from one another. For this can hardly be the community of amorous delight . . . but rather it is clear that the soul of each desires something else, which however it cannot explicitly utter but only hint at. (192b-c)

The lovers cannot explicitly utter what it is that they desire from each other, because what they desire is so utterly different that it can only be uttered by someone else. This, at least, would seem to be the reason why, at the very end of his tale, Aristophanes recounts the intervention of yet another figure—or is it rather a *hypothesis*, a supposition that suddenly makes its appearance here, to guide the story toward its happy end?

And if, while they lay together, Hephaistos was to step before them, tools in hand, and was to ask them: What is it then really, people, that you want from each other? And if they then had no answer, and he asked further: Is what you desire something like this, that you may be together as much as possible, and never part, either day or night? For if this is your desire, then I will melt and weld you so that you are one instead of two, and may live together as one, and so that when you have died, even in the underworld you will be dead not as two but as one. (192d-e)

Hephaistos, the god of binding and unbinding,[13] often pictured with his tools slung over his shoulder like a capital X, appears here on the scene to assure the binding that the lovers, it would seem, so desire, and also to guarantee the moral of the story, that both Aristophanes, and Freud, cannot do without. But if Hephaistos thus ties up the loose ends of the story into a seemingly neat knot, the lovers, it should be observed, remain silent. And since they cannot say what it is that they want, Hephaistos must do it for them. For he does not merely pose his question, he *imposes* the response, putting his answer into the mouths of the lovers just as Plato, according to Freud at least, put his story into the mouth of Aristophanes. Is this, then, the mouth that gives us the *true* sense of the story?

Hearing this, we know for certain, not even one (of the lovers) would refuse or indicate that he wanted something different, but rather each would be sure to have heard just what he had wanted to hear, what he had always yearned for, that is, by being close to, and melting into the beloved, to make two into one. (192e)

Does Aristophanes speak for Plato here, for himself, or for Hephaistos, who speaks for, and in the name of, the lovers? Will we ever know for certain? "Each would be sure to have heard just what he had wanted to hear, what he had always yearned for." This, Aristophanes concludes, "we know for certain." But does that not mean that all we know for certain is what we desire to hear?

The lovers, in any case, remain silent. They must be spoken *for*; but their silence speaks *to* us, through the voice of a narrator, about whose status we grow increasingly uncertain:

It must therefore be feared that if we do not behave properly towards the gods, that we will once again be rendered asunder, and have to go about like the figures carved out of tombstones, which are divided at the nose, and that we will then become just like split dice, each of which possesses its other half. (193e)

The fate of the lovers, Aristophanes makes clear here, at the end, is ours as well: the mark they leave us, imprint of the sun and its relation to the earth, of a violent intervention of powerful forces, is a signal that suspends us somewhere between symbols and "split dice," in the silence of a figure engraved on a tombstone. The danger with which the signal confronts us is that, like Nietzsche's "female," we shall be neither deep, nor even flat, but rather twisted, distorted, entstellt. And that we shall move about like Hephaistos himself, who, it should be recalled, is the only Greek god known to limp.

And perhaps it is this, more than anything else, that binds the Greek god of binding and unbinding, bearer of the great X, to Freud, who concludes his speculative way *Beyond the Pleasure Principle* with the following remark:

This is tied up with countless other questions which are impossible to answer now. We must be patient and await further means and occasions for research. Also ready to forsake a way that we have followed for a while if it seems to be leading to no good end. . . . Moreover, for the slow advances of our scientific knowledge we may take comfort in the words of a poet:
      "What we cannot reach flying, we must reach limping.
      . . . .
      Scripture tells us it is no sin to limp."

Again, it is the words of a poet (Rückert), philosophizing, that provides Freud with comfort. Or is it really a poet that Freud cites, here at the end of his speculative way? For, many years before, he had cited the same poet, and the same passage, but at a time when he was less concerned with death and with repetition than with the machine he was in the process of constructing, a machine that seemed almost ready to "fly" by itself. This machine, or more properly, this automat (Hephaistos, we recall, is said to have been the founder of automats) was none other than Freud's first attempt to elaborate a psychological system. As the "Project" drew ever nearer to completion, Freud wrote of his feelings in a letter to his friend, Fliess:

Now listen to this. One strenuous night last week, when I was in the stage of painful discomfort in which my brain works best, the barriers suddenly lifted, the veils dropped, and it was possible to see from the details of neurosis all the way to the very conditioning of consciousness. Everything fell into place, the cogs meshed, one had the impression that the thing was now really a machine which in a moment would begin to go by itself. The three systems of neurones, the "free" and "bound" state of quantity, the primary and secondary processes, the main and compromise tendencies of the nervous system, the two biological rules of attention and of defence, the indications of quality, reality and thought, the state of the psycho-sexual group, the sexual condition of repression, finally the conditions of consciousness as a perceptual function—that all fit together and still does. I can, of course, hardly contain myself for delight. (*Origins*, p. 129)

Freud, who can hardly contain himself, nevertheless wishes he had waited before sending his friend and first reader an early draft of his "machine," one that was still incomplete:

Had I only waited a fortnight with the communication to you, everything would have turned out so much clearer. But it was only in attempting to communicate it to you that the thing became clear to me in the first place. So it could not have been otherwise. Now I shall hardly find the time to give you a proper account. If only I had forty-eight hours to talk with you about this and nothing else [*und nichts anderes*], the thing could probably be finished up. But that is impossible. "What we cannot reach flying . . ." (*Ibid.*)

In the absence of the cherished friend, "first reader" and "representative of the others," Freud turned to the poet for comfort. And if the latter, repeating Scripture—*Die Schrift*—could tell him that it is not a sin to limp, Freud was far from limping in 1895. Rather, he was flying high: "Other neurotic confirmations deluge me. The thing is really true and genuine" (*Ibid.*). In 1920, however, in the absence of the Friend, Freud still sought solace from the poets, and confirmation from the neurotics. And in the "transference" of the latter—precisely, that is, in their refusal to confirm—Freud seemed to distinguish the true and genuine machine behind it all: the driving force of the repetition-compulsion, working automatically, flying, as it were, in the face of the pleasure principle. If the psychoanalytical machine might falter as therapy, it would fly as theory, as speculation, if need be. But the latter, like the automat, still needed a start from somewhere else—a start, which would also be a finish—and so Freud found himself on the way to an utterly different place, where he thought he discerned the authoritative voice of the poet-philosopher.

But if the figure he found there was indeed a "poet," it was no philosopher but rather their antagonist, a man of the theater, a storyteller with a sense for the absurd. And the legend he told only repeated what Freud himself had thought and written elsewhere, long ago; repeated, that is, but also and inevitably transformed.

*   *   *

And after the playwright had finished his story and after the actor had had his say, it finally came time for the philosopher to speak. And he promised to speak the truth about Eros, rather than simply to sing his praises:

For I shall hold no panegyrics, and could not do so if I wanted to. Rather, the truth is what I will tell you, if you are willing, not in the style of your speeches but in my own way, so that I don't make myself ridiculous. (199a)

Like the comic writer, the philosopher also announces that his talk will be different from the others; and like the former, he also fears laughter. But this time, there will be none. For what the philosopher has to say concerns the most serious thing of all, truth. And truth must be said in its own way:

See too, Phaidros, if you can use such a talk, if you can listen to the truth about Eros, but told in phrases and words that just happen to come to mind. (199b)

Having thus announced his "basic rule," which repeats, or anticipates, that which Freud will make the basis of psychoanalytic "free association," Socrates proceeds to tell, or rather to retell, the story told to him by a woman met long before when he was still a very young man.

And after he has finished retelling this story of love, a strange thing comes to pass:

Now after Socrates had spoken thus, the others showered him with praise; Aristophanes, however, was about to say something, because Socrates had mentioned his own speech in the course of his talk. But suddenly there was a knocking on the outer door, and it became very noisy, as though there were voices of people wandering about, and the tones of a flutist were heard. . . . (212c)

Notes

Notes

Preface

1. M. Foucault, "What is an Author?" reprinted in: *Language, Counter-Memory, Practice*, ed. Donald F. Bouchard, Ithaca, NY, 1980, pp. 133-35

2. These remarks are intended less as a critique of the Standard Edition, whose merits in introducing Freud to the English-speaking world can hardly be questioned, than as an indication of the price paid in rendering Freud clear and intelligible. As François Roustang observes, "Freud's writing loses all of its vigor and even its meaning in the majority of French translations, and even in the English translation of the Standard Edition, because the translators are interested only in rendering the overall meaning of a phrase defined by its syntax, and not at all concerned with the placement of words and with their repetitions. If parataxis must be respected in Freud's text it is because his writing *is* the very machine it constructs, because this machine . . . *is* his discourse and because therefore its parts cannot be displaced without rendering its functioning impossible." ("Du style de Freud," in: F. Roustang, . . . *Elle ne le lâche plus*, Paris, 1980, p. 35). To which I would add only that since the "machine" functions precisely *by displacing its parts*, its operation cannot simply be *respected* either, except perhaps by continuing, and reflecting on, the process of displacement itself. In a critical discussion of the Standard Edition's translations, see Bruno Bettelheim's 1982 article in *The New Yorker*, "Freud and the Soul," 1 March 1982, pp. 52-93.

Part I. Psychoanalysis Set Apart

1. Ernest Jones, *The Life and Work of Sigmund Freud*, Vol. III, London, 1957, p. 30.

2. Citations of Freud refer wherever possible to the Norton Library editions. Otherwise, the *Standard Edition of the Complete Psychological Works of Sigmund Freud in 24 Volumes* (London: Hogarth Press, 1953-66), with volume and page number, is given in parentheses in the body of the text. In almost all cases, however, I have retranslated the passages cited, and the reference to the Standard Edition is given as a contextual and comparative aide to the reader.

3. The IPA, in short, was to be *organized* much like a collective Ego, of which Freud observes: "The Ego is an organization. It is based on the maintenance of free intercourse

and of the possibility of reciprocal influence between all its parts." *Inhibition, Symptom and Anxiety*, New York: Norton Library, 1959, p. 24.

4. Jones, II, p. 143.

5. *Ibid.*, p. 145.

6. The problem of institutionalization has attracted increasing attention in the psycho-analytic literature of recent years. Within the context of the French experience, the study of François Roustang, *Un destin si funeste*, Paris, 1976, deserves special mention. Motivated no doubt by the problems he encountered as a member of the École freudienne, founded by Jacques Lacan (and dissolved by him in 1980), Roustang's study seeks to trace the institutional difficulties of the psychoanalytic movement to the relations of Freud to his followers.

7. "I felt the need of transferring this authority to a younger man, who would then as a matter of course take my place after my death. This man could only by C. G. Jung. . . ." ("On the History of the Psychoanalytical Movement," New York: Norton Library, 1966, p. 43).

8. Such a conflict-situation is typical of those investigated by Roustang, who concludes that they entail a complicity based on the shared need of Freud and his followers for mutual recognition and confirmation of their respective positions within the hierarchy. It is worth remarking a notable absence in the panoply of conflict examined by Roustang: that of Adler. This omission assumes particular significance in view of Roustang's conception of the kind of power-struggle that he sees as characteristic of the relation of Freud to his followers. Indeed, the conception of the subject that emerges in Roustang's discussion of these struggles seems far closer to that of Adler than that of Freud. Roustang's propensity for formulations such as "to desire for oneself," "to speak on one's own," "to write for oneself" all imply an autonomy of the ego (= self) that—paradixocally, given Roustang's Lacanian affinities—is closer to American ego-psychology than to Freud. The fact, however, that even one of the most independent and most critical analysts in the Lacanian tradition should thus employ what we have described as the "language of the ego" is less paradoxical than it might seem. For insofar as the Lacanian approach to analysis tends to establish an opposition and hierarchy between the "symbolic" order of unconscious desire and the "imaginery" order of the narcissistic ego, the latter can be easily treated as an object of polemics, thus obscuring the necessity of further reflection on the problem of narcissism. The lack of such reflection can then easily pave the way to the kind of lapse into the language and "standpoint" of the ego that one finds in Roustang's otherwise highly suggestive book. One of the aims of these studies, on the contrary, is to demonstrate how a certain narcissism forms the insurmountable, conflictual horizon of psychoanalytic thinking, and therefore how any attempt—be it that of Lacan (the Symbolic order of desire) or that of Freud himself—to map out a region "beyond" narcissism is ineluctably determined by what it seeks to transcend.

9. Letter of May 8, 1913, cited in Jones, II, p. 168.

10. S.E. 23, 250.

11. "The ego is, indeed, the organized portion of the id." *Inhibition, Symptom, and Anxiety*, p. 23.

12. Roustang characterizes the Freud-Jung relationship as one between tendentially paranoic (Freud) and schizophrenic (Jung) forms of thought, and suggests that Freud ultimately unified both into a "new type of theorizing (*Un destin si funeste*, p. 73). In the terms I shall elaborate in this study, this new type of theorizing is designated as the movement of *Auseinandersetzung*, the "setting apart" that emerges as the conflictual result of the "paranoic" effort to determine and to systematize, through the construction of opposition, and the "schizophrenic" tendency to displace and dislocate such determination.

13. If Freud's theory of the phallus and "castration" is informed by opposition *visible/invisible*—the psychological primacy of which his own discussion of the ego and its relation

to perception should have moved him to question — the fantasies discovered by Melanie Klein, involving the interior of the body, no longer privilege perception: "The interior of the body — the invisible — becomes the representative of the unconscious and of the super-ego," she writes in *Die Psychologie des Kindes*, Vienna, 1932, p. 215, note. The invisibility of the interior of the body distinguishes itself from the invisible moment in castration through the fact that it is not the attribute of a phenomenal object, the phallus, and hence merely a negative mode of visibility, but rather the *scene* of the phantasy itself.

14. "The shortest path to the fulfillment of the wish is one leading directly from the excitation produced by the need to a complete cathexis of the perception. Nothing prevents us from assuming that there was a primitive state in which this path was actually traversed, that is, in which wishing ended in hallucinating." S.E. 5, 566.

15. Any approach to Freud that tends to hypostasize "castration" — as is the case with that of Lacan (see Philippe Lacoue-Labarthe and Jean-Luc Nancy, *Le titre de la lettre*, Paris, 1973, who argue this convincingly) — will therefore inevitably hypostasize narcissism as well. Although he is often captivated by his own story, no one more than Freud has demonstrated the narcissistic character of such captivation, as well as its inevitability. No theoretical speculation is free from such narcissism, a fact that Freud's *writing* constantly takes into account (although not always, or most interestingly, at the level of explicit statement or reflection). For Lacan, by contrast, narcissism, by being identified with the quasi-ontological order of the "Imaginary," is represented as a step to be surmounted by the subject, at least ideally, in its accession to full maturity, i.e., the "Symbolic." Unconscious desire thus emerges in Lacan as beyond narcissism, essentially distinct from the "imaginary ego." The latter's "return," of course, is all the more implacable, as the history of the École freudienne demonstrates.

16. The "position" or "positing" (*Setzung* or *Stellung*) of the child in the primal scene is in fact threefold: in addition to the double, oppositional identification with active male and passive female, the child sets itself apart from both, precisely *as* spectator of a scene in which it nonetheless participates. The primal scene thus emerges as a prototype of the manner in which the subject sets itself apart, both in opposing itself to the scene it seeks to confront (or perceive) and in distributing or dispersing its self among the three positions just mentioned: active subject of desire, passive object, and active/passive spectator. In this process of Auseinandersetzung, identity — the organization and standpoint of the ego — emerges as the ambivalent, conflictual effect of an interminable struggle to alter alterity.

17. The space implied by this triadic topology is, as we shall see, very different from that "projected" by the ego in its *Auseindersetzung* with, and through, anxiety. If the latter can be designated as conforming to the traditional, Euclidean notion of space as homogeneous, continuous extension, the container (Aristotle) of bodies, each in its proper place — the space of Freud's topology is one rather of constitutive and conflictual *overlapping*. It is a space in which the process of setting apart from the other converges with setting apart of the self, as the following remark of Freud suggests: "We were justified, I think, in dividing the ego from the id. . . . On the other hand, the ego is identical with the id, and is merely a specially differentiated part of it. If we think of this part by itself in contradistinction to the whole, or if a real split has occurred between the two, the weakness of the ego becomes apparent. But if the ego remains bound up with the id and indistinguishable from it, then it displays its strength. The same is true of the relation between the ego and the super-ego. In many situations the two are merged. . . . We should be quite wrong if we pictured the ego and the id as two opposing camps . . ." (*Inhibition, Symptom and Anxiety*, p. 23). The ego, in short, is strongest when it is "indistinguishable from" the id or superego, and weakest when it differentiates itself from them. Freud's ensuing discussion of the struggle of the ego with the "symptom," its effort to integrate the latter's "alien body" and the resulting disintegration of the ego (what might be called its "de-corporation" following its attempt

to incorporate the symptom) provides a graphic model of the process of Auseinandersetzung.

18. What distinguishes the Freudian theory and practice of interpretation from all traditional hermeneutics is the place it assigns to conflictual forces, as the following remark from *The Interpretation of Dreams* illustrates: "It must not be forgotten that in interpreting a dream we are opposed by the psychical forces which were responsible for its distortion. It is thus a question of the relation of forces, whether with the help of our intellectual interest, our capacity for self-discipline, our psychological knowledge and our experience in interpretation we shall be able to master the internal resistances" (S.E. 5, 524-25)

19. Freud's description of the emergence of the secondary process indicates, at least in passing, that the primary process already entails a certain tendency to bind energy, and hence that the latter does not result entirely from the inhibition of the secondary process; indeed, such inhibition appears itself as the reaction to the tendency of the primary process to bind: "A second activity—or as we put it, the activity of a second system—becomes necessary, which would not allow the mnemic cathexis to proceed as far as perception and *from there to bind* the psychical forces; instead, it diverted the excitation arising from the need along a roundabout detour." (S.E. 5, 598-99, my italics). The simple opposition, binding/nonbinding, inhibition/noninhibition will therefore, in Freud's thinking, have to yield to the attempt to articulate the *different kinds* of bindings and inhibitions and ultimately to the development of the second topology, which is not merely a topology designed to account for ambivalence, but itself an ambivalent topology.

20. As we shall see, Freud's conceptualization of conflict will entail an increasing "conflictualization" of his concepts themselves.

21. *The Origins of Psychoanalysis*, New York, 1977, p. 421 ff.

22. "It is not repression that produces anxiety, for anxiety is prior to it; anxiety creates repression." *New Introductory Lectures*, 32, S.E. 22, 89.

23. For a recent and remarkable exception, see: Jean Laplanche, *Problematiques I, L'angoisse*, Paris, 1980.

24. Freud's first published essays on the subject of anxiety are: "On the Grounds for Detaching a Particular Syndrome from Neurasthenia under the Description 'Anxiety Neurosis,'" and "A Reply to Criticisms of my Paper on Anxiety Neurosis" (both 1895).

25. This and the following citations from *Inhibition, Symptom and Anxiety* refer to the Norton Library edition pagination, although the text has generally been retranslated.

26. "Negation," S.E. 14, 237.

27. The passage from *Inhibition*, cited in note 17, indicates that the difficulty in conceptualizing the ego relates to the necessity of representing the function of representation itself as the *effect* of a conflictual process, which in turn cannot be conceived of in representational categories. The English translations of "Es" by "Id," and of "Ich" by "Ego" tends to substantialize—and hence, to portray as representation—what in German are, first and foremost, linguistic terms. The narrative of "castration" is indicative of the aporetic attempt of the ego to represent itself by rendering its irreducible alterity as a negative mode of appropriation, that is, as "loss" or deprivation.

28. Freud's distinction between isolation and repression proper can be traced at least as far back as the seventh chapter of *The Interpretation of Dreams*, where he describes two types of "censorship," one "directed only at the *connection* between two thoughts," the other at the thoughts "in themselves." S.E. 5, 530-31.

29. An important aspect of this dislocation—although Freud is no longer concerned with it—is furnished by the physical accompaniments of anxiety: shortness of breath, sweating, heart palpitation etc. If the ego, as Freud suggests in "The Ego and the Id," is above all "a body-ego," the result of "a projection of a surface," the physical innervations of anxiety embody the transgression of that surface, and as such, incorporate the "danger" to which

anxiety reacts. In this sense, the body becomes the signal of the alterity that the ego, through anxiety, seeks to bind through its ambivalent and ambiguous cathexis of representations, and their temporal organization into a scenario.

30. If "reality" can be apprehended only through a process of repetition, or of "rediscovery" (see footnote 27); and if the "real" object to be rediscovered is not an object at all, but the excess of unbound energy (the trauma), then the latter can only be recognized as real by being *misconstrued*. The signal *is* this misconstruction, and hence, it is always tendentially a *danger*-signal. Since, however, conscious thought itself, as Freud asserts, can only "free itself . . . from exclusive regulation by the unpleasure principle" through the formation of signals (S.E. 5, 602), such thought must be conceived as the prolongation of the defensive process of "misconstruing" at work in anxiety. That this must also hold *a fortiori* for psychoanalytical thinking itself is what these studies seek to demonstrate — and to explore.

31. For a discussion of the problem of "apprehension" and of some of its theoretical implications, see: S. Weber, "It," Glyph 4, Baltimore, 1978, pp. 16 ff.

Part II. The Other Part

1. Freud's German expression is *Rücksicht auf Darstellbarkeit*: literally, "considerations of representability." But since the representational content of the dream only operates in the dream as elements of a "rebus" or hieroglyphic script (Freud), Lacan's proposed translation of Darstellbarkeit by "mise-en-scène" is preferable. Still more apt, I would suggest, is the term *scenario*, which calls attention not only to the scenic, theatrical aspects of the dream, but to its narrative moment as well. On the condition, to be sure, that it be stressed that the dream-scenario does not stop at the spectator or narrator who (re-)tells it.

2. My translation here, by comparison to that of the Standard Edition, restores the present tense in which Freud narrates this dream. This use of the present tense suggests the structural affinity that the narration bears to the dream narrated, which, as Freud emphasizes, always places itself in the present. If Freud relates the latter to the timelessness of the unconscious, one might add that the present constitutes the *pre-tense* of the dream as dislocated wish-fulfillment.

3. J. Lacan, *Les quatre concepts fondamentaux de la psychanalyse*, Paris, 1973, p. 25.

4. *Ibid.*, p. 26.

5. *Ibid.*, p. 28.

6. *Ibid.*

7. "I must confess that I am not at all partial to the fabrication of *Weltanschauungen*. Such activities may be left to philosophers, who avowedly find it impossible to make their journey through life without a Baedeker of that kind to give them information on every subject. Let us humbly accept the contempt with which they look down on us from the vantage-ground of their superior needs. But since *we* cannot forgo our narcissistic pride either, we will draw comfort from the reflection that such "Handbooks to Life" soon grow out of date and that it is precisely our short-sighted, narrow and finicky work which obliges them to appear in new editions, and that even the most up-to-date of them are nothing but attempts to find a substitute for the ancient, useful and all-sufficient Church Catechism." (*Inhibition*, p. 22)

8. Freud, "Negation."

9. Freud, *Origins of Psychoanalysis*, p. 298.

10. *Origins*, p. 297.

11. *Ibid.*

12. *Ibid.*, p. 298.

13. Page references in the text to this work refer to the Norton Library edition, New York, 1963.

14. Immanuel Kant, *Anthropologie in pragmatischer Hinsicht*, § 51, *Werke*, Vol. XII, ed. W. Weischedel, Frankfurt am Main, 1964, pp. 537-38.

15. *Ibid*.

16. J. Lacan, "Le stade du miroir," *Ecrits*, Paris, 1966.

17. This is perhaps why laughter and anxiety are so closely related: in both unbound energy is transformed, i.e., partially bound to convulsive, involuntary bodily movements, and thus partially incorporated by the ego.

18. Cf. S. Weber, "tertium datur," in: *Austreibung des Geistes*, ed. Fr. Kittler, UTB 1054, Paderborn, 1980, pp. 204-21.

19. S. Freud, "On Transformations of Drives as Exemplified in Anal Eroticism," S.E. 17, 128-29.

20. The German word, Instanz, generally translated as "agency," also and perhaps above all designates a tribunal, a court of appeals, a meaning that is particularly appropriate in regard to the superego.

21. E. Benveniste, "La nature des pronoms," in: *Problèmes de linguistique générale* (I), Paris, 1966, 256.

22. If one of the central, and most traditional problems of any theory of jokes, is the relation of wit and knowledge, Freud's discussion demonstrates the pertinence of the etymological derivation that traces *Witz* and *Wissen* to the term they share: *videre*.

23. The Standard Edition translates the German *Vorspiegelung* as *pretense*: "The pretense makes it possible that etc." Although this accurately renders the denotative meaning of the term, it abandons the connotation that here, as so often in Freud's writing, is of decisive importance.

24. A volume of essays recently published in France bears the suggestive title, "Is Psychoanalysis a Jewish joke?" (*La psychanalyse est-elle une histoire juive?*" Paris, 1981.)

25. See Eric Partridge, *The Shaggy Dog Story*, New York, 1954.

26. *Der Grosse Duden, Herkunftswörterbuch*, Mannheim, 1963, 785.

27. *Ibid*.

28. This joke was told to me by Jacques Derrida.

Part III. Love Stories

1. Jones, *Life*, III, 287.

2. J. Lacan, *Ecrits*, 659.

3. G. Deleuze, *Présentation de Sacher-Masoch*, Paris, 1967, p. 111 ff.

4. Deleuze, p. 114.

5. For a recent and notable exception, see J. Derrida's staging of *Beyond the Pleasure Principle*, in: *La carte postale*, Paris, 1980.

6. Concerning Lacan's distinction of "imaginary" and "symbolic," see my: *Rückkehr zu Freud: J. Lacans Ent-Stellung der Psychoanalyse*, Berlin, 1978.

7. J. Laplanche, *Vie et mort en psychanalyse*, Paris, 1970.

8. Cf. the analysis of primary and secondary processes in Part I of this book.

9. In his lectures on anxiety — see above, p. 172, fn. 23 — Laplanche has emphasized that the double function of consciousness, as receptor of impressions both from without and from within, requires us to construe it topologically not merely as a surface, but as having a certain depth — precisely what Freud suggests in *Beyond the Pleasure Principle*, as we shall have occasion to see. Laplanche therefore proposes that the psychic apparatus, as Freud conceives it, be compared to a kind of *bucket* or *trough* ("bacquet"). See Laplanche, *L'angoisse*, 178 ff.

10. Cf. Plato's *Republic*; see *Republic* III, 392-397b, where the distinction is made between *diegetic* and *mimetic* discourses, and the latter excluded from the Republic because

in it the poet "delivers a speech as though he were someone else" (393c) and thus, through mimesis, refuses to assume responsibility for his words. Overt narration is thus acceptable, whereas mimetic attribution of discourse to another must be condemned.

11. See, however, the discussion of the *Symposium* in Stanley Rosen, *Plato's Dialogues*, New Haven, 1968.

12. "The Ego . . . may thus be regarded as a mental projection of the surface of the body." *The Ego and the Id*, S.E. 19, 26.

13. See Marie Delcourt, *Hephaistos, ou la légende du magicien*. Paris, 1957.

Index

Index

Abfallsbewegung (secessionary movement), 7, 9, 14, 16. *See also* Adler; Jung

Adler, Alfred: systematic deviation of psychoanalysis, 5-6, 8-9, 14-15, 17-18, 20-21, 25, 33, 51, 53

Animism: form of narcissistic thinking, 12-13. *See also* Secondary revision

Anticathexis (*Gegenbesetzung*): mechanism of repression, 40-41

Anxiety, 48-60. *See also* Danger, Signal, Trauma

Aristophanes: in *Symposium*, 148-164 *passim*

Aufsitzer. See Shaggy Dog Story

Auseinandersetzung, figure of psychoanalytic thinking: and the *Urszene* (primal scene), 24-25, 27, 31, 32-34, 70-72, 106-9, 170-72. *See also* Setting-apart

Author: authority of, 149-50

Benveniste, Emile, 174

Bilderschrift: of dream, 28-29. *See also* Bildersprache

Bildersprache: figural discourse of Freudian metapsychology, 28; and language of jokes, 90

Binding (*Bindung*) of energy in primary and secondary processes, 37-38; and combination (*Verbindung*) in primary repression, 43, 122; and perceptual identities, 126-27, 172. *See also* Fixation

Castration: and observation, perception, 23-24; and anxiety, 56; as crisis of narcissism, 105; as narrative, 172

Cathexis (*Besetzung*): in primary and secondary process, 34-39; and binding of energy, 127-28. *See also* Binding

Combination (*Verbindung*): and primal repression, 43. *See also* Binding

Danger: and theory of anxiety, 51-52. *See also* Signal

Darstellung (presentation, exposition): category of representation dislocated by Freudian notion of *Entstellung*; 20, 31. *See also* Entstellung

Death drive (*Todestrieb*), 121-25; "silence" of, 129

Delcourt, Marie: Hephaistos as god of binding, 175

Deleuze, Gilles: "transcendental" character of Freudian speculation, 121-26, 129-30

Derrida, Jacques, xii, 174

Description: as category of Freudian epistemology, 21-22, 33. *See also* Observation, Interpretation

Disfiguration: one of aspects of Entstellung, xiii, 20; and anxiety, 54. *See also* Entstellung, Dislocation

Dislocation: another aspect of Entstellung;

177

xii, 20; dream as, 30; and anxiety, 54; essence of dream, 77. *See also* Entstellung, Disfiguration

Distortion. *See* Entstellung, Disfiguration, Dislocation

Dream: a model dream," 69-74. *See also* Interpretation

Ego: 13-18, as "compromise formation," 19; "Standpoint of" and narcissistic thought, 8, 22, 25; and castration-anxiety, 54-57. *See also* Narcissism

Entstellung: disfigurement, dislocation, distortion, xii-xiii; dream-narrative as, 20; and psychoanalytic topology, 21-25, 30, 31; constitutive gesture of ego in anxiety, 54, 58; dream as, 66-68; and *Witz* (joke), 86, 101, 160

Ferenczi, Sandor, 5

Fixation: and verbalization in repression, 44. *See also* Binding, Combination (Verbindung), and Repression

Fliess, Wilhelm: 63; as first reader, 84-86, 162-63

Fort!/Da!: as game described by Freud, 95-99; as speculative game played by Freud, 137-39, 148, 152, 157

Foucault, Michel: on difference between science and discursive practice, xi-xiii, 169

Hephaistos: god of bindings, in *Symposium*, 161-62. *See also* Binding

Hypercathexis (*Überbesetzung*): one of two mechanisms of repression, 40-45. *See also* Anticathexis, Signal

Inhibition: in primary process, 37-39; and joke, 93, 112

Institutionalization (of psychoanalysis), 4, 170. *See also* International Psychoanalytic Association (IPA)

Interdiction (*Versagen*): of "translation" in repression, 44. *See also* Repression

International Psychoanalytic Association (IPA), 3, 169

Interpretation: dream as, 21-22; in dreams, 66-76, 82; nontraditional character of Freudian Interpretation, 172. *See also* Description, Observation

Isolating: described, 58; practiced by Freud, 73

Joke (Witz): relation to psychoanalytic theory, 84-86; and analogy, 87-88; laughter, 88, 100, 109; discontinuous temporality of, 89; principle of economy in, 91; as jest (*Scherz*), 93; third person in, 101-4; *Zote* (smut). *See also* Shaggy Dog Story

Jones, Ernest: 4; on death drive, 121-25

Jung, Carl Gustav, 5-6, 14-15, 21, 25, 33, 51, 170

Kant, Immanuel: theory of wit as analogizing, 88, 174

Klein, Melanie, 23, 171

Kraus, Karl, 84

Lacan, Jacques: xii; on dream-navel, 78-82; theory of mirror-stage, 96-97; on death drive, 121, 124, 171, 172, 173, 174

Lacoue-Labarthe, Philippe & Nancy, Jean-Luc, 171

Laplanche, Jean, 125, 172, 174

Laughter. See Joke

Narcissism: in secondary revision, animism: 8-16; ego and play, 97; castration as crisis of, 105; in jokes, 114; in speculative assumption of death drive, 125; and repetition-compulsion, 132-33

Narration: as integral part of dream, 20, 29. *See also* Entstellung, Stories

Navel of dream (*Traumnabel*): as figure of Freudian hermeneutics, 75-82

Observation: as aspect of psychoanalytic theory, 20-26; in the speculative assumption of a repetition-compulsion, 136-37. *See also*: Bildersprache, Description, Interpretation

Partridge, Eric: on the etymology of the "shaggy-dog story," 174

Psychoanalyst, the pleasure (desire of), 131

Perceptual Identity (*Wahrnehmungsidentität*): in primary process, 36-37; and binding, 126-27

Phobosophie, 12-13

Plato: *See Symposium*

Play: pleaure of, in Witz, 92; Fort!Da! as game, 95-96; and narcissistic ego, 97; and verbalization, 128. *See also* Fort!/Da!, Narcissism

Pleasure: as function of narcissistic ego, 128

Primal Repression, 43. *See also* Repression

Primal Scene (Urszene): 18-19; as Auseinandersetzung, 24

Primary/Secondary Process: set apart, 34-39; as "theoretical fiction," 38

Rank, Otto: theory of birth trauma, 51-53

Reizschutz (protective shield), 143-44. *See also* Trauma

Repetition: in theoretical discourse of metapsychology, 59-60; 122, 126, 129, 137; *Symposium* as, 150-53. *See also* Repetition-Compulsion

Repetition-Compulsion: in transference, relation to death drive, 130-35.

Repression, 39-48. See also Anticathexis, Hypercathexis, Primal Repression, Translation

Rosen, Stanley, 175

Roustang, François, 169, 170

Schreber, Daniel Paul, 108

Secondary Revision (Elaboration), 8-12. *See also* Systematization

Set(ting) Apart: in psychoanalytic topology, 25; of writing, 32-34; spatial consequences of, 171. *See also* Auseinandersetzung.

Sexuality: as substitution, 105

Shaggy Dog Story (Aufsitzer), 100-120. *See also* Jokes

Signal: as hypercathexis, 42; in repression, 48; in anxiety, 53; as product of ego, 54; as "X" in Freudian metapsychology, 59; as temporizing-temporalization narration, 144-45; as misconstruction, 173. *See also* Narration, Stories, Trauma

Socrates, 164

Speech-Associations (verbalization); in repression, 46

Standard Edition, xii-xiii, 76-77, 89, 169, 173-74

Stories (story-telling): infantile sexual theories as, 24; castration as, 56; of repetition and death, 134-35; as articulation of Freudian speculation, 138; of life, 139-40; of consciousness, 141-43; as disfigural representation, 147; castration as, 172. *See also* Narration

Strachey, James, 76, 89. *See also Standard Edition*

Superego: as the "third person" of joke, 107-9

Symposium (Plato), 69, 148-61

Systematization: of psychoanalytic thinking, 8-20. *See also* Narcissism, Secondary Revision

Thallus, the meaning of, 81-83

Topology: psychoanalytic topology marked by overlapping, 25; by the displacement of place, 146-47; as Auseinandersetzung, setting space apart, 171; and binding, 172

Transference: institutional, 5; in psychoanalytical discourse, 27; in assumption of death drive, 130-31

Translation (*Übersetzung*): as hypercathexis (*Überbesetzung*) in repression, 45-46

Trauma: in anxiety, 53-59; 143-45

Wisstrieb (urge-to-know): 22; develops from *Schautrieb* (scopophilia), 111, 123

Witz. See Joke

Writing: as Auseinandersetzung, 32-34

"X": unknown of metapsychology, 27; as "reality" of "danger" and signal of psychoanalytic thought, 59, 140, 147, 160-62

Samuel Weber, who teaches in the Humanities Center, Johns Hopkins University, was a member of the faculty of the Free University of Berlin for many years. He has also been a visiting professor at the University of Strasbourg and the University of Minnesota. He is the author of *Unwrapping Balzac: A Study of "La Peau de Chagrin"* and *Rückkehr zu Freud: Jacques Lacans Ent-Stellung der Psychoanalyse.* A founding editor of *Glyph: Textual Studies,* he also edits its German counterpart, the yearbook *Fugen. The Legend of Freud* is an expanded and revised translation, by Weber, of his *Freud Legende,* published in Germany in 1979.